Why We
TEACH

Why We TEACH

Sonia Nieto
Editor

Teachers College, Columbia University
New York and London

Published by Teachers College Press, 1234 Amsterdam Avenue, New York, NY 10027

Library of Congress Cataloging-in-Publication Data

Why we teach / Sonia Nieto, editor.
    p. cm.
  Includes bibliographical references and index.
  ISBN 0-8077-4594-4 (cloth: alk. paper)—ISBN 0-8077-4593-6 (pbk. : alk. paper)
  1. Teaching—United States. 2. Teachers—United States—Conduct of life. I. Nieto, Sonia.
LB1775.2.W494 2005
371.1—dc22   2005043076

ISBN 0-8077-4593-6 (paper)
ISBN 0-8077-4594-4 (cloth)

Printed on acid-free paper

Manufactured in the United States of America

12   11   10   09   08   07   06   8   7   6   5   4   3   2

Contents

Preface

While administrators, policymakers, businesspeople, and politicians have all had their say about teacher quality, teacher recruitment, and teacher resilience, the voices of teachers themselves have been largely missing in these discussions. Yet who better to tell us about the lives of teachers? I conceived of this book as one way to hear what teachers have to say about their motivations for coming into teaching, and their thoughts about the profession itself.

Why We Teach includes reflections by 21 teachers who work in U.S. public elementary, middle, and high schools in a variety of settings (mostly urban, and a few suburban, schools). Some are new to teaching, others have been in the profession for a decade or more, and still others are veteran teachers with more than 30 years' experience. Most teach students of diverse ethnic, racial, linguistic, and social class backgrounds, and their own backgrounds are also diverse in terms of ethnicity, race, gender, social class, sexual orientation, and other differences. I have known and worked with some of them for many years; others I have never met face to face. Some were recommended to me by friends and colleagues as teachers who would have interesting stories to tell.[1] I read about others in the newspaper. Some I happened to meet by chance at meetings. While I was not looking for only "stars," my major criterion was that all the teachers share a passion for teaching, whether it was acknowledged publicly (one, for instance, is currently a state Teacher of the Year) or not (one is a brand-new teacher, just graduated from college). But having worked with thousands of teachers in many schools over the years, I am convinced that teachers such as these can be found in all schools. These are teachers who care about kids, who love what they do, and who would choose to do it over again. Some are also frustrated, angry, and concerned about the state of public education today and, in this way also, they reflect the sentiments of many teachers around the country.

In asking them to tell their stories, the only guidelines I gave the teachers was to answer the central question that is the title of this book, and to stay within a specific length. I didn't propose any particular format or suggest what they should include. These teachers are different from one another in many ways. In fact, if I were to gather them all in one room, I know that the conversation would be interesting and respectful, but certainly they each would have their own ideas to contribute to the conversation. They are not "cookie-cutter teachers" or, to use the words of Judith Baker (one of the teachers in the book), "template teachers." Not surprisingly, then, the results of their essays are also varied, providing numerous explanations, from heartfelt to poetic, about why they teach. Some mention incidents with specific students (all of whose names are pseudonyms—unless otherwise noted—to protect their confidentiality); some recall an initial experience that led to their choice to become a teacher; some describe anecdotes from yesterday or from 30 years ago that have stayed with them and that keep them energized. Some express tremendous disappointments—for reasons from political to personal—yet even for these, teaching has remained their mission.

The book is organized into six parts: The first is an introductory chapter that focuses on my reasons for engaging in this project. The middle four parts contain the meat of the book, the teachers' essays, with a brief introduction about each teacher. I have organized the teachers' essays into four general themes: "Taking the Long Way"; "To Make Sense of the World"; "To Help Students Name and Claim the World"; and "To Become More Fully Human." The teachers' essays may reflect one of these themes more than others, but these are necessarily overlapping and complementary themes. There are no doubt many ways in which I could have organized the book, and I make no claim that this is the best. But in reading and rereading the teachers' essays, these four ideas seemed paramount: that not all teachers are "born to be teachers" or get to teaching through a direct route; that teaching helps them make sense of the world; that helping students claim their place in the world is a key reason for teaching; and that teaching helps them become more fully human. I provide a brief explanation of the themes at the beginning of each part.

In Part II, I consider those teachers for whom the decision to teach was made more or less serendipitously or even accidentally, or those who took the long road. Although many of the teachers in the book decided to teach as children or early in life, this is not the case for all teachers, and the stories of the five teachers in this section provide intriguing insights into why and how they came to the conclusion that they should teach.

Part III includes essays by teachers who explain how teaching has helped them to make sense of the world. Whether seen as a spiritual journey, political commitment, craft, or vocation, these six teachers describe how teaching has given them a way to understand their role in life. In Part IV, six teachers describe teaching as a way to help students find their voice and their place in the world. This is no small task, especially given the dilapidated and abandoned urban schools—schools that offer little hope for many of those within their walls—in which most of them work.

Part V includes essays by four teachers: two who are fairly new to the profession and two who have been teaching for many years. In their essays, they provide vivid descriptions of how teaching makes them "more fully human." What they mean by this varies, but what is clear is that teaching for them is a way of serving the public good and of contributing to positive change in the lives of young people.

The final chapter is my attempt to make sense of the many perceptions provided through the teachers' essays.[2] I do so by suggesting five major qualities—which are necessarily overlapping—shared by people who choose to teach, and I conclude with some implications for policy and practice at various levels. Of course, not all teachers in all contexts will find themselves in these pages, and there are no doubt some reasons that people teach that I may not have included in my analysis. But it is my hope that many teachers indeed will see their own motivations and passion for teaching echoed in these pages. I hope that those of us who care about teachers and about public schools will find something useful in the book as well.

In these times of shrinking support for public education, it is my wish that *Why We Teach* will help shift the focus of the conversation about teaching from blaming and accountability to support and

acknowledgment of the role of teachers. I love working with teachers; it is what I have devoted the past 30 years of my life to doing.
But even more important, I care about the future of public education and the future of our nation's children. I believe that the work
of teachers is essential in ensuring both, and it is with this thought
in mind that the teachers and I offer this book.

ACKNOWLEDGMENTS

Numerous people have helped bring this book to fruition. Chief
among them, of course, are the teachers whose essays you will read.
Most teachers do not have the luxury of spending time on reflection and writing; they go from one whirlwind day to another, with
barely time to pause. Yet all of these teachers took time from im-
possibly busy schedules to write their thoughts about teaching.
Many of them thanked me for having the opportunity to think more
deeply about their work because they rarely have the time or space
to do so. In fact, thinking about who they are and what they do is
an opportunity so rare as to be nonexistent in the lives of some of
them. Of course, they *do* think, but usually not about themselves:
They think about their students, colleagues, and administrators,
about the students' families, about what strategies to use to help
students engage with learning, about developing curriculum that
will energize them, and so on. But rarely do they have the time to
think about themselves, their work, and why they do it. I am grateful
to them all for having done so, and I know that many readers around
the country will be the better for having read their thoughts.

In addition to the teachers, I am grateful to a number of other
people who helped me think about and complete this book. First
among them is Brian Ellerbeck, senior editor at Teachers College
Press, who first approached me with the idea for this book. Having
worked with Brian on two previous books, I was eager to do so but
at first reluctant to take on yet another project in the midst of a very
busy life. But shortly after our initial conversation, and after staying awake one night thinking of the many possibilities for the book,
I was hooked. I thank Brian for his ideas, his support, and his uncommon good sense and creativity. Working with the other members of the staff at Teachers College Press, from President Carole Saltz

to all the production and marketing people, is always a joy, and I thank them as well for moving the process along.

Patty Bode, teacher, research assistant, colleague, friend, and author of one of the essays in the book, provided me with feedback, help on some of the introductions to the teachers' essays, and countless other tasks. For this, and for her constant help and support, I am also grateful. Finally, I want to thank Angel, my husband and best friend of many years, without whom life would be infinitely poorer. His sharp eye caught many things that mine did not, and the book is improved because of it. For reading everything I write and for giving me exceptional feedback, I am always grateful to him.

PART I

Introduction

Why do people choose teaching as a career? What is it that entices them to spend their days engaged in learning with other people's children? Why do they decide to go into what are frequently demanding situations, sometimes in poorly funded and rundown schools? Why do they choose teaching rather than other professions that would give them better compensation, higher status, and more respect?

Today, these questions take on greater urgency than ever. The rapid turnover of new teachers, the changing demographics in U.S. classrooms, the widely touted "achievement gap" between White students and students of color, and the national insistence on "highly qualified teachers" all contribute to a situation where retaining the best teachers and encouraging others to enter the profession are essential. In the end, the answers to these questions say a lot about who we are as a nation, what we value and believe in, and how we educate our young people.

Although for over a century our nation has advanced the ideal that a high-quality and excellent public education is the birthright of all children, our schools cannot fulfill this ambitious and noble purpose unless all of us—parents, policymakers, and the general public—commit ourselves to sustaining education as a public trust and a promise to future generations. Teachers are at the very center of this matter and it is only by understanding the motivations and inspiration of teachers that, as a nation, we can hope to accomplish the lofty goals of public education.

The intention of this book is to focus on what teachers think about the issues that define teaching in today's classrooms. In Chapter 1, we address the conundrum of teaching by first considering the current context of education.

Chapter 1

Public Schools and the Work of Teachers

T here are approximately 3 million teachers in U.S. public schools. They work in grades kindergarten through high school, and they teach everything from art to science to physical education and reading; some teach all of these things or some combination of them, and many see more than 100 students a day. They teach in small schools and large, in urban, rural, and suburban schools, in racially and culturally diverse schools, as well as in less diverse settings. They have from zero to 40 years of experience, and most, if given the chance, would choose teaching all over again.[1] When asked, many say that they became teachers for reasons that sound old-fashioned and that seem at odds with the current national obsession with bureaucracy, accountability, and high-stakes testing: In general, they view teaching as a "calling" and they are driven by a sense of service. For instance, in a survey of nearly 1,000 new teachers (with 5 years' experience or less) conducted by Public Agenda, 96% said that they loved teaching and 72% declared that contributing to society and helping others was paramount to them. In most cases, they became teachers out of a sense of mission, for love more than money. Their responses, taken together, define an idealistic group of people who share at least one significant quality: They have a passion for teaching, a quality that, according to the report, is "palpable, vastly unappreciated and a valuable asset that money can't buy."[2]

Teaching is hard and stressful work, and it provides relatively low compensation and, in most cases, little autonomy or support. Teachers work countless hours in the classroom and out: The average teacher spends 50 hours a week on all teaching duties, more than those in many other professions, and they get an average of 32 minutes for lunch. They spend nearly $500 a year of their own money for classroom supplies, and their salaries are less lucrative than those of other professionals requiring similar credentials.[3] They teach too many kids, and they have too little time to do so. They sometimes face unresponsive bureaucracies, listless students, and seemingly disinterested parents. *Why do they do it?* This is the question at the center of this book.

A SHIFTING POLITICAL CONTEXT IN EDUCATION

To understand why people become teachers, we first must understand the context they enter. These are hard times for public education, which increasingly is characterized by a mean-spirited and hostile discourse, one with little respect for teachers and the young people they teach. Currently, the most common buzzwords in education are borrowed shamelessly from the business world: The school is a "market," students and families are "consumers," and teachers are "producers." In this discourse, "accountability" is proposed as the arbiter of excellence, teacher tests are the answer to "quality control," and high-stakes tests are the final judge of student learning. As a result, public schools are challenged by countless privatization schemes, including vouchers, tuition tax credits, "choice," and charter schools, even though such alternatives traditionally benefit students who already enjoy economic and other privileges, while they further jeopardize those who do not.

In the current context, there is also an increased focus on schooling as job training, and education as a vehicle to serve limited self-interests and consumerism. Less attention than ever is paid to education as a way to expand the human spirit and create a better world. Moreover, public schools are no longer viewed as the one place where children of all races and social classes can expect to be educated—however imperfectly schools ever did this, at least in the past, there was a shared vision that schools had the *responsibility* to educate all children.

Paradoxically, while these are challenging times for public education, they are also hopeful times. In fact, two current and competing discourses concerning public education are evident: One is the "official" discourse, embodied in the language of the federal No Child Left Behind legislation and other mandates with a focus on accountability, standards, credentials, and testing, accompanied by punitive measures meted out to students and teachers for failing to live up to them. The other is what one might call the "discourse of possibility," a way of thinking about teaching and learning embraced largely by teachers and others who view public education as, on the whole, an elusive and unfulfilled but nonetheless significant goal in the quest for equality and social justice.[4] This "unofficial" discourse is visible in many schools as well as in books and articles that focus on the positive and uplifting work that teachers do and that champion teachers who defy the current damaging climate in education.[5]

These, then, are difficult but also promising times for those who view public education as the last and, in many cases, the only hope for fulfilling our society's stated ideals of sustaining democracy through public education. Schools can serve this purpose, however, only when all children have access to teachers who are competent and caring and in schools characterized by fairness, enthusiasm, and high expectations. It is little wonder, then, that a great deal of attention has been focused lately on the quality of the teaching force. But what does it mean (to use the language currently in vogue) to be a "highly qualified teacher"? Given the rapidly changing student body in our classrooms, this question needs to be addressed with an understanding of the changing demographics in our nation.

A CHANGING DEMOGRAPHIC CONTEXT

Our country today is a far different place than it was even half a century ago. As of the year 2000, people of color made up 25% of our total population, a 5% increase from just a decade earlier. The growing racial and ethnic diversity has been accompanied by a growing linguistic diversity: Currently, 18% of U.S. residents speak a language other than English at home, with Spanish the language spoken by half of these.[6] Also in 2000, the number of foreign-born or first-generation U.S. residents reached the highest level in U.S. history, 56 million, or triple the number in 1970. And unlike previous immigrants who were primarily from Europe, only 15% are now from Europe, with over half from Latin America and a quarter from Asia.[7]

Not surprisingly, the nation's public schools are also very different from what they were just a few decades ago. Although not yet a majority, the number of children in our public schools representing backgrounds other than European American is growing rapidly: Whites still make up more than half of all students, but it is a dwindling majority at just 61.2%. Blacks now make up 17.2%, Hispanics 16.3%, Asian/Pacific Islanders 4.1%, and American Indian/Alaska Natives 1.2% of students in public schools.[8]

Regardless of the growing diversity in schools around the country, and despite the desegregation movement that began over 50 years ago, racial and ethnic segregation is on the rise. Students in U.S. schools are now more likely to be segregated from students of other races and backgrounds than at any time in the recent past. In fact, according to researcher Gary Orfield, for Blacks, the 1990s witnessed the largest backward movement toward segregation since the 1954 *Brown* versus *Board of Education* decision, and the trend is continuing. Moreover, Latinos now have the dubious distinction of being the most segregated of all ethnic groups in terms of race, ethnicity, and poverty.[9]

Poverty too continues to be a serious problem in our nation. Due to a booming U.S. economy, the percentage of people living in poverty improved later in the 1990s from its low point of 14.5% in 1994. But poverty is again on the increase, and it is especially bleak among people of color: While Whites represent just over 9% of the poor, Blacks are over 22% and Hispanics over 21% of those living in poverty.[10] These numbers also point to a chronic problem in terms of teacher retention: The turnover rate for teachers in high-poverty schools can climb as high as 50%, creating even more uncertainty and unpredictability in such schools.[11]

At the same time that the number of students of color, those who speak languages other than English, and those who live in poverty has increased, the nation's teachers have become more monolithic, monocultural, and monolingual. The percentage of White teachers actually *grew* from 88% in 1971 to 90.7% in 1996, while during those same years the number of Black teachers decreased from 8.1% to 7.3% and the number classified as "other" decreased from 3.6% to 2.0%. By 2001, the number of teachers of color was still less than 11%, with Black teachers at 6% and those classified as "other" at 5%.[12] Complicating the issue further, although there is a crucial need for teachers of all backgrounds to teach poor students of color in urban districts, fewer than 6% of education graduates nationally express a desire to teach in such districts.[13] Given this situation, it should come as no surprise that researchers point to a major gap in the research on how best to prepare teachers to teach students of diverse backgrounds.[14]

WHY TEACHING MATTERS

It is now an established fact that the quality of teaching matters, and it matters especially to the most vulnerable young people. One widely cited study found that students who are assigned to several highly effective teachers in a row have significantly greater gains in achievement than those assigned to less effective teachers, and that each teacher's influence has effects that spill over into later years.[15] Yet Black and Latino students, who could benefit greatly from having qualified teachers, receive a disproportionate amount of poor teaching and are much less likely to have certified teachers than are White students, among many other disadvantages.[16] Consequently, in a review of dozens of studies in the late 1990s, researchers Linda Darling-Hammond and Beverly Falk suggested that until schools address the enormous inequalities in students' access to qualified teachers, other reforms would have little effect on student achievement.[17]

Given this reality, we need to think about what it means to recruit, prepare, and retain teachers to work with students who in most cases are vastly different from them in background and experience. In this book, the focus is on teachers *not* because they alone are responsible for either all the good or all the bad that happens in public schools. It would be simplistic in the extreme to believe this was the case. Indeed, if we were to place all our hope—or all our blame—on teachers, it would be tempting to overlook the deeply entrenched structures, policies, and practices still prevalent today, not only in schools but in our nation as a whole, that caused the problems of inequality in the first place. Problems of economic inequality, institutional racism and other biases, poor and inadequate health care and housing, underfunded schools, and insufficient instructional materials also need to be confronted, and teachers are not responsible for these problems. We might even say that without structural changes in schools and in society in general, teachers can have only a limited impact.[18] But as a nation, we cannot afford to sit around and wait for these structural changes to take place. They do not appear to be happening any time soon and, in the meantime, too many young people are being lost. The times call for working on what *can* be done to help keep the most caring and committed teachers in our public schools, and this means looking carefully—and skeptically—at what it means to be a "highly qualified teacher," to use the current discourse.

BECOMING EFFECTIVE TEACHERS OF ALL STUDENTS

What does it mean to be an effective teacher of *all* students? Put another way, how might we best characterize excellent and committed teachers, especially those who teach students who attend our nation's most troubled and least supported schools? And how can we do so without falling back on clichés, stale formulas, or mechanical checklists? Tackling this puzzle may help us prepare new and continuing teachers more successfully to meet the challenges of teaching students of backgrounds that differ from the majority, the most rapidly and dramatically growing segment of our public school population. At the same time, exploring this question may in the end shed light on what it takes to help *all* students reach their potential.

In spite of the prevailing notion that teachers are simply technicians who know how to write lesson plans, prescribe prepackaged programs, discipline students, and evaluate them through rubrics, benchmarks, and tests, teachers are also professionals and intellectuals. This means simply that tests, checklists, or other such procedures cannot adequately determine what it means to be a good teacher; these systems are frequently incomplete and inappropriate. Instead, in this book we suggest that qualities of excellent teachers can emerge through reflection, investigation, collaboration, and study.[19]

Numerous educational researchers over the years have tackled the question of what it means to be a successful teacher of students of diverse backgrounds.[20] A synthesis of this literature suggests a number of common characteristics that describe highly qualified teachers. These include, of course, strong subject-matter knowledge and pedagogical effectiveness, as well as excellent communication skills. In addition, in general such teachers:

- connect learning to students' lives
- have high expectations for all students, even for those whom others may have given up on
- stay committed to students in spite of obstacles that get in the way
- place a high value on students' identities (culture, race, language, gender, and experiences, among others) as a foundation for learning
- view parents and other community members as partners in education
- create a safe haven for learning
- dare to challenge the bureaucracy of the school and district
- are resilient in the face of difficult situations
- use active learning strategies
- are willing and eager to experiment and can "think on their feet"
- view themselves as lifelong learners
- care about, respect, and love their students

Taken together, these qualities define teachers as enthusiastic lifelong learners who are deeply involved in their work and who defend both their students' right to an excellent education and their own rights as intellectuals and professionals. Their own growth is clearly important to such teachers, yet less than 1% of all the money spent on public education is used for professional development, a situation that would never be tolerated in the business world.[21] In spite of the comparisons between public education and business discussed earlier, research and development in the business world are of paramount importance, while in public education little consideration is given to the need for these activities.

In addition, far too few of the professional development activities in either university teacher preparation or inservice education—courses, workshops, field placements, and so forth—focus on the skills or qualities identified by researchers as characteristic of excellent teachers. Not many courses, for instance, help teachers learn to challenge school bureaucracies, or teach them strategies for learning about the identities of the students they teach. And although issues of difference and bias are now more prevalent in teacher education programs than they were a decade ago, they are still left largely unexamined in many teacher education and inservice programs.[22] Also, practicing and prospective teachers rarely have the opportunity to delve into research that considers the work of teachers and schools in a broader sociopolitical context, or that presents educational reform in a critical and comprehensive way.[23] Yet this is precisely the kind of research that could open their eyes to different perspectives and critical understandings.

THE CONUNDRUM OF TEACHING

Public education is at a crossroads today. Historically viewed as an essential partner in creating and sustaining democracy, today the link between the two is tenuous. Sadly, the words of John Dewey sound strangely out of place in this day and age: In 1916, Dewey wrote that our society, like every other society that has ever existed, was replete with inequality. He turned to the schools to help remedy this situation, writing, "It is the aim of progressive education to take part in correcting unfair privilege and unfair deprivation, not to perpetuate them."[24] Yet today, many people are losing hope in the possibilities of public education. This hopelessness is understandable: Too many youngsters are being failed by schools, too many families are disappointed with the broken promises of equal and high-quality education, and too many good teachers are tired and burned out. They are overworked, underpaid, and underappreciated, and they rarely experience the support and public acclaim of other professionals.

Not all teachers are excellent, of course. Some should never have entered the profession, and some who remain in the classroom, for all intents and purposes, left it years before. Some teachers damage children, sometimes irreparably, and others are simply biding their time until retirement. But most people who enter the profession do so for unselfish reasons; they want to contribute to society and they view teaching as a good way to do so. This book is about those who stay the course or intend to, who care deeply about who and what they teach, and who know that they touch the future. Some are experienced professionals, while others may appear to be naive and young. But all of them know that they make a difference. We can all learn from these teachers.

As you will see as you read the essays in this book, the core message here is one of hope, both for the teaching profession and for public education. The intent of the book is to focus on teachers who embody quintessential values of teaching, values that may help redirect our national attention away from such distractions as privatization and high-stakes testing to what really matters in teaching: not test scores, not rubrics or benchmarks or "best practices" or teacher tests, but students and teachers and the future of democracy in our nation.

PART II

Taking the Long Way

Not all teachers decide to enter the profession when they are young children, or even by the time they leave college. For some, the decision comes after graduation, and sometimes many years later. In certain cases, they cannot find a job in their field and decide to try teaching. Others may realize that, years after fighting the idea of becoming a teacher, it is the only job that really interests them. For others, the decision is made long after being in another profession, one perhaps less satisfying or rewarding—although probably better compensating—than teaching.

The five essays in this part demonstrate what it means to take the long way to teaching. The first, "The Accidental Teacher," by Jennifer Welborn, is the story of someone who actually tried to *avoid* teaching as a career. It proved to be, however, the inevitable choice for her. The second essay, by Judith Kauffman Baker, says it all in the title: "I'm Not Sure I Want to Be a 'Teacher.'" In it, Judith, a veteran teacher, muses on how grueling, and how gratifying, it is to be a teacher. In the third essay, Bob Amses reflects on his first 2 years of teaching and explains why he decided to change gears after a successful career as a cameraman. "On Re-Becoming a Teacher," by Laila Di Silvio, explains how the author was essentially discouraged from becoming a teacher by one of her own teachers. Her eventual decision to enter the profession in spite of this advice was made out of a strong conviction rather than out of convenience. The final essay in the section, "Waiting Tables and Juggling Motherhood: Taking the Road Less Traveled," recounts Patty Bode's rather circuitous route to becoming a teacher by combining her love of art and commitment to social justice in one place: her middle school art classroom.

Chapter 2

The Accidental Teacher

J<small>ENNIFER</small> W<small>ELBORN</small>

J ennifer Welborn teaches science in middle school. We first met when she took a course with me several years ago, and I was immediately impressed with her quiet presence and strong commitment to equity. As a student, she gave a great deal of thought to the issues we discussed in class, many of which concerned controversial topics. But whatever the topic, Jennifer was clear about one thing: Teaching is fundamentally about fairness and having high expectations for all students. In the years since we met, I've often heard from others about Jennifer and about the innovative work she and the other members of her team in the Amherst Regional Middle School have done on the social construction of race. As she recounts in her essay, her awareness of the topic began when she read a book about scientific racism as a graduate student. In 1994 she received a "World of Difference Teacher Incentive Award" from the Anti-Defamation League for her work in this area.

In her essay, Jennifer describes how she was a teacher twice before she finally committed herself to the profession. In fact, for years she tried to escape teaching each time after leaving it. But, given her love of science and her fondness and talent for working with young people, it was inevitable that she should become a teacher.

I've taken many a twist and turn in my career path to becoming a middle school science teacher, including two stints in private schools and a job with a college textbook publisher.

Perhaps it was my 7th-grade science teacher, Mr. Fegley, who fueled my innate interest in science and showed me how exciting a science class could be in public school. I majored in forestry/wildlife in college and fully intended to be a Ms. Marlin Perkins, a featured scientist on *Wild Kingdom*. Or, perhaps, I would become a park ranger or research scientist. I never, ever, ever considered teaching.

After contemplating a career in medicine to work as a pediatrician, I took my father's advice to visit a career counselor. I spent 2 days talking and filling out forms and surveys. It was the ultimate "What Color Is Your Parachute?" experience. I took that Myers-Briggs test that not only matches your interests with a profession but also matches your interests with other people who are in various professions. After 2 days of waiting, I was to finally hear what the counselor thought I should be doing with my life. He announced that, after much careful analysis, it was clear to him that if I hadn't already done so, I definitely should consider being a TEACHER!

I couldn't believe my ears. I hate to admit this but I actually cried. *Oh, no . . . not a teacher. Not again.* But I could avoid it no longer. I needed to get back into teaching.

I've been in the classroom for 10 years this time around. Obviously, people see me as a teacher. I even call myself a teacher now. However, in reality I see myself as always *becoming* a teacher in the same way that I am always becoming a runner. I don't think I'll ever get there. I don't want to feel that I have all the answers. I'm still learning and trying to be the best I can be in this incredibly challenging and rewarding career.

I teach because, as the career counselor pointed out, teaching suits my personality. I love being on the move, being flexible, negotiating, multitasking, helping, listening, creating, laughing, and loving. I am passionate about being with kids, helping them learn or unlearn things, and perhaps changing their lives in subtle and not-so-subtle ways. Being with young people, particularly young adolescents, suits my personality. They are fun, refreshingly honest and open. They are sincere and unpredictable. They are always forgiving.

Kids generally like coming to my class; perhaps it's because I like having them there. I like teaching science. It's fun for me. On my best days, I believe kids are learning science. On my worst days, I believe I have at least provided a safe and welcoming place in my room for all kids. Later, when I see my students in town, or working in stores, I still have a connection to them. I care about them and I think they know that.

Teaching as a career also suits my lifestyle. I am now a mother of two kids. It would be dishonest of me if I did not admit that one of the reasons why I teach is to have time off to be with my kids. I love it when we have matching holidays, snow days, and summers off. I also love the cyclical nature of the job. There is a clear beginning and a clear ending. Every year, a teacher and her students get a fresh, new start. That's pretty unique to the teaching profession, I think.

I teach because it gives me a purpose. Teaching gives me a really good reason to get up and try my best every day. I may be naive, but I believe that what I do day in and day out *does* make a difference. Teachers *do* change lives forever. And I teach in public school because I still believe in public school. I believe that the purpose of public school, whether it delivers or not, is to give a quality education to all kids who come through the doors. I want to be a part of that lofty mission. The future of our country depends on the ability of public schools to do that.

I teach because I believe in the affective as well as cognitive outcomes of education. I realize that even though I may feel that teaching is an impossible job, a job I will always "jog" through, I have the opportunity each and every day to help kids feel like competent, important people. They may not always like science. In fact, for any number of reasons, they may not even learn a lot of science in my class. But I still have the power to positively affect my students' perceptions of themselves as capable and worthy people. I teach because I believe I help kids enjoy coming to school, enjoy learning, and feel good about taking risks and challenges.

I teach because I know teachers are role models. We have a powerful influence on students. I said earlier that I decided to pursue a degree in science because of a positive experience I had in 7th-grade science. My teacher, Mr. Fegley, positively influenced my desire to pursue a degree in science by showing me that it is important to *do* science, not just read about it. Science is a way of knowing. It involves trial and error, messing around with things and experimenting.

As a middle school science teacher, I realize that each and every day I am showing both my male and female students that women can be competent scientists. I am showing them that teachers are people who do not have all the answers. I am showing them that it is okay to take risks and make mistakes. I also am showing them what science is, and what it is not. That is my "hidden curriculum."

I believe teaching is the most challenging but also the most rewarding career there is. There are the rewards that one sees in a year: Kids grow a lot in a year, cognitively, behaviorally, and socially. Sometimes the growth is incremental, sometimes it is enormous. Growth in any area is extremely rewarding for me. I can say honestly that in 15 years of teaching, I have never seen one of my students *not* grow in some small way either cognitively, socially, or emotionally. Like a gardener, I consider the subtle growth of a tiny shoot as rewarding as the dramatic growth of a long vine.

Then there are long-term rewards. Middle school students go through a lot of changes. Some of them are quite dramatic. They are constantly becoming who they will be as adults. One of the most rewarding aspects of teaching is seeing my students—even some of my reluctant scholars—years later, mature and confident in who they are, acknowledge me and give a friendly hello and smile. "Teaching is an impossible job." One of my colleagues (who is a brilliant, master teacher) said this to me and it made me feel, somehow, relieved. It acknowledged something that I had felt for over 20 years. Yes, teaching is an impossible job and it's okay to feel as if you are always becoming a teacher. It's okay to feel like you are never on top of the profession. It's okay to feel like you're jogging even though others believe you are running. In fact, the challenges of the profession also make it interesting and compelling.

There is no end to the demands placed on teachers, particularly public school teachers. Teachers are constantly challenged by external demands to do more and more administrative work. They are challenged by a stream of paperwork, which ends only on the last day of school. They are challenged by large class sizes, lack of money, lack of support, heterogeneous classes, multiple learning styles, and an increasing number of kids with social/

emotional issues being mainstreamed into regular education—all of this within a context of local, state, and national standards, and while attempting to prepare kids for the 21st century. They are challenged by helping students cope with cookie-cutter standardized tests, even though some of them have learning disabilities that prevent them from succeeding on this kind of assessment. Some of the external demands seem so unrealistic and unattainable that they are beyond challenging; they are overwhelming.

Other challenges are internal. I am always striving to do the best I can in this demanding profession. Many nights I lie awake wondering how I'm ever going to make sure that I'm addressing each and every kid's learning style and individual strengths while helping them work to improve their weaknesses. How will I ensure that each of my students is getting enough of my attention, liking school, and not being bullied, while learning skills that will help him or her be successful, feeling appreciated and respected, and being appropriately challenged: In reality, I can't do all that. That's what makes teaching impossible. It is also what makes it interesting.

On many occasions people have asked me, "Are you still a teacher?" When I hear this, it makes me think that people must think that, since I've been teaching for years, I must have it down pat and I'm ready to move on. Or perhaps they think I'm too "smart" to stay in teaching (someone actually did say that to me once). People never ask a doctor, a lawyer, or even a carpenter whether he or she is *still* a doctor, lawyer, or carpenter. When I get that question, I realize that many people have no idea how difficult it is not only to teach, but to do it well. They have no idea how "smart" you have to be, to be a good teacher.

Yes, I'm still a teacher because every year I am expected to meet the needs of 90 students who are counting on the fact that I will be able to do that—and it never gets any easier, no matter how many years I've tried. In fact, the more I teach, the more I realize how much I need to learn. I need to learn more about cooperative learning, peer editing, integration, differentiation, writing across the curriculum, reading strategies in the content area, mediating, counseling, advising, rubrics, looking at student work, exhibition, and "best practices" in general. It is because of those challenges that I continue to teach.

I like teaching science. It's hands-on and interesting for many kids. But I want my students to do more than just have fun in science. I want them to come away with some big ideas they can apply later on in real-life situations.

I feel it's important for kids to know that science is one way of knowing—a way of gaining knowledge about the material world. The scientific method has strengths, but it also has weaknesses. There are limitations to what science can explain. It is actually those weaknesses that I want my students to fully understand. I want them to learn to be skeptics. I want them to be able to determine the validity of scientific data. I want them to differentiate between good science, bad science, and pseudoscience.

For example, every science book explains the steps of the scientific method in the first chapter. After students learn the steps of the scientific process, there may be a few questions, but generally, that's it. Students are never really challenged to think about the strengths and the limitations of the scientific problem-solving model. The rest of the book goes on to describe an endless array of "facts" with accompanying vocabulary. Sometimes, the vocabulary can be quite intimidating. I read once that the number of vocabulary words in a biology textbook is more than the number of words in a first-year language course.

Students rarely are asked to apply the scientific problem-solving steps to solve a problem of their own or to use them to design their own experiment. They simply are asked to perform cookbook-like experiments to verify a hypothesis that they have already read to be a "fact." Traditional textbooks never teach kids explicitly about the characteristics of a good experiment. To me, this is what science is all about: It is about setting up an experiment, gathering data, drawing a conclusion, and evaluating the strengths and weaknesses of an experiment. It is about recognizing hidden variables and sources of error. It's not about loads and loads of "facts."

Ever since I was young, I have felt strongly about issues of social justice. My parents were active in the civil rights movement. They took my brother and sisters and me to countless marches on Washington. I remember seeing Detroit burning from the race riots. I grew up recognizing (as best I can as a "White" person) some of the inequities in America and believing that it's important to work to create social justice in one's life.

In graduate school, I read *The Mismeasure of Man* by Stephen Jay Gould for the first time.[1] I stayed up all night reading it. I could not put it down. The book deals primarily with scientific racism and the concept that race is a social construct. Racial categories were created in Europe about 300 years ago. However, it was actually the Greeks who developed this idea of a "great chain of being," a preordained, natural order of people. In this great chain of being, Whites were at the top, perceived as the most highly evolved. Various groups were beneath Whites, meaning less highly evolved. In *The Mismeasure of Man*, Gould brings to light the fact that during the past 200 years, prominent scientists attempted to "prove" racial superiority by measuring skull size, arm length, and many other body parts of various groups of people. Data that did not fit a preconceived notion of White superiority were discounted, erased, or thrown out. The book also addresses the use of the IQ test as a sorting device, which was never Alfred Binet's intent. I was thoroughly shocked by what I read. Up to that point, I had not considered the role of science in establishing, perpetuating, and even legitimizing racism.

That weekend I began to develop a unit on scientific racism that I have taught every year for the past 10 years. Each year, I spend quite a bit of time on it when my students learn about the scientific method and experimental design. I explicitly teach them about the characteristics of a good experiment. Then I contrast this with examples of scientific racism, which is bad science. I do this because I want my students to learn that while human variation is real, racial groups are not based on genetic differences between groups of people. The mapped human genome presents overwhelming evidence of this. Racial groups are socially constructed. That is, racial categories were created by people. There is no "race gene," that is, one gene that is present in one group of people and not another. In fact, there is more genetic variability within a so-called racial group than between members of different so-called races. Racial groups cannot be measured. The groups change over time and place. Emphasis on the salient aspects of racial grouping varies with context and culture.

I also want my students to realize that science is not the objective pursuit of knowledge that it is professed to be. I want them to understand the limitations of gaining knowledge through experiments. I want them to understand that data may support a hypothesis that is not valid to begin with. I want them to know that correlation does not imply causality. I want them to know there are hidden variables that may affect an experiment. I want them to know about researcher bias. I want them to know all this so that when they read in the newspaper that "minority SAT scores are down," they know that these data must be due to social, economic, and political inequities in our society. They are not due to genetic inferiority.

Eighth graders are fully capable of understanding these concepts. In fact, middle school kids are passionate about issues of justice. I believe it's important for kids to understand how and why racial groups were formed and how racial grouping affects individual people both positively and negatively. I want them to know the concept of White privilege. I want them to think about the automatic advantages and disadvantages that racial grouping brings to individuals in our country. It is through this knowledge and dialogue that students can understand the complexity of racism in our country.

As a science teacher, I am hopeful that my students will go out into the world and work to eradicate social, political, and economic inequities that manifest themselves in racial disparities. This may sound like a lofty goal. However, last week I attended a community-wide meeting organized by the school system in my town, in which many people were invited to discuss issues of social justice in our community. From across the room, I noticed two students taking part in this important conversation. They were the only kids in the room of about 100 people. When they turned, I recognized them as former students of mine. They looked at me and smiled in a knowing way. In all my years of teaching, that moment was the most rewarding of all.

I end where I began. A major reason why I teach is incredibly simple: I teach because I like it. I like the pace, the challenges, the rewards, the kids, the colleagues, and the subject matter. At this point in my life, I cannot think of anything I would rather do. Teaching is a compelling profession. I've come back to classroom teaching three times in my life. I'm here now for the long haul.

Chapter 3

I'm Not Sure I Want to Be a "Teacher"

JUDITH KAUFFMAN BAKER

Judith Baker teaches English in a Boston high school. She brings an analytical perspective and deep insight to everything she does. Sharply critical of American education, Judith says, "I am convinced that education is largely a sham. Poor kids aren't liberated by schools; rich kids are privileged by them. . . . I am not so much building a school as fighting a system." She comes to this work, she said, more from a "social justice framework" than an "educational framework." Judith is also critical of the educational fads and bureaucratic solutions so common in urban and other poor schools. She describes such schools as being in "template heaven," where models are imposed on all sorts of things, including writing, one of the subjects she teaches. But for Judith, teaching writing—or anything else, for that matter— is much more organic than that. For her, young people need to be taught to solve their own problems and make their own way if they are to really learn.

Judith's social justice work extends far beyond her own school. As part of her long involvement with South African educators, she and several colleagues at her school have developed a sister school project in South Africa where they have brought sorely needed resources to several schools. She says that the Boston teachers have received much more in return. Visiting there last year, they were deeply moved by the struggles of their teacher colleagues in South Africa. In one of her emails to colleagues at her school, Judith described the visits to South African schools:

> At every school, we were embraced with a warmth and enthusiasm that exceeded anything we've felt elsewhere. Children who sing and dance for us with such beauty that as the saying goes, makes grown men cry. We never got used to it. And then the teachers danced and sang even more beautifully—can you imagine the staff of ANY Boston public school getting up and dancing and singing in four-part harmony off the cuff for visitors?

Judith came to teaching somewhat by accident. Having studied economics at Harvard University, she never dreamed she would become a teacher in an inner-city high school. Her essay explains how this happened and how she has reluctantly, after over 3 decades, taken on the title of "teacher."

In 4th grade, after reading down the shelves in my rural small-town library in New York State, reading all the mysteries, the few science fiction books, finishing off the promising biographies, and all the kids' books, I decided to move on to Hemingway, a name I'd heard somewhere. *For Whom the Bell Tolls* sounded good so I headed to the desk with that and several other now long-forgotten titles. The librarian loved the company of bookworms and she wouldn't have done anything to hurt me. That's why, I suppose, she wouldn't let me sign out Hemingway. "Not old enough for that," she said. Only the intercession of my 8th-grade friend, who, I figured, had read every book in the library that had arrived before last week, convinced her to let me try it. I can still see the librarian at her high desk, shocking me with her denial, my friend coming from the right side of the room to plead my case, my victory propelling me home to the back porch to read the book in one day.

Over the next several years I read my way around adult fiction, Dickens, Steinbeck, and even *Lady Chatterley's Lover*, with no further objections. But somewhere early in high school, I suddenly didn't want to read anything—or listen to anyone—on any subject of importance to me. I was gripped with the fear that I might not be able to have my own thoughts once I listened to someone else's. I started hearing other people's ideas coming out of my mouth. I needed to figure out what *I* thought, and I got very scared that I would have no original ideas.

I changed from the kid who tried to read the Durants' history of philosophy to someone who wanted to decide between George Wallace and Stokely Carmichael with no one else's input. I shocked my history teacher, a liberal Democrat living in that conservative territory, by declaring for Wallace, not wanting to hear his reasons why I was wrong. I really didn't want to know what my teachers thought. Later, when my parents would call me in college, begging me not to get arrested in whichever civil rights protest loomed, I again found myself unwilling to listen. I had to think for myself.

My schooling was in an era when most teaching was rote. My world history teacher didn't bother making us buy the textbook. He required only a small green paperback with the New York State Regents tests of the past 10 years. He pointed out which questions were perennial favorites of the examiners and drilled us on the answers. I never learned who Constantine was, but I still know that C = C, that wherever there is a question about Constantine, the answer will be Christianity. Our English teachers told us what the main idea of every book was, and our "understanding" was tested with multiple-choice and fill-in-the-blank questions. It was only 20 years later, when my English department finals committee was trying to write the four possible answers to "The theme of *Julius Caesar* is . . ." that I seriously questioned the teacher's role in setting a required interpretation of a text. I knew that I resented being told the proper interpretation of just about anything, but it still seemed normal that a teacher would see her pronouncements as legitimate.

In 9th grade, I came to the jarring realization that in rote learning, failure may work better than success; that is, that making an error in a drill was the best way to remember something. I've forgotten most of what I memorized in biology but I'll probably never forget that evaporation is a *cooling* process, because I filled in "heating" on the blank and lost five points. I told the teacher later that I should have received credit for my answer because heating caused liquids to evaporate, and therefore evaporation was a heating process. No, he responded, "the answer is evaporation = cooling, please remember that." I'm still not sure which upset me more: being told I was wrong or hearing the message that my thinking was unnecessary. At any rate, I think now that I came to an accommodation with school: that as long as I could just memorize the answers and didn't have to believe anything in particular, I could do my thinking outside of school, and give the teachers what they seemed to want. I could just forget about explaining my own logic to the biology teacher, and in return I would maintain a good measure of privacy.

Then, for a few months during my junior year, I stopped ignoring my teachers and risked listening to one of them. She was a maverick, of course, and she was fired halfway through the year, ostensibly because she refused to stop wearing her sneakers to school. What lured me into "listening" to her, I think, was that she surrounded us with the real things—real operas playing in the background, real art books full of Michelangelos and Titians, science books with diagrams of airplane engines, real poetry, Plath and Ginsburg and Leroi Jones and Walt Whitman, if my memory is trustworthy. We memorized the beginning verses of *Canterbury Tales* but we didn't have to take a vocabulary quiz on it. She seemed content to let us work, and I'm not sure how, but I'm sure she encouraged us to think. I tried writing that year, and she didn't criticize the silliness of my emerging thinking. But I stopped bothering after she left.

In my high school, we sometimes were told to write in class, usually in answer to an "essay question." Of course, these "essays" were long answers where a phrase wouldn't do, like repeating the economic causes of the Civil War. But once or twice we were asked to write a page-long essay. This frustrated me very much because a few of my friends seemed to know how to write and I didn't, so this was a battle I figured I could not win. As bad as it was for me, my painter friend, a brilliant artist even at age 5 when I first met him, couldn't figure out what a sentence was until late in high school. Caught up in the folk song era, our group all tried to write poetry, and he discovered that he could write lovely poems effortlessly, and that he actually had a great deal to say. This must have been enough to convince him and his teachers that he wasn't dumb after all, and he's probably a perfectly fine writer now—I know he's a great painter. But no teacher I can remember ever really helped either of us learn to write.

I say all this about my own schooling because I am trying to decide whether to accept the label *"teacher."* Do I want to be a teacher? I came to urban teaching with a passion for social justice activism—not for pedagogy or literature or the history I was hired to teach. I was 22 and determined to "work with kids." I didn't think I had much in common with their other teachers and I was very ambivalent about the schools themselves. I didn't believe a school could be respectful to kids of color. Course content excluded them almost completely. Our literature anthology included no one like them in 1971 and the history text was blatantly demeaning. The schools were almost totally segregated racially, and there was a widespread feeling that White teachers were in physical danger in schools like mine. I knew that I wanted very much to assist in the conscientization, the awakening, that was swirling around the urban community in which I worked. I hoped to create something for the young people stuck in the desperately unequal school where I taught that would empower them, equalize something for them. I felt I had to take sides, and I, like many of my generation, was determined to take the side of the students. I had rejected all teaching except the loosest and freest and was very conflicted in the role of teacher, so I decided I would be a teacher, but I wouldn't act like one.

Luckily, I was far from alone. Two thirds of the teachers in my school were under 25, most of us fresh from antiwar or civil rights or lifestyle movements. I had plenty of company; the sides were getting blurred. We were severely criticized for being radicals— "She's a communist, but she works hard," was the way one of my department heads introduced me to everyone—but we did bring a new look to "teacher."

Still, teacher remained a troubling title for me to accept. Even if I could disconnect rote learning from my teaching, the role of teacher was hard to wrench from didacticism and authoritarianism. I still found myself framing everything in the classroom, and setting myself up as an authority in ways I had rejected as a student. I didn't understand it at the time, but now I think that any culture of teachers asking young people questions, even open-ended questions, is potentially a form of rote learning.

Yet the teaching I hear about in professional conferences, even the teaching I see in teacher-hero movies, seems to involve teachers asking questions or, as some say, "setting" the questions. What troubles me about teacher questions, my own as well as those of my colleagues, and the endless barrage of questions in the ever-expanding test culture, is that other people's questions interrupt a person's thoughts and define the mental territory a student is allowed to enter. Just as I don't want to be like my hometown librarian who was tempted to limit what I could read, I am worried that we teachers constantly interrupt the kids' own thinking—to the point where thinking becomes subordinate to, often limited to, guessing what the teacher thinks on the topics that the teacher is thinking about. If this goes on for many years, the K–12 interruption of thought must be truly debilitating. "Think this" and "think about that" are not-so-subtle incursions into a vulnerable, precious mental territory. I might feel that I'm just asking the student to tell me whether she agrees with Morrison about a certain point, but the message of thousands of such guidings cannot help but be, "Stop what you are daydreaming about and think about *this* thing that *I, your teacher*, find important."

I remember clearly that when the writing movement started sweeping over us in the 1980s, we teachers constantly were asking students to state their opinions in class. *What is your opinion of Huckleberry Finn? What is your opinion of Ronald Reagan? What do you think about girls playing professional basketball or becoming fighter pilots?* And so many of my colleagues would lament that many students had no opinions. But my students also would say, "I don't have an opinion on that topic." And we would complain that this writing thing was not going to work because kids would rather fill in blanks than write essays. But what was really happening was that the students were not thinking about their opinion of the book. Each was thinking her own thoughts, and we hadn't been asking, "What do you notice?" We were boxing in the thinking, damming up those streams of thought or honoring only one type of thinking.

Now, 20 years later, I am still in the only job I have ever held, and I have to admit that I am a teacher. After 33 years in this job, it is very hard for me to maintain the separation that I sought when I was 22. In order to reconcile myself to this role, I've tried to cut out aspects of pedagogy that I believe are most injurious to learners. One such deletion is that I've tried to stop asking questions—test questions, homework questions, "raise-your-hand-and-answer-this" questions—and I've tried to make questioning the domain of the learner. Another is that I've tried to make my students responsible for *noticing* what is important in a text. *They* have to find the ideas, the facts, the vocabulary; *they* have to draw the inferences that lead to what's important and what's connected. It doesn't always work. I cannot always resist the impulse to show my students how to think about our text of the day. But when I am truest to my beliefs, I try hard not to interrupt or direct their mental momentum.

Instead of many questions, I try to stick to one basic question: "What do you notice?" Instead of assignments, I have one main activity, aside from reading texts and writing formal papers: "Try to balance your attention between what this particular author says and what your mind says." My job is to provide great texts, to set up situations in which students are pressed to consider problematic and challenging ideas. But my job is not to set either the questions or the answers. And in the best of times, my job may not even be to set the texts.

Has it worked? Have I found a role as teacher that I can both believe in and also believe works? I am not sure, but I try to study my classroom as carefully as I can to find evidence one way or the other. I also ask my former students, many, many of whom I see because I live in the same neighborhood as they do, "What worked for you?" and "What do you still remember?"

Much of the feedback is encouraging, but there is one experience that points up questions I am still pondering. I had a succession of four brothers in my English class, recent immigrants from a country where rote learning reigned, all but one of whom are now medical doctors. The first brother demanded that I "teach" and stop asking him to teach himself. He transferred to another teacher's class, which he greatly preferred to my "noticing" class. The second brother put up with me, grudgingly at first, and seemed by the end of the year to begin to enjoy the freedom to think what he liked. The third brother was several years removed from the old country, and didn't mind that I wouldn't answer all his questions. But at the end of the year, the first draft of his valedictory threw me for a loop. He had written the every-high-school valedictory with no whiff of voice or conviction. It wasn't that he consciously sought to write what he thought would be acceptable to others or what was expected. Rather, he had internalized the most conventional of thoughts—I felt he was thinking other people's thoughts. Six entire versions later, he finally wrote his own thoughts, a personal, challenging, and intelligent speech, and something he later felt was the one high school experience that prepared him to face the rigors of medical school. The fourth brother, a charming young man, had no interest in school, and I found him unreachable as a student.

This family forces me to realize that my own convictions and interests are no sure guide to those of the young people who find their seats in my classes. My fear of being a teacher comes at least partly from my experience as a student, and it is not based on any reliably universal experiences.

It would be silly for me to say that after 33 years teaching in high schools, I am not a teacher. The role grew around me as I grew into it. I accepted some of its generally accepted attributes, while I purposely rejected others—and an objective outsider would, I am certain, report that I did not always choose well. But if I could live up to the standards I wish I could meet, I would say now that there are four things that characterize the teacher I would like to be. I would trust my deepest convictions and base my teachings on them, even when the larger community, and my own employers, disagreed. But I also would study my students carefully, hoping to get the clues that would guide me away from destructive, harmful attitudes and practices, knowing too that students are different and they change. I would try to be critical of my own experience and not generalize it to my students, not ever falling into "it worked for me, so it will work for them," or losing sight of the certainty that as much as I *do* know them, I also *don't* know them and must continue to pay attention. I would try to notice. And last, I would seek the community of others who dare call themselves teachers. I would go back to my hometown teachers and make my peace with them, and I would try to listen to teachers just starting out, and I would see that this job is too hard for any one of us to do well enough alone.

Chapter 4

Who Invited That *Guy?*

Bob Amses

Quiet but fun-loving, it is easy to imagine Bob Amses in a classroom with kids. Although he is serious about many things, he also exudes enthusiasm and playfulness, qualities well-suited to his chosen profession of teaching young people. But Bob was not always a teacher. For years, he was a cameraman, a profession that brought him satisfaction while also giving him the flexibility to spend time with his young children. Yet he had a nagging feeling that this was not all there should be to life. He had been thinking about teaching for a long time, and 5 years ago he decided to take the plunge and immerse himself in a teacher education program to become certified as a teacher. He says that he loved every minute of it: the readings, the discussions in class, the excitement of learning new things. He brought this same energy to his first job as a 4th-grade teacher in a Phoenix public elementary school.

In his essay, Bob writes about the roundabout road that brought him to teaching and the rewards he has already reaped as a result of becoming a teacher just 3 years ago.

"No, I'm not out of my mind!"

That became my stock answer to the question of why I became a teacher, and, believe me, I had a lot of explaining to do in the summer of 2000, when I was gently nudged into my new profession by ripples of change so tiny that I barely noticed it happening. I'd spent more than 20 years in the television/film industry as a cameraman, and all of a sudden I realized that my life had become incompatible with my career. Everything was suddenly complicated. I felt spread too thinly over the many areas my life had expanded into since becoming a husband and father. As my children grew into elementary school age, they became more involved in sports and social activities. I started missing too many of those "can't miss" events that I swore I'd never miss when I became a dad. As I hung up the phone in some hotel room in Florida after my daughter shared the experiences of her first day in kindergarten, an overwhelming feeling of disconnection made me take a hard look at what I really wanted from life.

I had a very cool job. As a documentary cameraman, I did a lot of traveling and had the pleasure of meeting fascinating people and exploring interesting social and physical phenomena. Each documentary was a wonderful learning experience for me—sort of the, "Gee, I never realized that . . . " feeling you get when you see a good PBS or Discovery Channel documentary, but even better because I got to see it all firsthand. I also worked as an assistant cameraman and camera operator on movies, TV shows, and commercials. The hours were long and the conditions were often tough, but I was doing what I'd wanted to do ever since I was a child. I was making good money and excited about my work.

So what happened? It would be easy to say that things changed, but that's a little too clichéd and simply not the case. The events in my life just ran their course like they do for all of us, but over time I had changed, my priorities had shifted, and I found myself on shaky emotional ground. I realized a couple of things. First, there is a big difference between what I do for a living and who I am as a person. This epiphany occurred somewhat abruptly as I realized that my life had become a balancing act, and the equilibrium between my professional duties and my responsibilities as a parent had become increasingly difficult to maintain. I felt that I was constantly choosing between my job and my family, and I became reluctant to accept projects that took me away from my wife and kids. As a freelancer, I really couldn't afford the luxury of turning down projects unless I had a really good reason. And so the simple ringing of the telephone took on new and disturbing implications. What had once been the sound of opportunity knocking had become the knell of potential separation. I was missing the picnics, puzzles, bike rides, soccer games, and all those other daddy things because when work was offered, I was compelled to take it. My saving grace was that I never lost sight of the fact that I had options, and I considered several. But there was one that was just so obvious to me that my decision was nearly immediate: teaching.

I never thought I'd end up teaching, especially after spending about half my life in another career that I really enjoyed. But I've never second-guessed myself because I'm just following my interests, and that's what life is all about. My experiences over the past 10 years have profoundly altered my views of who I am and what my possibilities are. Becoming a father marked the beginning of my foray into teaching, years before I ever consciously considered taking on the task of "educating" young people. What I've witnessed in my own children's development provides the foundation for everything I do in the classroom, and my lifelong experiences as a learner have sharpened my perspective of the teacher/student equation.

With teaching, I'd found that elusive *something* that challenged me intellectually, philosophically, emotionally, physically, and as I'd find out too late, financially! But the important thing is that with one simple decision I'd restored order to my life. My 10-year-old son and 8-year-old daughter took me shopping for a new backpack with lots of cool compartments for books, pens, and pencils, and sent me back to college.

And I can't even begin to tell you how much we all enjoyed the experience. I loved my classes, I loved researching and writing papers, I loved the concepts and terminology, I loved practicum work in classrooms, and best of all, I loved having homework because I could pull up a chair next to my children and we'd all work together. My wife was totally supportive (except for introducing me as "my husband Bob, who's going through his midlife crisis"), and I'll always remember the dinners she'd make and deliver to me when I was chained to the computer or immersed in reading. The excitement of changing direction in life was not lost on me at all, and it was both thrilling and personally rewarding to rebuild my skills and knowledge for the new challenge.

This much I do know: Life is funny because we may travel different routes but we arrive at the same place. I've been told that I entered the schoolhouse through one of the side doors, and that's a pretty fair judgment. I never had great ambition to be a teacher. My previous work experience did little to prepare me for teaching. My formal education wasn't exactly suited to teaching. Yet here I am, feeling more and more comfortable in this new role because it seems to be evolving at precisely the same rate that I'm growing into it. That's cool.

I consider my greatest strength as a teacher to be precisely what many perceive as my greatest liability: I'm an outsider. And I hope I stay that way because my lack of traditional teaching experience has allowed me to model my approach to learning on a lifetime of real-world experience and observations of people learning the skills and information they need to be successful in their chosen endeavors.

Learning is a survival skill that comes naturally to us. Learning is change, and change comes in all shapes and sizes: baby step, quantum leap, fine-tuning, and complete transformation. Change also can be either positive or negative, and sometimes it's difficult to make that distinction. As a teacher I try to never stray too far from the idea that I am in a position to help people make themselves more capable, that my students "change" over our time together, and that my attitudes and behaviors significantly contribute to those changes.

Of course, I'm kidding myself if I honestly think that everything I do makes kids somehow "better," because I'll be the first to admit I've had some real disasters! There have been days and even weeks when I've had to confront my failure to contribute to positive change in my classroom. I presented information poorly, or I chose an activity that didn't achieve the desired objectives, or my mismanagement foiled my own best intentions. But freeing myself from this twisted wreckage underscores precisely what I love about teaching: Through my mistakes, I learn how to be better.

Over my short experience as a teacher, the most important lesson I've learned from my interactions with students, parents, colleagues, and administrators sounds like anathema, yet it is the key to my survival and growth. It's *not* all about the kids. Sure, it's *mostly* about the kids, but to deny the existence of teachers' physical, emotional, and intellectual balance as vital components of the education equation is short-sighted, naive, and even dangerous.

I'm the father of two wonderful children, and I want my kids to have teachers who aren't afraid to try new ideas, teachers who impart the value of their own life experience into the education process, and teachers who are excited about what they do. Teachers are role models, and kids spend a lot of time observing who we are and how we operate. If our greatest hope is that they become lifelong learners, then that's exactly what *we* need to be. The process has got to be rewarding for all of us. We need to grow and develop as a result of the choices we make, and it's absolutely crucial that we each identify our strengths and use them to maximize our potential, while at the same time realistically and pragmatically confronting our shortcomings. This is what learning is all about, and this is what excites me about teaching.

I consider myself a very lucky guy because when circumstances in my life called for change at *precisely* the moment that change proved most transforming and liberating, I was able to make the move. I got hired immediately after completing my studies. The principal may have wondered whether she'd fallen short of her goal of hiring "a mature male teacher" when I giggled as I was handed my very own set of keys to the school, but she'd already signed the papers. Too late—I was in!

A 4th-grade class had been created for me from three overcrowded existing classrooms, and I was hired right after Thanksgiving. I had 3 days to get ready, and I remember the very first thing I did when I arrived in my classroom on Saturday morning. I made sure no one was around before dimming the lights and playing with *my very own overhead projector.* I'm not kidding. Overhead calculator ... Wow! Overhead pattern blocks ... Cool! Overhead dice? ... No way! Within an hour, I had the whole family in there playing with all my cool stuff.

And to this day my excitement hasn't waned. Whenever the supplies arrive from the district warehouse, I tear into them like it's Christmas morning. Felt-tipped pens in three different colors, white board markers in both primary and pastel tones, industrial strength hole-punches and electric pencil sharpeners are just a few of my most prized possessions. I even go to OfficeMax on weekends to scope out exciting new colors in index cards, file folders, and Post-it notes. Yeah, I think my transition is complete.

Now that I've been at it for a little more than 2 years, it's interesting to compare my expectations going in with the realities I've confronted on the job. I should've known better. In teaching, expectations are a moving target, or a set of moving targets. I'm surprised at how little I was prepared for the actual day-to-day operation of the classroom. This was no longer just volunteering in the classroom, or interning for college credit, or student teaching. No one was there to hold my hand, or prop me up when I got wobbly. I had all my grand ideas ready: *Individualized, student-driven learning?* Check! *Real-life application?* Got it! *Emphasis on higher order thinking?* I'm all over it!

And . . . it was a complete disaster! No pace, no rhythm, students either bored stiff or running around the room hurting themselves and one another. Oh, the humanity! There I was, clipboard in hand, "Good morning class, and which five of you will be spilling hazardous chemicals on your partners during science today? Got it, thank you. Excuse me, Jarrett, I don't think William *likes* his head pinned between the door and the wall like that, and I think he'd tell you how it makes him feel *if only he could breathe.*"

It bottomed out on February 14, 2002. *The St. Valentine's Day Massacre* is what I've called it ever since. The kids were perfectly behaved for the first hour of school, and then they asked if they could have their candy. They presented a compelling case: The *other* teachers *always* let them have their candy early in the morning so that "we don't lose our appetites and miss out on a healthy lunch." Oh, of course, they must be right, I thought. So I let them have their candy. By the time the parents showed up at 11:00 for the official celebration, an entire table of kids had chocolate smeared all over their clothes, two kids were slumped in the corner crying, a couple of desks had been dumped over, and the floor was covered with candy wrappers and crumpled up valentines. And all this happened during math! But that was only the beginning. By the end of the day, the casualty list had grown to about 16, including three who vomited (two after eating a *healthy lunch*), and another three who never even made it to lunch and were taken home (hopefully, they vomited there) by their parents at the conclusion of the party. Two of my students spent the afternoon in the nurse's office, and I caught one kid sleeping off his chocolate hangover under a table during afternoon reading time.

If you were to come into my classroom today, you'd still see it tacked up on the wall as a reminder. The lesson plans for February 14, 2002, obscured by a huge red X, and in gigantic red letters the single word that explains to the world my Valentine's Day policy for all eternity, "NO!"

Somehow I survived, but survival demanded that my "system" evolve at a harrowing pace, with the absolute highest priority being that I went into each day prepared with enough work to keep the students busy for 7 hours. It worked, but it wasn't very good for them or for me, and that's NOT how I'd imagined myself as a teacher. More than a little demoralized, I resigned myself to the fact that my own utopian ideals were the first victims of my regime!

As I've gained experience, however, I recognize that I never abandoned my ideals at all. I just had to shove them out of the way for awhile so I could survive the transition. I learned an important lesson almost immediately: *Be yourself.* Teaching is an interactive, interpersonal experience that requires personality and communication. Initially, I tried to emulate the methods of my colleagues and I failed miserably. If I have any hopes of connecting with my students and helping kids connect with their world, I've got to be myself and do things my way. Teaching is based on trust, and when students see me as a real person who genuinely wants them to succeed, strong bonds are formed. On the other hand, if I'm "acting" as the teacher, the kids "act" as students, and a host of stereotypical behaviors present themselves. I think that's one of the reasons that first year was so tough. Our insecurities sometimes can get the better of us, and we're just too willing to take too much advice from well-intentioned colleagues helping us get through. Unfortunately, this keeps us from learning valuable lessons on our own. It's great to have the support of colleagues, but growing into the job requires that we experience the confusion and disorientation that force us to prioritize, build on our successes, and develop a system that works.

Coaching sports was a devotion of mine long before I began teaching, and the similarities between coaching and teaching were central to my decision to become a teacher. As a result, my philosophy of teaching and learning is founded on many of the same principles that govern coaching. When I combined these ideas with the fact that so much learning and development take place in the absence of "teaching," I began to explore the many ways teachers support learning beyond direct instruction. I came up with a system for the classroom that is completely reflective of my philosophy of "teacher as coach."

I've explored the analogy, and the deeper I go, the better it seems to fit. Every school year is like a new season, and each year I have goals and objectives that determine my broad strategies for the year. I can go into the year with a "template," but I can't get too specific until I'm introduced to my personnel. Over the first 3 or 4 weeks of school, I evaluate and assess students to determine strengths and weaknesses, and establish some kind of starting point for my "team" as well as each of my "players."

The real "season" starts about a month after school begins. The first units in all the content areas have been completed, and I've collected a lot of data that indicate how my team shakes out. This is like the first couple of games of the season. After this phase of the season, the template really starts to come together as I adjust goals based on actual performance, and I modify instructional practices to effectively achieve the new goals.

Sometime before mid-season, it becomes obvious that the team either has a shot at the championship, has a chance to make the playoffs, or is mired in one of those "rebuilding" years. By this time, the coach knows his personnel and program inside out and can really go to work to maximize the season's outcomes. This is the most important time of the year because the template is matched to the team's personnel and expectations.

From mid-season until the end of the year, the team can operate at maximum efficiency because its members are executing a template designed specifically for them. Identifying their strengths, applying those strengths to realistic team goals, and increasing the proficiencies of each individual in relation to personal goals—that is a blueprint for a successful school year.

As a teacher, I'm doing everything I can to establish and maintain an environment in which students can grow, explore, and create. I nurture understanding and compassion between the students, and also between adults and students. I want kids to feel safe and to take chances with their learning, secure in their understanding that curiosity is a perfectly natural impulse. Sometimes that leads us down the wrong path, but even that's a learning experience because we get answers to our questions. I treat my students as capable human beings in search of knowledge and experience. My conversations with them go beyond "teacher talk" and get to the core of who we are as people. It's meaningful dialogue and productive discourse. I give them free rein to take advantage of every learning opportunity that comes along either in or out of school.

But when it comes to learning, that's their deal entirely. And here's where the true essence of the coaching analogy hits home. I can't "learn" for them any more than the coach can go out to the mound and pitch for his team. I apply whatever expertise I have directly to those areas we've identified as opportunities for growth. I provide perspective, that other set of eyes that "see" what the student may have difficulty perceiving. I encourage and motivate with observations and feedback. But ultimately I have to get out of the way and let my students develop the tools that will make them lifelong learners.

The greatest thing I can do for my students is to place the responsibility for learning squarely in their hands. Watching young people grow and find their depth is another incredibly gratifying benefit I've derived from teaching. The most compelling sense of closure to our brief time together doesn't show up on any tests or score sheets or essay booklets. There's just something in the eyes of each and every one of the kids that tells me that I made a difference. Some kids come right out and say thank you, and that melts me every time. But whether or not a single word is exchanged in parting, that look in their eyes reflects the power and purpose they've created within themselves. I glimpse a little piece of the future as they walk out the door. Deep within my being, I know that my eyes are giving me away too, because I'll emerge far better for the experience.

I teach because teaching is connection, and connection is definitely a two-way street. Learning unleashes incredible force, and not only am I energized by that, but I want to know *why* it happens and *how* we can consistently create the conditions to make it happen again and again. Teaching challenges me on every level and forces me to concentrate my abilities and energies to see what kinds of incredible outcomes are possible. Teaching presents me

with fascinating problems to solve, and complex personnel param-
eters to manage over the long and short term. Teaching requires
that I experiment with a multitude of variables and build a program
that produces results. Teaching might just be the highest order I'll
evolve to, and I'm okay with that because I've barely scratched the
surface. I feel like I'm in that transcendent frame of mind where
every answer I produce uncovers only more questions to explore,
and who knows where that will lead?

Chapter *5*

On Re-Becoming a Teacher

Laila M. Di Silvio

aila Di Silvio is a creative and committed teacher, but before becoming a teacher, she was a Peace Corps volunteer in Zambia where she focused on community health education. It was through this experience that her initial goal of becoming a teacher was ignited once again. Laila returned to graduate school to get her certification, more convinced than ever that she was meant to be a teacher. For the past 3 years she has worked in urban schools, first a high school and now a middle school, teaching history and social studies. She also has been an advisor to Gay/Lesbian/Bisexual/Transgender (GLBT) students at these schools.

The past 2 years have been filled with dramatic personal changes in Laila's life, both painful and joyful, changes that made teaching even more challenging than usual. In her essay, Laila reflects on what her students have taught her and how they have helped sustain her. She also describes why she chose teaching in the first place, why she has re-committed herself to it, and how she came to realize that teaching, although enormously significant and meaningful in her life, could not become her entire life.

It is disheartening. Roscoe is suspended again. He is the student my husband hears the most about this year. I can't help it, I take his stories home. Often they are actually quite funny, but lately they have been full of frustration, both Roscoe's and mine.

Roscoe constantly makes me ask myself the question I struggle with most as a teacher: When is one student's behavior just too much to tolerate? The special education teacher on my team maintains that the answer is when you can't get through your lesson. Sometimes I don't get through my lesson because of Roscoe. Recently, I have been taking a hard-line approach. It seems to have been working and Roscoe has mostly good days in my room. His grades have started to reflect his new attitude. About a week ago though, Roscoe decided to hurl his eraser at another boy in the class. He missed his target and hit another unsuspecting child. I don't think he knew I saw him. I wasn't meant to see him; for once it wasn't a ploy for my attention.

As a teacher, I've learned not to take things personally. It would be just too hard and I would burn out within a few years. Besides, what my students need most is a steady, consistent adult in their lives, preferably one with a big heart. Yet I was especially disappointed with Roscoe's behavior that day. We had spent a great afternoon after school just the day before. Roscoe and Antonio, who often gets into trouble himself, had voluntarily stayed for extra help. They worked hard and we had extra time to just chat. These two boys, who drive me nuts some days, are in love with Harry Potter. They are too cool to carry backpacks to school, but they insist on reading Harry Potter books secretly. I love seeing new sides of students, and this discovery made me incredibly happy.

So I decided to share my dilemma with Roscoe and Antonio. I too was addicted to Harry Potter and had devoured the first book. I had the third book of the series in my possession and was anxious to jump in. I explained to them that I knew that I should go to the library to find the second book but I just couldn't wait. They were horrified that I was contemplating skipping the second book! But they empathized with my plight. It was the very next day that Roscoe threw the eraser. What can you do?

I worried the entire 3 days that Roscoe was out of school. I didn't even particularly enjoy the relative calm in my classroom. I suspect, however, that my students did. Many of them like it when it is quiet. As I said earlier, it is a question that I often wrestle with: When are the actions of one individual student just too much?

Students often come back from suspension especially unruly. They have been cooped up for 3 days, unable to talk to anyone, forced to sit at the same desk, and even required to eat lunch in the same room. I know I wouldn't like it very much. So I was concerned with how Roscoe might behave when rejoining our class. All I could do was wait and see what a new day would bring. When he returned, Roscoe motioned to me at my door during homeroom. He wanted to speak to me privately. As it turned out, he had been thinking about me too. He had brought me his copy of the second Harry Potter book to borrow. It was a marvelous moment.

I loved reading that second book as little clues about Roscoe's life popped out from the pages. Using his museum stub as a bookmark reminded me that there is a lot more to students than what I see daily in my classroom. Will Roscoe and I have run-ins again? I'm sure we will. But it is these small steps forward that I relish and that keep me teaching.

I love my students as unique individuals. It may take me awhile to open my heart, but to date I have been able to love them all. When I began teaching, I had thought that my educational philosophy and will to make a difference would be my driving force. I had not yet realized that my students, not as a group but as individuals with distinct stories, would give me the impetus to continue teaching.

I am not sure when I knew that I wanted to become a teacher. For me it was definitely a process. I come from a family of educators so perhaps teaching has always been a part of my reality. I do remember after my first semester in college going back to visit one of my favorite teachers. I told him that I wanted to become a teacher. Without mincing his words, he told me he thought this a very bad idea. In his estimation, teaching was a terrible profession to enter. He thought I was too young to make this decision. And so, for a few years, I took a different course.

Post college, I joined the Peace Corps, in the public health sector, working alongside mothers and their young children to promote good health practices. While a volunteer, I had lots of time for reflection, introspection, and self-growth. It was a wonderful time in my life. I realized that I enjoyed the educator in "Community Health Educator" a whole lot more than the health part. So after more than 3 years in Zambia, I decided to go back to graduate school to become a teacher. My disenchanted high school teacher actually gave me a huge gift. By temporarily changing my course, I came to teaching with the knowledge that I was *consciously* choosing to teach rather than merely falling into the profession. This knowledge helps me day in and day out to stay strong. And teaching has never been easy. If it ever were to become easy, then I probably would be in the wrong place.

It was thus with a bit more world experience as well as the visceral feeling that I was in the right place that I came into teaching. I relish the title *teacher*. It is an honor to be entrusted with the education of so many children. And it is the little indications that I am getting through to a student that keep me going day to day. When I step back, I realize how lucky I am. The fact that I have the ability to make a real difference in a child's life, is amazing. However, I also fear the repercussions of saying something that might really hurt a child. That I have this power scares me. I am only human; I have bad days too.

I often have thought about writing an essay on learning how to teach. I would call it "Teaching with Latirah."

Latirah was a student in my "F" period class. This group was filled with some pretty smart, although not necessarily book smart, students. Refusing to sign her first-quarter progress report, she threw it on the floor. I was totally unprepared for her actions. I tried to cajole her, but after one or two attempts, I picked up her progress report from the floor and taught my lesson. I needed more time to decide what to do. Finally, I opted to go to Latirah's counselor, a man I knew she liked. I didn't want to go to her assistant principal, as it was too early in the year to lose her. When the counselor talked with Latirah, she repeated what she had told me. She said she wasn't a "D student" and that was why she would not sign her progress report. In the end, Latirah agreed to sign her progress report, but only after vocalizing that she was going to show me that she was a "B student." True to her word, Latirah earned a B that quarter.

About February that same year, I had another sticky situation with Latirah. We were working in groups; I don't even remember the project. But I do remember she was irate with me. She declined to work in the group I had assigned. Every muscle in her body was engaged in her refusal. I ignored her for awhile and got the other groups going. Then I asked to speak to her privately in the hall. Latirah told me she thought I was picking on her. She felt I had put her in a "slow" group intentionally because I thought she was "stupid." I became angry myself. I raised my voice, incensed that it didn't occur to her that I thought she was "smart" and a "leader" and that is precisely why I put her in that group. Latirah barely looked at me. Given her options of taking an F or participating in the project, she decided to go back and join her group. But she did so only after shedding one huge, round, silent tear.

Latirah had so much spirit and I feared that I had cracked it. I went home that night feeling I had done something horribly wrong. I spent a sleepless night agonizing over my every word. I replayed that scene at least a hundred times, regal Latirah shedding a tear before choosing to work with her "stupid" group.

Latirah did become the group leader and her group got an A. I am still not sure I did the right thing, but Latirah and I reached a tentative understanding that day in the hall, and the rest of the year went more smoothly. I knew she was constantly aware of what I was doing and watching my every move. She smiled when I planned an activity that helped engage our demanding class. She continued to voice discontent when she disagreed with my actions, but we never had another escalation of tempers. I think that out there in the hall she saw that I was human too, and in a pivotal moment decided that I cared.

Latirah made me a better teacher. She forced me to reflect on my teaching practices. As a result, I made some visible changes, but many more took place inside my heart and mind. I rarely assign groups anymore. It is just too dangerous. I learned that students read my hidden subtext and that what they read is not always the intended message. I've decided that, for groupwork, it is best to draw individual popsicle sticks, each with a student's name on it. Students thus see that groups are formed randomly and fairly. "Fair" is a very important word, especially now that I am in the middle school. I don't think I have to treat every student the same to be fair. Doing so, in fact, would be quite inequitable. But I do need to convey that I care about each and every student. I work hard to achieve this goal. In wanting to address each student's needs, I constantly face the same question: When is one child's need for attention a detriment to the learning of his or her peers?

A current student of mine, Shawn, stayed with me after school the other day for extra help. He almost never speaks in class unless

I ask a direct question, and then his hand might shoot up. His grades had been progressively slipping throughout the quarter and he was looking at a D+ on his progress report. I have to confess, I hadn't even noticed that his grades had slipped so drastically. Shawn talked for the entire hour and a half we were together. It seems he had been dying to talk to somebody about school, the movies he wanted to see, his family, and so on. I never would have known this need had he not stayed after school and been so willing to speak. We smile at each other every day now and I make a point of catching his eye at the start of class. I try to go around the room and smile at each of my 100 plus students daily. How many Shawns are there in each of my classes?

I am now in my third year of teaching and each year has gotten easier. I don't think I will ever forget some of the characters from my first year of teaching. I dreamt nightly about my students that year, well into July. Latirah featured prominently in my dreams as did Travis, a boy who slept, not literally but figuratively, through most of his classes. He was always just so exhausted. There were no medical issues, at least none that were known. It seemed that it was the weight of life that slowed Travis down. But one day he woke up.

I remember clearly the turnaround. We were discussing the use of mascots in sports teams, and I had invited some guest speakers to address the issue. He did not view the racial stereotyping of American Indians as pernicious; to him, these mascots were just funny. On the other hand, when he saw fictional caricatures of the "Chicago Chicanos" or the "Washington Whities" in class, he perceived them as blatantly racist. It concerned him that he, someone who identified as both African American and Cherokee, might be slighting one of his cultures. He asked our guest speakers tons of questions to try to understand why this was. For weeks, he would bring up the concept of "dysconscious racism," a term coined by Joyce King that I had introduced them to. According to King, dysconscious racism is a form of internalized racism that tacitly accepts the status quo. In other words, it is a type of unconscious racism that results from a failure to question the validity of White norms and privileges.[1] This became a powerful concept for Travis.

Travis also started coming to visit after school. He asked me to write him a letter of recommendation for a summer program that targeted 9th graders who would be the first in their families to go to college. His other teachers noticed a difference too. Who knows if this change would have happened without the words and stories of my guest speakers that day? Teaching can be so powerful and it is our students who channel this power.

Even in my short tenure as a teacher, I have already had a truly "off year." My second year of teaching made me question what I was doing. In retrospect, I think I shut down when my father was diagnosed with cancer. It became all-consuming and I didn't let many people in. I sort of drifted through last spring, probably doing a reasonable job, but without very much feeling. Because I was going through the motions but failing to nourish the relationships I had built with my students throughout the year, my classroom began to feel lifeless. I chose to do a lot of reflection over the summer. I remember it was with some relief that I read Tracy Kidder's book *Among Schoolchildren*[2] about a local, urban, passionate teacher. I really related with the central character and I took notice that she too had had a bad year. I also re-read my students' summative evaluations about our school year. I was touched by their honesty and the adjectives they picked to describe me. They let me know that I was strict but also fair. Through their eyes I was "positive," "fun," and "intelligent," qualities I aspire to. As always, it was my students who helped me remember why I teach.

I decided to give myself a break and I returned to teaching this year with an open heart. I have not had an easy year. In the space of 3 weeks my father passed away, I got married, and my husband and I moved into a new apartment. I had to miss a lot of school this fall. Yet, I think this roller coaster ride has made me a better teacher. For one, I let my students in. I never attempted to burden them with my issues but I did try to be honest and candid. They responded in kind, not prying but leaving many little clues that they cared. One student drew me a gigantic poster of a lion. On it she wrote that drawing helps her feel better when she is down and that she hoped that her drawing would make me feel better too. It was endearing to find these cards and notes hidden among the piles of paper on my desk.

Returning to the same classroom this year, I have had the pleasure of seeing last year's students all grown up. It is a gift to continue to have a peephole into students' individual lives, if from a different vantage point. Sometimes, I am glad I am no longer their teacher but I still enjoy checking in. Francesca and Lauren are doing a History Day project on a theme we debated in class last year. Keishawn's dad continues to get called into school, but Keishawn is no longer the jumpy boy who could not stay in his seat. Abe sends his condolences about my father on the part of all my former students. Dolores shyly ask me if I changed my name when I got married and if I would bring my husband to the school dance. Demaris demands to know why I never ate lunch at her table last year.

I feel proud, sad, happy, and amused with my students' words and actions. But the important thing is that I feel again. In a middle school, one year can make a huge difference. It certainly has for me. I am clear again about why I teach.

As I suspected, my relationship with Roscoe continued to be a tumultuous one. Compared with what I knew he was going through at home, his classroom antics seemed mild. He was moved into emergency foster care, a common occurrence in his life. Roscoe did not make it through the year. By March, he was spending up to three periods daily in my room; he had been asked to leave other classrooms as a result of his unruly behavior. While not always an angel during our own class periods together, Roscoe seemed to accept a tacit agreement that he could spend additional time in my room provided he complied with my class rules. But he could not hold it together for the entire school year. Roscoe threatened another teacher, for which he received a 30-day suspension.

I never saw Roscoe again, as an extended family member came back into the picture and moved him to a neighboring community. I would like to think that maybe he got a fresh start at his new school, but realistically I accept that it may prove to be yet another disjointed chapter in his unstable life. Roscoe will have to forge new relationships all over again and it is my hope that in doing so, he will win his way into another teacher's heart.

Chapter 6

Waiting Tables and Juggling Motherhood: Taking the Road Less Traveled

PATTY BODE

Patty Bode never stops: Always in action, she is a whirlwind of activity whether in her art classroom, helping to organize a Latino art exhibit or her middle school's yearly assemblies to commemorate African American History Month and Women's History Day, presenting a workshop about her research at a national conference, or cooking a meal for a sick friend. In addition to this dizzying display of energy, Patty also has taught  undergraduate and graduate courses at a number of colleges and universities and, for 9 years, was the director of a highly regarded summer arts camp.

Patty's incredible vigor—what her colleagues call "Patty Bode energy"—is immense, but it's not just her energy that is impressive. Most impressive is that it is focused in the service of a commitment to young people, the ideals of social justice, and a profound belief in the power of the arts to nurture the lives of all human beings.

Patty's art classroom is the epitome of an antiracist and multicultural space. This is not a once-a-month activity for her; instead, every lesson is imbued with it. To do this, she is engaged in constant research and learning,

49

thinking about not only how to make her lessons appealing in artistic terms, but also how to engage all her students—who are from many different backgrounds—to become more open, more comfortable with difference, and more willing to take a stand for justice.

For the past 6 years, I have been an art teacher in a public middle school. Prior to that, I was an elementary school art teacher, a day care provider, and the director of a summer arts camp. Each endeavor holds its own set of objectives and challenges, but my motivation and passion are consistent. Despite the tragedies and inequities the world offers, my students and I find ways to learn while we are laughing, and we always go back tomorrow, to learn more.

My students bring fully who they are to my art room every day—that is why I teach. We make art together while they generously laugh at my jokes, announce a baby sister's birth, worry about our government's decisions, wonder which foster home they will stay in tonight, study for bar mitzvahs, dream of pro basketball careers, and all the while, try so desperately to fit in. Listening to one another's humanity in all our similarities and differences motivates our art making and learning, and my teaching.

Growing up in an urban neighborhood in a big Irish-Catholic family of seven sisters, two brothers, and what seemed to be countless aunts, uncles, and cousins, taught me that life is never very orderly or predictable (great preliminary training for an art teacher). My mother kept a chalkboard near the kitchen sink so she could drill us on our phonics, handwriting, and multiplication tables while she was scrubbing potatoes and dishes. From a very early age, academic achievement was linked in my mind to my mother's singing, scolding, praising, and praying. She instilled in each of us high expectations, respect for teachers, and a deep, passionate love of learning. I distinctly remember arguing with my sisters about who would get to be teacher when we played school—and now three of us are career public school educators.

I had this exchange regarding school and teachers with my dad on a weekly basis. He would ask:

"Did you go to school today?"

"Yes."

"Did you learn anything?"

"No—nothing really."

"Then I guess you have to go back tomorrow!"

I fell for this repetitive joke week after week. Despite my empty response (he still relishes the memory), I loved school as a child. The classroom always made sense to me. I knew what to expect, yet it was full of surprises. Now, from the perspective of a teacher, my dad's joke emphasizes that we don't always know when we are learning. Of course, this is not an original idea. John Dewey often said that we learn not simply by *doing* but by reflecting on what we do. It took awhile for this idea to sink in, but I figured out that some of my most important learning happened when I didn't know I was learning. I learned as much from the memories as I did from the experience.

In the whirlwind of daily chores, homework, family meals, quarrels, and corny jokes, I found visual art as a way to make sense of the tragedies, joys, and menial moments of childhood. After the nightly rituals of dinner, dishes, and homework, I would sneak down to the basement and open my paints (purchased with my paper route money) to explore color, brushstroke, dimension, and drawing. While exploration was fruitful, I craved instruction in drawing technique and color theory. Later, in my teenage years, that craving was filled by dedicated teachers.

I remember every teacher from elementary through high school. Most of my so-called art classes in elementary school consisted of construction paper and scissors, often with a holiday theme on a Friday afternoon. The first time I actually had an "official" art class in my Catholic school education was in 7th grade, with Ms. Schumacher, who also taught English and Spanish. She was magical. On the first day of art class, she asked what we knew about color. Then she explained the difference between color as light and color as pigment, pointing out the science and the poetry in the concept. She wore colorful long skirts and wild earrings. She had curly black hair past her hips and she laughed a lot.

Sometime in 7th grade, with Ms. Schumacher in art class and Mr. Murphy in religion class, I made the connection between my ideas, my art, my expression, and my visual world. Ms. Schumacher assigned an art project in which we were to express our beliefs. At the same time, Mr. Murphy assigned a project for religion class in which we were to connect our beliefs to our everyday world. My beliefs, like so many young people's, were shaped by the socio-political context of my environment. Throughout my youth, my family's financial struggles paralleled the labor struggles of my father's career in the fire department. The Vietnam War had dominated my childhood. I was in 3rd grade when both Dr. Martin Luther King, Jr. and Senator Robert Kennedy were assassinated. In my 5th-grade year, the Kent State shootings, just 40 miles from my home, killed four students, permanently paralyzed one, and injured eight others. My junior high school years unfolded in the Nixon era.

In response to Ms. Schumacher's assignment for my 7th-grade art class, I created a collage with painting, drawing, text, and photos from news media. One of the photos was from the Kent State shootings, of Mary Vecchio as she kneeled over the bleeding body of Jeffrey Miller as photographed by KSU student John Filo. (That AP photo, reproduced countless times in the popular press and media, also hung on my mom's kitchen bulletin board for years.) It was a piece of the visual culture of my childhood, my geographic region, my family's politics, and the startling reality of misguided government actions. I also used the art project—with the permission of both teachers—for part of my religion class project. It was my first, albeit unintentional, integrated curriculum design. I felt the power of using art and academic work to connect my visual, political, social, and spiritual worlds. For me, that project connected art making with understanding and using art for social justice, and it continues as a thread in why I teach: to provide students with the tools for reshaping, revisioning, and recreating their worlds.

Of course, not every piece of junior high art was a revelation. In addition to my struggle to paint my ideas, questions, and beliefs, I also painted plenty of sunflowers and impressionistic landscapes. I was trying out realism, abstraction, expressionism, and political commentary, and I also was inventing my own methods along the way.

For quite some time it seemed unlikely that I would transition from standing in front of a painted canvas to standing in front of a classroom. I took a circuitous route to become a teacher. It took me 13 years to achieve my bachelor's degree and teaching certification. In what is now sociocultural hindsight, I see that in an attempt to negotiate my working-class background with my college aspirations, I became a mother while I was still an undergraduate student.

After my first 2 years of art school, I briefly entered and exited a too youthful marriage and gave birth to my first son. With an unending well of moral support from my family, as a young, single mother I struggled to complete college. While re-entering college part-time, I took my first position in public schools as a paraprofessional in a special needs classroom. I was awestruck by the teacher, Mrs. Joan Tonelli, who to this day is the model of patience and commander of high expectations for every child in her classroom in Cleveland Heights, Ohio. I wanted to be like her. In Mrs. Tonelli's class, I lived the daily routines and miracles of school life in a classroom for children with autism. Mrs. Tonelli's talents had an enduring effect on my classroom practice.

During the time that I worked in Mrs. Tonelli's class, I also was waiting tables and juggling motherhood. I met Mark, my spouse (now of 22 years), and we married and added one more child to our family. In between restaurant work and parenthood, I continued my education, one course at a time, at Kent State. After moving our family to Massachusetts and 13 years of undergraduate work at three different institutions, while under the tutelage of many professors who believed in me in spite of my somewhat chaotic life, I graduated from the University of Massachusetts with a BFA and a teaching certificate in art education. The motivation to achieve that certification was fueled by my teachers along the way; my mom and dad, Ms. Schumacher, Mr. Murphy, Mrs. Tonelli, and far too many more to name.

All these teachers created a space where students who were afraid, feel safe, become confident, and find out how much more there is to know. These were qualities that I aspired to instill in my students. However, while creating a sense of safety is essential to learning, and nurturing curiosity is central to teaching, there was something much more tangible I learned from these individuals. I knew from my own struggles to develop skills in my childhood basement that young artists need the keys to unlock their skills. It is the effort and tenacity of my students to develop skills and expand their critical thinking that are rooted in the heart of my classroom.

I teach to help students develop skills to express themselves and deliver the message they want to convey. Every child I have ever met from kindergarten through high school has wanted to increase his or her skills, whether the medium is crayon wax or digital software. Yet skill development in isolation can be mechanical and emptyhearted. Drawing on my memory of Mr. Murphy's assignment to connect my beliefs to my everyday world, since my early years of teaching art I have worked to integrate skill development with student voice, social awareness, and multicultural, antiracist goals.

One story that illustrates my efforts toward these goals started when I was teaching a landscape lesson in a 4th-grade art class. Two boys, Andrew and Damon, were sharing a paint tray. I demonstrated a minilesson to the class about mixing tints and shades of color, emphasizing the importance of arriving at their own decisions for color combinations. The lesson was going smoothly; the air was filled with the audible "creative hum" of a productive classroom of self-directed, motivated students. Then Andrew and Damon started a little competition about whose tree paintings were "better." Andrew started chanting: "My color is better than Damon's color, my color is better than Damon's color, my color is better than Damon's color . . . "

While I was making my way across the room to intervene, I was shocked to see Damon leap and tackle Andrew to the floor. I pulled the boys apart before anybody was seriously hurt, but before sending them to the principal's office, I escorted them to my red carpet square, our "problem-solving spot" in the room. There, everybody gets to take turns speaking, uninterrupted. While Andrew was brushing off his pants and giving Damon the evil eye, Damon fought back tears to tell me: "Andrew was making fun of my color. He was teasing me about my skin."

Andrew indignantly protested. "I was not! I was teasing, yeah, but not about that—I was talking about your tree."

At that moment, I knew both boys were stating the truth. From Andrew's European American perspective, the topic was landscape colors. From Damon's African American perspective, the topic was race. They were sociopolitically positioned to see the world this way, and it was my job to help them see into one another's worlds.

Every teacher knows that Andrew should not be teasing anybody about anything and Damon should not be using physical force instead of words. But this scenario beckoned me to work beyond conflict resolution strategies and get to the heart of the issue, which, it appeared to me, was the history of institutionalized racism.

Damon, Andrew, and I talked over the situation. We talked about *context* and how certain words and ideas are understood or misunderstood. We talked about historical abuse of privilege and power. We discussed words and ideas that have been misused and how today's misunderstanding may be part of a long history that started before we were born. We talked to the principal and arranged for Andrew and Damon to help me prepare a new art lesson instead of missing recess for fighting.

The next day we put our landscape lesson on hold, and Andrew and Damon helped me hang dozens of magazine photos of children's faces on the bulletin board. They also helped me mix paint to match the skin color of each face.

When the class entered the art room, I used a twist on my memory of Ms. Schumacher's first question, and asked, "What do we know about skin color?" On chart paper, we made a list of what we know and what we noticed in the photos: People have many tints and shades of skin color (vocabulary from our landscape lesson!); some families have different shades and tones in one family; when exposed to sun, some people get darker brown, others get red and sunburned; skin color has different tints and shades in different places on our bodies. More questions ensued. Next, we made a list of what we wonder and want to know. Why are some people darker or lighter than others? What's in our bodies to make the skin color? Does geographic region influence skin color? If geography makes a difference, why are there so many people of so many different skin colors in our town? Why do some people call other people names about skin color? Why does it hurt so much when those names are used? What are some words that are helpful and not hurtful to describe skin color and race? Why is it uncomfortable to talk about skin color? The list grew and grew.

To integrate the discussion of skin color and paint color, I hung four pieces of construction paper: yellow, red, black, and white. We discussed how those color words have been used to describe people's skin and compared the colors of the construction paper to the colors of the people in the photographs. We noticed that nobody matched those construction paper colors.

Next, I demonstrated how to mix red, yellow, and blue to make brown, and emphasized the importance of the color brown. We need brown to make every skin color of all 6 billion people on the planet! We all have some brown in our skin! Damon and Andrew traced their hands on a big piece of paper at the bulletin board. Then they demonstrated paint mixing techniques to achieve various tones of skin color. We all went to our art tables and traced our own hands and tried to mix paint to match our skin color. Students ran around the room holding up their hands and arms to one another, discussing the various tones. They held their paintbrushes next to one another's skin to give advice about adding more red, yellow, or blue. The classroom bubbled with excitement as each student struggled and finally succeeded in mixing his or her skin color.

After our painting activity, when we hung our hand images on the board, we looked at our chart paper with our list of questions. One thing we noticed was that we felt more comfortable talking about skin color now; the art activity had given us some language and tools to approach a difficult topic. To answer the questions from our chart paper that required more research, we enlisted the help of the classroom teachers and the librarian to research our questions about physiology and melanin, as well as historical events and political language used to describe racial groups and cultural groups. We asked the guidance counselor to help us learn about what to do with hurtful feelings. Eventually this project turned into a fully developed 4th-grade unit integrating science, math, language arts, and social studies through art.

The following year when the 4th graders became 5th graders, I invited them to lead a school-wide art lesson in which everybody in the school—each student and all adults from custodian to principal—would paint their hands and learn about skin color. I have written elsewhere[1] about a 1st-grade class working on a similar unit. This lesson has become the springboard of my year-long curriculum. In recent years, I have been heartened to see many curriculum videos, books, art supplies, and other packages that address the topic of teaching about skin color—certainly an indicator of the need for clear, frank, safe discussion of race in our public school classrooms. Some of the prepackaged materials are helpful, but mostly, with students in kindergarten through senior year, in college courses, and in staff development workshops, I still refer to the lessons I learned from Damon and Andrew.

When the Twin Towers crumbled and the phrase "Islamic terrorist" dominated the news media, we asked, "What do we know about Islam?" We studied tessellating patterns and their inception in the Golden Age of Islamic mathematics, we researched Persian miniature paintings inspired by the literature, and we studied the art of various contemporary painters who identify as Muslim. We made a list of phrases beginning with the word *Islamic,* such as *Islamic beliefs, Islamic artwork, Islamic culture, Islamic families,* to counter the phrase *Islamic terrorist* and to explore how much we could learn about our list through visual art.

In a topic closer to home, when a local developer threatened the environment on our local mountain range, we asked: What do we know about the mountain? We studied paintings of the site and hiked to the top to create our own sketches before writing letters to our local officials about the importance of land conservation. In response to current world events, we ask questions about the war in Iraq by studying Picasso's *Guernica* and comparing it with historical paintings about war as well as current news photographs and video about the war. We ask what we are learning from each image, what we want to know, and what we want to communicate through our art. As classroom conflicts or world events bring up questions, we answer them by studying art, critically viewing our visual culture, and developing skills to give meaning to our answers.

Damon, Andrew, and all my other students remind me over and over again, like my dad's joke, that there is always more to learn today and even more to learn tomorrow. While my curriculum changes and develops with current events, student interest, and other content-area integration, I still open each school year, or each academic quarter, with variations on the skin color hand painting activity. Through this introductory lesson, students see that art is created in a social and cultural context and that art making is meaning making. Students notice and wonder, and they see their teacher learning and asking.

My skin color art lesson tells me so much about my students, but more important, it tells my students why I teach: to create a classroom that is deliberately antiracist, where respectful dialogue, critical thinking, and lots of messy art making are required.

PART III

To Make Sense of the World

Oe's role in life, whether defined as a profession, a craft, or a vocation, helps people make sense of the world and of their place in it. Teaching is no different. Through teaching, people name themselves and reveal what they stand for. This is true whether one teaches kindergarten or high school physics. Unlike other professions, teaching is fundamentally a social activity; it concerns itself above all with connection with others. Whether we view it as a craft or a science, as intellectual activity or creative endeavor, teaching is first and foremost about relationships. It is these relationships that are at the heart of teaching, and it is through them that teachers find out who they are.

The essays that follow demonstrate how various teachers make sense of the world through their teaching. Sandra Jenoure, retiring after 32 years as a science teacher and coordinator, has bittersweet memories of the past 3 decades. But one thing she is certain about is that the children she has taught all these years deserve and need an excellent education, although they do not necessarily receive it. Stephen Gordon, another highly valued teacher, is also retiring, after 35 years of teaching English in the Boston public schools. In the past several years, Stephen has given a great deal of thought to what kept him in the classroom. In his essay, he shares many of the reasons for his long and ongoing commitment to teaching, to the English language, and especially to the young people of Boston.

Sometimes the desire to teach grows out of teachers' search for identity. This is the case with Katina Papson, a young high school art teacher who specializes in photography. Katina uses a photography metaphor to define teaching, and her life, as light and darkness. Ambrizeth Lima, a high school teacher of Cape Verdean students in Boston, often has struggled with the injustices her students face. She portrays teaching as both a political and a spiritual journey and explains the many ways in which it is so. Ayla Gavins, a teacher for the past 12 years, compares teaching to being on a moving train: It is equally exhilarating and unknowable, and it opens new horizons for her and her students. Elaine Stinson, a 4th-grade teacher, views teaching as one way to demonstrate a commitment to making learning meaningful and joyful for all students. In her essay, she describes the ways in which she teaches "outside the lines" so that the children in her class can find more enjoyment in school than she did as a child.

Chapter 7

Looking Back in Wonder

SANDRA JENOURE

S andra Jenoure has been working as an educator for the past 32 years. Her own identity as the daughter of immigrants led her to teaching. As a child, she learned that education could make a tremendous difference in her life, and she wanted to make that kind of difference for her own students. She loved science and she was determined to inspire the love of science in her students as well.

Filling various roles in a number of schools in Harlem, Sandra has been a classroom teacher, science cluster teacher, and science coordinator. In this, her final year in the system, she was a science instructional specialist, believing that this position would allow her to make positive changes for a greater number of children in the New York City public schools. It meant leaving the children she has loved and served for over 3 decades, a decision that was not easy to make. She is still not certain it was the right one.

In the months before her retirement, Sandra has given a lot of thought to the politics of education, a mix she considers lethal. She begins her essay by looking back: in wonder at her own career and everything it has brought her, and in disappointment at a system that has served so many children badly.

During the 32 years I have been a teacher in New York City, the children in this city have always needed strong, committed educators, people who know how children learn and care about all the children of the city. Learning is not a business, it is personal; teaching also should be personal and not a business. When children's lives and futures are at stake, we must all make their success our personal endeavor. Science is a good example of how students in New York City are not succeeding. Our students are unsuccessful in science mostly because they are not being taught science. This means that there will be fewer and fewer mathematicians, scientists, and engineers of color who have come through the New York City Department of Education.

I grew up in the Bronx, in a neighborhood that encouraged girls to ride bicycles, roller skate, and play with marbles. As a child, I had a Lionel Train Set and my very own set of Lincoln Logs. At that time, girls were not supposed to do those things, but not being allowed to participate in those kinds of activities keeps you from ever entering the world of science.

I spent my summers in the country exploring. Catching fish, frogs, and turtles was an everyday experience for me. Hiking, climbing mountains and trees, and camping and cooking out were the things I most looked forward to. I've been on this road all my life, the road to scientific literacy. The encouragement to explore I received as a child is the foundation for my life as a science teacher.

There are many other reasons for my growth as an educator. My student teaching experience was wonderful. It wasn't reality, though. I was not exposed to the politics of a school building, or to the politics of education, for that matter. I had chosen to work in East Harlem at PS 108, the school where a friend of my parents was a teacher. I had wonderful role models as cooperating teachers and my demonstration lessons were well prepared. But the classes in that school were small: The 1st grade where I was assigned had 15 students and my 5th-grade class had 20. I observed the students and classes a great deal and I learned how to teach reading using the method of one commercial program. I also learned how to perfect my handwriting, how to line up a class, not to talk until I had the children's attention, how to decorate a bulletin board, and how to write on a blackboard. These are important skills for a teacher to have, but they are by no means sufficient. Student teaching does not prepare you for the teaching and learning of children.

One of my early observations about the educational system in New York City was that it is unequal. My own children went to public schools that provided all the materials necessary for their education: computers, science materials, new books. In contrast, in East Harlem, my students didn't have what they needed. I learned that if I wanted those things, I had to get them myself. *I* had to make my classroom equal. I also learned that if I wanted my students to have a voice, *I* had to make sure they were heard.

When I graduated from college, I was hoping to be able to stay in PS 108 but there were no positions available. My college supervisor heard of another school in the district that was looking for a bilingual teacher. I met with the principal and I thought the interview went well. I would not be starting with my class on the first day of school. Instead, I would have 2 weeks of workshops on how to teach the bilingual class—an excellent idea if there had been quality educators as workshop facilitators.

I was so scared on my first day. I really had no idea what to expect or what to do. I walked into a political cauldron that first day. I was taking the teaching position of a monolingual teacher who had been "excessed" due to lack of funds. Is bilingual education necessary? That was the cry! But all I wanted was to teach.

A school aide handed me the teacher's guides for math and reading, and the assistant principal gave me 25 first, second, and third graders as my first assignment, along with a paraprofessional to help me. I had an English dominant class, which meant I was to teach in English but also teach them to read in Spanish. It was the beginning of bilingual education in New York City and I was lost. I had no idea where to begin or even how. None of my education courses had dealt with teaching Spanish or teaching Spanish reading.

So here I was: first teaching assignment, a multilevel group, a paraprofessional, parents, political intrigue: Oh, and did I mention that I had to learn to use a different English reading program with a totally different approach than the one I had worked with as a student teacher? Not enough books, not enough materials. Tables and chairs mismatched, some too small for the 3rd graders. No one said, "Welcome." No one said, "What do you need?" No one said, "How can I help?"

But there were some caring people in that school. The speech teacher and the guidance counselor befriended me. Mrs. Giordano, the guidance counselor, took me by the hand and saw me through my first year. She was getting ready to retire and I was just starting. She taught me how to teach reading, math, and social studies using the commercial programs of the school, and she sat with me during preps and lunches.

One of the first things that Mrs. Giordano taught me was that New York City had many resources, wonderful places to take your class for great social studies and science learning experiences. This was a federally funded program and we had money to hire buses. So my class and I went on trips. The first place I took my class was the camp where I had spent summers as a child. This was the beginning of our science studies. The students had never seen real cows. It was such a learning experience for both my students and me. Afterwards, we read, wrote, and did math around science.

Even though I am Hispanic and I speak Spanish, the lives of my students were foreign to me. I had never really understood what poverty was. I did not know neglect. Carlos, one of my little boys, waited outside the school for me every morning. He was unkempt and often fell asleep in class. Later, I found out that he came early with his little brother, and the school secretary fed him breakfast (this was before free breakfast and lunch were served in schools). She brought them clothing and made sure they had notebooks and pencils. I learned that more goes on in schools than education. I learned that you also needed to be involved in the lives of your students in a compassionate and loving way. Being a teacher meant you gave of yourself.

That December the parents of East Harlem closed all the schools, kept their children home, and picketed in front of the schools. For a week the children had no classes; teachers came to work and were turned away. The parents wanted a better education for their children. They wanted smaller classes and books and materials. My first year was a learning experience. It was enough to send anyone else into the job market again. But once I was in my classroom I enjoyed what I was doing. I loved my students.

Ooops! I'm "excessed." I had to change schools again. This time I was back at PS 108, working in another federally funded program, teaching the Distar reading method to 1st and 2nd graders deemed behind in reading development. I pulled the students out from their regular reading program and taught them using a completely new reading program. I saw 25 students daily. There were two parapro-fessionals working with me, and of course I had to teach them the program also. I had 2 weeks of professional development for this new program. The students progressed, but at the end of the year they had to return to their classes and their regular reading program.

The following year I was allowed to stay at PS 108 but not in a bilingual class this time. Instead, I was given a 4th-grade class of 25 students labeled as "low-performing." I loved them all. Each one presented a different problem. Attendance, for instance, was a major dilemma. I will never forget one student, Margarita. She told me she couldn't learn and not to even try to teach her. She came to school on Tuesday, Wednesday, and Thursday. On Monday and Friday, she was always absent. In conversation she told me that on Mondays she had to do the laundry with her mother and on Fri-days she had to do the grocery shopping with her. At various other times, she had to go along with her mother on other appointments: medical, welfare office, and so on. Her mother did not speak En-glish. As the oldest of five children, these were Margarita's respon-sibilities. It was also the life of many of my other 9- and 10-year-old students.

I decided that I would give the students an extra incentive to come in every day. Students with the best attendance would be able to take the trips I had planned. For Margarita, it meant com-ing in for a whole week and on time. The first week of the pro-gram, Margarita managed 4 out of the 5 days. The second week she came in all 5 days. The week of the trip she was in 5 days also.

The first trip was to the Statue of Liberty. I had never been to the Statue of Liberty and neither had my cousin, Barbara, who was one of my chaperones. Of course we had both lived in New York all of our lives, but still it was the trip of a lifetime for all of us. Believe it or not, it was also our first time on the Staten Island Ferry. It was exciting. At that time we were still allowed to travel all the way up to the inside of the torch and we went inside the crown. Barbara led the way; I brought up the rear. Some of my students were quite large and the spiral staircase is quite small, so we made many stops along the way to the top. The view was spectacular and the educa-tion we all received was phenomenal. After that my students' at-tendance improved greatly, and so did their behavior. Our motto that year was, "I know we can." I often read *The Little Engine That*

Could to them. If we could make it to the top of the statue, we could do anything.

We also went to the Ringling Brothers' Circus, a Mets baseball game, various museums in New York City, the Bronx Zoo, and the Botanical Gardens. One time I was absent for 3 days (an impacted wisdom tooth) and my students misbehaved. The assistant principal's office was right next door to our classroom and she had to work for her money those 3 days! When I returned she said to me, "The next time you're absent, call and let me know ahead of time so I can be absent also." We also had a nice lesson on dental hygiene and wisdom teeth. I brought the tooth in for "show and tell."

At the end of the year, we celebrated attendance, promotion, and the education we had all received. All my students were promoted to 5th grade. We all cried. But once again, at the end of the year, I found myself looking for a job. Along with my last check, I was given a letter that said my services were no longer needed, not because I had not done a great job but because there were again cutbacks.

Another teacher was told to go back to her appointed school and she asked me if I wanted to take a drive with her. It was a drive of a lifetime. We drove up to 117th Street between First and Second Avenues to PS 155 where Mrs. Lavinia Mancuso was the principal. I walked into the office and Lavinia greeted me with, "Do you have a license?" "Do you speak Spanish?" "Do you want a job?" My answer was yes to all of the above. Lavinia said, "Wait here." She went into her office, called my former principal, came out, and said, "You're hired."

I say it was a drive of a lifetime because Lavinia was the best role model and the most supportive person I have ever worked with. There are some supervisors who believe that children come first. Lavinia was one of those. She led by example. She made it her mission and in turn it became our mission to give our students the best education possible. It was at PS 155 that I was allowed to blossom and flourish. It was there that I took advantage of many opportunities. It was there that I made lifelong friends. Through Lavinia I also learned that learning is lifelong. We were a school of teachers who believed in continuing education; we attended workshops, institutes, and graduate school to hone our skills. At each step, there was Lavinia to encourage us, to push her fledglings out of the nest.

Every chance we got we attended classes. Classroom teachers attended Teachers College writers workshop institutes with Lucy Caulkins. Lavinia attended graduate school and received a master's degree in computer engineering. We celebrated together, partied together, and mourned together.

We were a small school, only about 400 students. We were an oasis in the middle of burned out buildings and tenements. In the beginning our students were mostly Puerto Rican. We celebrated their Puerto Rican heritage and taught them to read in both English and Spanish. We wrote grants every chance we got and each and every time we were awarded the money. We made sure our students were exposed to all facets of education. We had a computer lab for our students, and each classroom had at least two classroom computers and printers. We had a state of the art library. Our students took dance lessons with Alvin Ailey's dance group and, years later, 2 of them were invited to join the group. Classical artists, dance groups, orchestral groups, theatrical groups all visited our school and performed for our students.

By 1982 I decided to go back to graduate school for a degree in administration and supervision. I thought that I might want to open my own school or perhaps be a principal in one of the schools in East Harlem. During my studies I had to do an internship and Lavinia said, "Sandy, you like science. Why don't you do your internship in the development of a science curriculum for our school?" She gave me an "out of the classroom" position as the science cluster teacher. With this position, I had to move to a smaller room, give up teaching an official class, and take on the science instruction for all the students of the school. Lavinia showed me a closet where all the science materials were stored. For me, it was a toy store.

At that time, neither the New York State Education Department nor the New York City Board of Education had an updated core curriculum. The last time New York City had updated its science curriculum was in 1966. I still have some of those books. So, here I was with all the materials in the world but no curriculum. In contrast, today we have national, state, and city performance standards and a state core curriculum, but so many of our schools have no materials.

I decided to continue in the field of science curriculum development instead of becoming a principal. In those times, you had to have political connections for principal positions. Some people actually were paying for the positions. This was a great disillusion to me and I no longer wanted a school of my own or even an assistant principal's position. Politics and education: How does that combination help our children?

I also went back to graduate school. This time I received an MS in environmental studies. The year before, I had met Talbert Spence, the man who was to become my science mentor and lifelong friend. I had brought my class to Wave Hill, the most beautiful location in the Bronx. At the time, it was an environmental center to which you could bring your class. There the class would learn about forest ecology, estuary ecology, the life of insects, and how to care for our environment in general.

When it came time for me to set up programs for my school, our experience at Wave Hill came back. I sought out Spence. Before having met him, I was beginning to flounder again. I felt so strongly about wanting to teach science, but I didn't know where to begin. He came to my classroom and helped me set it up, organizing the materials I had. No one in the school had used the science materials, purchased by the district 7 years before, so I had a closet full of materials.

Spence gave me my first colony of mealworms. He got me involved in taking workshops at Wave Hill and other places. He encouraged me to attend all the workshops and institutes given in science around New York City. Along with the workshops came money to buy supplies or books. The Workshop Center at City College, which is a center for educational change, was important to my metamorphosis. I went there to learn the methodology of teaching science. I learned by doing, very different from listening to a lecture. There was a new pedagogy, methodology, and content to learn. It was an educational revival for me. My own children got to attend most of the outdoor workshops and they too learned on the job. Spence has a picture of my daughter at the age of 2 in a snowsuit digging for insects. She is now 24. I think I overexposed her to science. She's a mathematician.

Throughout the city, there were other teachers who also loved science. It was a time when New York City was beginning to write its own science curriculum and I gladly joined that group. We collaborated, writing curriculum for grades K–6. We tried out our lessons, honed our skills, and then took our show on the road. My students got to try out new ideas and they were open to all types of exciting lessons.

Science education was revitalized nationally as well. I was constantly looking for new ways to financially support my classroom. Coincidentally, federal legislation allocated money for science education. There was research to be done and new programs to be developed, and I was always there, bringing new ideas and new materials to my classroom and my students. We took part in pilot projects and we got to keep the materials, including computers and other technology of the times.

My classroom was a place of excitement and great interest. We had five aquaria that contained guppies, goldfish, tadpoles, and turtles. In my science classroom, the students constantly were experimenting, reading, writing, and asking questions. They learned how to care for the animals and they learned responsibility. They kept journals, did research, and worked cooperatively. Over the years, my students have taken part in three different videos: a *3–2–1 Contact* video on the surface tension of water, a *Voyage of the Mimi* video on integrating technology and science, and a *Batteries & Bulbs* video that focuses on materials management but really looks at how science should be taught in an elementary classroom.

I was always concerned that my students have all the information necessary to compete with other students around the state. New students learned early on, "Don't ask Ms. Jenoure for answers. She's not going to give them to you. We have to find the answers ourselves." It was about inquiry, and we were all on the road to scientific literacy together.

By the end of my last year as a science cluster teacher, my classroom had a technology center with six computers, three printers, a scanner, Internet connections, software, and a TV and VCR. We had a red-eared slider; two colonies of mealworms; land snails, pond snails, goldfish, and guppies; shelves full of science-related books; and a garden around the corner from school.

Getting ready to teach a class is exciting, and watching the students think and problem solve while doing the activities is even more exciting. My most treasured present from a student was a shell she had found. She said she saw it and knew I would love it. She was right. There is also nothing like a student running up and saying,

"Ms. Jenoure, please take this," and handing me a shopping bag. "My mother was going to cook it." I looked inside the shopping bag and there was a red-eared slider. Corissa knew the turtle would be safe with me.

In 1992, I was nominated for "New York State Teacher of the Year." I won, for the first time ever, the designation of "First Runner Up." Now PS 155 was really on the map. My students and I were videotaped during lessons. We took part in nationwide projects. We had our own website where you could see our ongoing science experiments.

I know it's easy to sit back and listen to the gossip in schools. "These kids can't learn," is what you hear. The truth is they can and do. We have to see and believe. There are great obstacles, of course. Teaching is not easy. There are so many incompetent administrators. There are many uncaring teachers. The political obstacles are almost insurmountable. But the truth is that an excellent, caring teacher can excite children to learn more. I believe that empowered students love learning and it was my responsibility to excite them.

Although I will be retiring this year, I am not leaving education completely. I can't. I'm going to continue working with teachers in the hope that there are some educators among them with the love of learning and children.

Chapter 8

Teaching to Affirm

STEPHEN GORDON

A high school teacher of English for 35 years, Stephen Gordon has been a coach for other teachers for the past 4 of those years. He is retiring this year but will continue to provide professional development support for new teachers. He says that thinking about retirement has been hard. It is not easy to "let go," especially because he is concerned about the sustainability of the collaborative nature of his work with students and teachers.

In his career, most of it in the Boston public schools, Stephen has had many roles: teacher, mentor to new teachers, workshop leader, inquiry group member. In all these, he has struggled to make sense of the world through his teaching. For instance, he is sometimes perplexed, sometimes incensed by the intractable bureaucracies in schools, bureaucracies that chip away at the job of teaching. He is also exasperated by the focus on "best practices" and other seemingly surefire answers to the complex problems of urban schools. In spite of it all, in a recent email, Stephen wrote that he is a teacher because he is "entwined in the rich lives of adolescents, an adult who represents a way to be in this often unjust world." In his essay, he explains this and some of the many other reasons he has for being a teacher.

THE QUESTION

Teaching has been my chosen profession. I have spent my work life as an English teacher in junior and senior high schools, and for the past few years I have been a "coach" for fellow teachers. I believe in students and teachers; I have loved teaching for and with them; and I judge I have been good at it.

Teaching has meant working in city school buildings surrounded by adolescents and adults who faithfully have decided to spend day after day together as students and teachers. This commitment seems similar to recurring attendance at church or temple. By walking into their schools every day, students and teachers hope to become better people. Writing about my decision to work in these urban schools allows me to explain why I have engaged in this intellectual, political, and spiritual struggle.

Although I say I chose to do this work, I believe "character is fate" and, as T.S. Eliot wrote, "in my beginning is my end." So how did I come to teach and why did I continue to do it?

THE PROBLEM

My work choice stems partially from my character and family experiences before I decided to teach—my beliefs, emotions, and ethics. My character and parents, therefore, partly explain why I teach, a necessary but not sufficient explanation. My father, for example, believed in the power and beauty of language, the obligation for people to develop their minds, and the need to work for social justice. To write about why I teach, therefore, names both the family realities I brought to teaching and those that flooded my life in school with students and colleagues, including the hours after school and at 4 a.m.—at all times driven to seek consequential experiences for students and teachers so that I might feel successful at my chosen craft.

No sentences, however, can fully "explain" why I teach; they merely generate words that recur in trying to understand why people teach, and finding these best personal and public words can be difficult. And they always are insufficient. Nevertheless, I see my explanation as perhaps a poem with three stanzas. One stanza can explain in an abstract way why people teach, the big words teachers have in common, abstract words and ideas that, when drained of their abstractness, leave shared moments that we agree affirmed, rewarded, and taught us why we teach. Words such as *love, learning, political commitment, social justice.* Another stanza will contain more personal words that express my more private lexicon of emotions and thoughts that sustain my work, cheer me on, keep me going, make me feel that I am doing the right thing with and for my students. And the final stanza will be the narratives of what actually happened in classes with students and teachers that, without agreed-upon interpretation, nonetheless "explain" why I teach.

BEYOND EXPLANATION

Teaching has enabled me to meet my lifelong need to feel useful and appreciated. When I hear "Mr. Gordon" yelled by a former student from a car at a traffic light, or when former students come to visit me at my school, I feel good. And when I meet them on the subway or in a store where they are shopping or working, immediately I am glad to see them. Most important, they have recognized and greeted me: They have felt the desire to call my name to share a moment with me. Meeting former students makes me feel I have done right by them, that they remember that I cared about them, that I respected their identity and intelligence, their hopes and difficulties. In this momentary meeting, I once more feel the joy and privilege of having been their teacher.

ONE ANSWER

A part of me teaches in the sense that as a master craftsman I know more than others, and through some method to be determined, I can impart, transmit, and transfer to my students what I know and can do. One goal for my identity as *teacher* has been to determine what I know and can do that has been sanctioned as worthy in the culture. These are the tools, dispositions, and cultural capital students need to "learn" to become functioning members of this culture, able to participate in the literate, political, and artistic institutions of the society, not merely to be passive, wallet-opening consumers.

I am a teacher when, as an adult similar to a parent, I try to find the quickest direct instruction to inoculate students with knowledge, even when I doubt the transmission model of learning. For example, like children acquiring language, students need to know the names of entities that parse the world. This side of teacher creates naming-day in Eden and I become Adam. I must fulfill my responsibility to my students and their parents by giving students the terms valued by the culture they have been born into, the language they will need to survive and grow in society. Then, their responsibility will be to decide whether these names mean what the culture asserts.

I believe in the power of language. A teacher can help students find the "right" words to make realities clear to themselves and others. I want my students to talk and write to find their words; and they must expand, qualify, and explain their thinking, challenging themselves to search into what D.W. Harding calls the "hinterland of thought," the intimation of understanding that the thinker perceives only dimly. Harding likens this emerging region to the sails of a ship coming onto the horizon of our consciousness; we can see only the tops of the sails on the horizon, and it is our job to make these ships—our thoughts—come fully into view as words. As a teacher I can help students express the ideas they can only partially see. I also believe we all experience what Eugene Gendlin called "felt sense": We feel the truths of our lives and use these emotions to drive our search for the best words to name and give meaning to our experiences. And I believe Nietzsche's assertion: "That which we have words for we are already beyond," although my reading of Holocaust literature reveals the limitations of this statement. Harding, Gendlin, and Nietzsche suggest to me that we are inundated by life's wordless realities, and our found words are the life preservers we use to make it safely to land. Teachers can preserve the lives of students by eliciting and validating the words that can both motivate and sustain their growth.

Working with students and teachers, I am involved in the struggle of adolescents and adults to discover and state their words, found on their own or elicited by me; and we then examine these words to see whether they are true for themselves and others.

SOME AUTOBIOGRAPHY

Growing up in New York City, I attended public schools. After I graduated from City College of New York in the mid 1960s I worked at the New York City Department of Welfare as a case worker. Client problems were intractable to me, and I had little effect, and after a year at this difficult job I began my English teaching life with 7th and 8th graders at Junior High School 52 in Manhattan. After 2 years, realizing I knew little about English, I went to graduate school in Boston, and then, after 2 years working as a textbook editor in Boston, I decided to return to teaching. I did so because I realized that teaching English was something I liked to do, difficult work I realized I was good at. But these résumé facts are the sequences of my decisions, not the causes for my choosing to spend my work life with urban students.

My background led me to teach for educational justice. I taught at a Boston high school because my father was a union organizer in the 1930s and in his house I learned about social and economic injustice that fell heavily on the poor and people of color who lived in cities. When I see students not working up to their capacity, I tell them that they are fulfilling this culture's demeaning belief that they cannot achieve. Moreover, the wealthy do not want them competing for positions at colleges and jobs "reserved" for their children. I teach to empower my students, not to succumb to the culture's lowest expectations.

MORE ANSWERS

Growing up can be hard, and adolescents need a positive presence in their lives. Becoming an independent man capable of making sense of my inner and outer worlds was hard for me, and I wanted to help young people get through these turbulent years. Similarly, becoming a successful teacher is hard work, and as a coach, I can advocate for teacher knowledge, craft, and development.

As a teacher, every day I seek to create experiences that affirm school, special words and activities that happen only in classrooms. I work to create conditions and opportunities for learning, responsible for deciding what is worth doing in a way that will be memorable and significant, fostering engagement and student participation in learning. As a teacher I represent what is worth studying, understanding, exploring, and knowing in the world. As an English teacher I must find the authors that create worlds and tell us truths to consider, encouraging students to write and speak their own truths and then sharing them in our classroom community.

Having the experience of authors who transformed my life, I want students to find published voices for themselves to provide models for their creation of thoughtful and artful forms. I encourage students to play with language, seeing language as art, recognizing that literature, like music, plays with patterns that are emotional and aesthetic. My students should know the significant literary voices of their cultures and the important literature of our inherited poets and novelists. I teach to show how writing and literature are essential, whether Toni Morrison or Shakespeare or Rumi or Martin Espada or . . .

I teach to be part of an intellectual tradition that includes so many deeply committed and engaged intellectuals, a designation I sometimes think our country derides. Growing up in my father's Jewish, Russian, socialist household, I learned to nurture ideas, to search for words and learning expressed in the truths and emotions of poets, philosophers, and novelists. When I teach, I belong to my father's intellectual tradition. Ideas sustain, motivate, engage, and enrage—why I teach.

I now work with teachers as a coach for the same reasons I worked with students. Teachers too need to examine their thoughts, beliefs, and actions to find centering truths that can inspire and sustain their work life.

THE STORIES

When I teach I am entwined in the rich moment-to-moment lives of adolescents, an adult who represents a way to be in this sometimes unjust world, a teacher who tries to show the importance of our lives in the specific minutes of our acts and words. Students grow when they see and hear adults who model the role of learning and understanding. A teacher often cannot know what a student has learned, but we must act as exemplars for students to infer how to survive and overcome. And sometimes we have memorable experiences that affirm our commitment to teaching.

Breaking up a Fight

I walk up to the second-floor landing at my school and two African American girls are yelling at each other. My years of teaching tell me that, judging from the tone and content of the words, they are close to fighting. They move toward each other and I instinctively move between them. They continue to yell at each other, pushing against me, their hands reaching around me to try to hit each other. I hold my ground, preventing the fight as they push against me. Another teacher comes along and we physically separate the students. A week later the headmaster calls me to the office to speak to the mother of one of the students who was involved in the fight I prevented. The mother looks at me and says, "Thank you so much for stopping the fight. My daughter could have been hurt." She hands me a package wrapped in tissue paper. I open it in front of her. It is a beautiful traditional shirt worn in Nigeria where she and her daughter are from.

Listening to Students

In the fall of 1993 I am doing teacher research through the Urban Sites Network of the National Writing Project. As an English teacher at midlife, I am trying to know how students perceive themselves and me in our classroom. I ask students to identify my words and deeds that encourage or discourage their learning, their mastery of writing, and their identities as students, deciding which assignments and classroom procedures enhance their involvement in their own learning. I am asking them to evaluate, suggest, and criticize what their teacher does day to day. To elicit their evaluation, I write "learning letters," in which I summarize what I have tried to teach, expressing my views on the previous 2 weeks and indicating what I plan to do in the future. Then I ask my students to respond to my letters, telling me what they think they have learned and the problems they have encountered.

A student writes:

> . . . I'm learning a lot with what you are teaching. The two-sided journal
> helps me out a lot. This helps me to understand stories that seem
> difficult. It helps improve on my comprehension skills too. With sentence
> combining, the new trick you showed me was very excellent. Your
> techniques showed me a different way of handling the problems. Now it
> is easier.
>   I think we should do more things that relate to SAT work, just to
> help people prepare for it, because that's our next step into life. On
> stories that we have the two-sided journal we should always read the
> story aloud so everyone can get a clear understanding of the story. It
> would help us as a class where we can discuss a point or someone's
> point of view.
>   I think that you are doing a great job, but I think you are getting
> frustrated too easily. If someone is talking, I think you should handle it
> much stronger. Sometimes I think that some people are getting away
> with murder and you're not doing anything. But you must be strong and
> not let them get to you like that.

Letters to Students

Classes and students can be exhilarating and also depressing.
Teaching is infinitely renewable, so a bad day can be followed by a
good day. Some of this is accidental, part of the rhythm of life with
adolescents, but sometimes I could not accept this random reality.
When sufficiently upset with individual students, I would write
them letters detailing my disappointment. Like students every-
where, they had their own agendas, which sometimes included
carrying on intrusive conversations and not doing the assigned work.
Feeling responsible for students' lack of engagement and attention,
I wrote to them so they could understand exactly what I wanted
from them. These letters made me feel better, that I had done something for the students and myself, and the letters usually led to a
change in student attitude and behavior—and mine also. For example, I wrote to one student:

> Dear ——,
>   I am writing to you because I am concerned about your perfor-
> mance in English. I recognize that you seem bored, uninterested in
> much of the class. I regret this. Unfortunately, since this is a senior class,

containing many students—including yourself—who will be applying for and perhaps attending college next fall, I feel responsible for doing as much as I can to prepare them for college.

I admit there may be more interesting ways to prepare prospective college students, and I need to learn them. I am open to suggestions for maximizing learning and interest.

But what about you? Your lack of involvement will lead to your not improving your ability to write, read, and respond to literature. My experience has revealed that many students lose interest because they are having trouble understanding and completing the work. Once they can do the work, they find the class more acceptable.

Since I taught you in 10th grade, I know that you are a competent student who can do most work. But I also know that you have developed some attitudes which hurt your chances to learn as much as you can. For example, yesterday you had your head down on the desk when we were reading "The Trap" together in order to try to get into this long story. For some reason, you dropped out. I believe that there are other ways that may get more student involvement in starting a story, and I'm working on them.

I hope you can become more involved and successful. Keep in touch. Don't let this get away from you.

Sincerely,

Mr. Gordon

After writing these letters and reading student responses, I felt I had done the right thing as their teacher.

THE ANSWER

As I end I am reminded of an experience that seems to answer the question one more time.

My colleague June Robinson and I co-taught a "transition" English class for 9th-grade students who needed more work on reading and writing. June and I had asked students working in groups to read and comment on poems we had given them. We circulated among groups, and then we talked about poetry: who likes it, who writes it, and lyrics of music. June asked whether anyone had memorized poetry. Tashia raised her hand just high enough to be noticed.

I asked her, "When did you have to memorize a poem?"

"Last year, in 8th grade," she answered.

"What poem?" June asked.

"'Phenomenal Woman' by Maya Angelou."[1]

"Recite it for us," June requested energetically.

"No," she said in a low voice, not wanting to become the focus of all our eyes.

"You can do it," June coaxed supportively.

"Please. I love poetry," I added.

Tashia reluctantly got up and walked to the front of the room. She began:

Pretty Women wonder where my
secret lies
I'm not cute or built to suit a
Model's fashion size
But when I start to tell them
They think I'm telling lies.
I say
It's the reach of my arms
The span of my hips
The stride of my steps
The curl of my lips.
I'm a woman
Phenomenally
Phenomenal woman
That's me

She continued through the next three stanzas. And we all watched and listened. I felt tears well up in my eyes, for here were 20 students and two adults experiencing the reason to be in school: to hear poetry, to be moved by language, to be together in a place where young men and women express the words that they have taken to their hearts—beautiful, powerful words of identity, hope, and learning. I knew that life was usually filled with exhausting struggle and alienating injustice, but for now I was in a sacred, life-affirming place: a classroom filled by Tashia's strong voice and chosen words.

I knew this was why I teach.

Chapter 9

Teaching Through Light and Darkness

K<small>ATINA</small> P<small>APSON</small>

A high school art teacher for the past 4 years, Katina Papson currently teaches photography and foundations of art at Amherst Regional High School. Her family background has profoundly influenced her work: a mother from Ecuador and father from Greece have given her the languages and insights of living in a multicultural society. As a result of her early experiences, Katina is deeply committed to social action through the arts, a commitment she has demonstrated through multiple experiences in her young career. At the high school, for example, she facilitates a student-initiated multimedia social justice theater group that especially encourages participation by students who previously have been marginalized or silenced. This project, now an institution in the culture of the school, provides a venue for students to meet, discuss, write, and direct their expressions of social and political issues, culminating in multimedia performance events. Katina's belief in youth vision and voice places her students at the center of this work.

Beyond the school walls, Katina taught an after-school photography program for teen girls for several years. The program focused on bringing forms of expression to girls in underserved communities. As an indefatigable champion of youth arts, Katina also directs an alternative summer arts camp for teen youth. In her own work, Katina is an artist in photography, working in both traditional darkroom and digital media. She is keenly interested in the opportunities that technology affords arts in social action and is considering graduate work in this area. In her essay, Katina uses a photography metaphor to describe her view of art and her vision of teaching.

Contrast has always caught my attention. Growing up, I was a careful observer of my world, always looking for differences. My environment appeared like a stage and I remember learning my most profound lessons while watching the show and dreaming up what was really happening between scenes when the lights went down. Even as a child, I began to develop questions about my culture, race, and sexuality. These were my first steps toward true learning. Good-hearted and sensitive parents from two different cultures enabled my unique personal growth. Exposure to the arts provided a world where I embarked on cultivating a better understanding of my identity, and participating in the arts granted me the space to create and explore differences.

My earliest memories have sparked an urge to aid others in their own inquiries through explorations of contrast. As an artist and teacher, I believe youth is where character, questions, and desires are born. Memories that illustrate my own experiences as a young learner begin to best tell the story of why I embark daily on the challenge of teaching youth.

I was a quiet child, intently watching and noticing all forms of life, as many children do. I observed by listening, often from the safety of my mother's lap. Nothing was more comforting than listening to my great-uncle playing the piano by ear on Christmas Eve in Queens, New York, while everyone sang *El Reloj,* an old romantic bolero "from home" about seizing moments and the necessity of having love in one's life. At loud, late-night parties where the Ecuadorian family, my mother's side, chatted until all hours with scotch on the rocks and cigarettes in hand, I fell asleep against my mother's vibrating chest to the hum of their stories, sing-alongs, and boisterous laughter. Living in New York City, my cousins and I always sensed that we were living the life our parents had always dreamt about. A good education in the United States meant opportunity. We felt so lucky.

As I grew older, I was curious about parishioners at my family's neighborhood Catholic Church. At this early point in my life, contrast was most apparent. My biggest question was whether or not I fit into all of it, mostly because of the makeup of my immediate family. My Spanish-speaking Ecuadorian mother and Greek Orthodox American father were 24 years apart in age. Our biracial and bilingual family and unique parent team made my brothers and me stand out in our tightly knit Catholic community. This play of opposites resonated in my family, parish, neighborhood, and school. No one explained why it felt strange and uncomfortable to be the only family that looked and sounded different. I grew anxious and uncertain about this obvious disparity and my relationships within it. I strongly questioned the disparities as my teen years approached.

RECORDING AND REVEALING:
LIFE STUDIES IN BLACK AND WHITE

I loved art mainly because my mother did. She frequently brought my younger brother Andreas and me to the Metropolitan Museum of Art in Manhattan. As my interest in the arts grew, my father became my one and only photography teacher. From the age of 7 or 8, I took what he called "interesting" family pictures. Having seen my innate love for the medium, he bought me my first camera, a Polaroid. For hours, my dolls sat for me while I captured them—next to the goldfish bowl, in front of my baby brother, on the old living room couch. The process of recording these objects and relationships inspired me. I wanted to study details of every moment, frozen into that small shiny square of an image. Which ones were contrasting? Which were the same? I played games with the pattern on my mother's apron and compared it with the texture of the chain link fence behind the neighborhood boys' basketball court. Hiding behind the camera and watching for a moment of insight became somewhat of an exploit, a mission for more differences. There was something out there that I needed to know, something that would answer the questions I had about who I was. The camera made me determined to seek relationships and spaces with the hope of finding within it my true identity.

In high school, I continued to make photographs on my own. I pursued photography in college as a major and I basked in the black and white image and the magic of the darkroom. Light became more evident as I studied all kinds of photography and art history, relating back constantly to my childhood, family, and current life and relationships. I soon realized that photographers throughout history were mostly male. But the head of my university's photo department was female and she had paved the way for my induction to mostly male-populated classrooms. Theory, criticism, and feminist photography inspired me. The camera became a microscope, a research tool not only for self-identity and reflection, but also for critical examination and questioning of relationships, postmodern theories, and expression.

Although archiving my life seemed to occupy all of my interest, I found myself teaching in a public high school in western Massachusetts 2 short years after graduating from college. I slowly gained experience. At the end of the 2004 school year, I had been teaching for a total of 4 years. While my current job as a high school art teacher consumes most of my time, I continue to enjoy teaching after-school arts and social justice theater programs as well as directing summer arts programs. It's a pleasant surprise that my passion remains while I do a job I never imagined having.

TEACHING RELATIONSHIPS: SELF-IDENTITY, COMMUNITY, IMAGE MAKING, AND POLITICS

Like most new teachers, I was immediately concerned about whether my students would like me. I was teaching Photography I classes at the high school and, although I knew it was a popular course, I remained anxious. When the bell rang, my 22-year-old self sat poised on a stool, attendance book in hand, ready to come up against teenage personalities galore. I calmed my nerves with the fact that I had youth on my side and knew enough about popular culture and music to get by as a "cool" teacher. I vowed to always be myself, but still I had many questions about my role in the classroom. I cared deeply for my students even before we met and I wanted to see them have power over their own education. Is there a healthy, professional way I can show them I love them and have faith in their abilities to advocate for themselves? How do I facilitate strong relationships and communities of trust in my classroom while teaching within a traditionally hierarchical school system? How can I help my students express their *own* ideas and emotions through photography and art?

Most students responded well to my creative and energetic style, although I quickly realized there was almost always a group who stayed in back of the room despite my incessant and heartfelt invitations to join the rest of the class. We met in a circle and some youths refused to sit together that way. More often than not, these were students of color, or students who were marginalized because of institutionalized labels on their learning or emotional disabilities. This initial observation of passive nonparticipation and contrast in my classroom caused me to think intensely about teenage identity, the larger institution of public education, and my role as a teacher. How could I help youth of all backgrounds and experiences feel at home enough to learn despite their "difference"?

I began discussions with the students to gather a better sense of what they were feeling and thinking. The young people in my classroom expressed concerns about their own education. They explained that they live and are forced to learn by a bell, follow a grid, obey strict rules, and always do what they are told. As a group, we talked about freedom, oppression, power dynamics, and censorship. The students in the back of the room began to contribute either by speaking up or creating images that spoke for them. Small communities began to build. My assignments transformed in order to accommodate my students' needs to explore their own personal politics. My original concerns and questions still remained but through open discussions, nonjudgmental listening, flexibility, and love, I saw a change in how my students seemed to feel in my classroom.

I continued to encourage critical observation. As young artists, my students began to study gender, self-image, the media, and relationships through their cameras' lenses. The personal and the political went hand in hand. Powerful images intended to raise awareness and explore opinions came flooding from them. By posing questions and allowing dialogue around problems concerning the students' lives, I found a whole new layer of relationship to my students. We were able to "study" these issues together through our conversations and explorations. We were working to advance our ideas of how to create noticeable social change in the arts.

Imaginative problem solving and critical analysis helped the students become less dependent on me. They began to participate more fully in their education. I began to find a way to create a true democracy in my classroom. Paulo Freire, a social theorist, speaks to how such educational reform works to combat common patterns of school subordination and domination. I relate closely to his philosophy that to be a good liberating educator, you need to have faith in human beings, and you need to love.[1] In my small classroom, while teaching technology, school rules, and basic visual art aesthetics, I have discovered ways of altering traditional standards of teaching in order to better accommodate the needs of young people. My students have shown me autonomy, character, wit, clarity of thought, kindness, and initiative.

I have realized the greatest contrast exists between students and teachers in a conventional classroom situation. My intention is to function within that setting while discovering the "grey" areas, the areas where students find voice and help one another learn by sharing their personal lives and perspectives. There is where everyone is learning. There, in that circle of young creative minds, is a revolution.

Chapter 10

Teaching as a Spiritual Journey

AMBRIZETH LIMA

Ambrizeth Lima came to the United States from the Cape Verde Islands as an adolescent. Having been a student in the Boston public schools, she knows how difficult the transition to U.S. school and society can be for her Cape Verdean and other language–minority students. As a result, she feels a special responsibility to help them navigate what can be treacherous waters both in and out of school. In a chapter she wrote a number of years ago for a book on the politics of bilingualism, Ambrizeth described her experiences as a young immigrant in the U.S. public schools.

> I felt different. But again, I was fifteen, an age when everyone feels different, especially if one is experiencing culture shock, language shock, and every other kind of shock one might think of. . . . A part of me died in my new school. I became mute—or perhaps people around me became deaf. I became invisible, or maybe people lost their sight.[1]

Ambrizeth is no longer either silent or invisible. In that same chapter, she wrote, "I believe it is my ethical and moral responsibility to advocate for my students. As a former bilingual student and current bilingual teacher, I would be remiss if I remained quiet."[2] Currently a doctoral candidate at Harvard University Graduate School of Education, Ambrizeth continues to teach part-time in the Boston public schools. In her essay, she likens teaching to a spiritual journey, one in which she can be both energized by the beauty of teaching and unsettled by its power.

There are days when I believe I was born to be a teacher. I walk easily through my lesson planner and I produce units at the speed of light. Creativity oozes off my pores! I forget the impending onset of varicose veins as I waltz through the desks and place a gold star on every student's work. Other days, well . . . things just aren't the same. I would like to think it is the winter blues. We people from the tropics (I am originally from the Cape Verde Islands) have a thing about getting the right amount of sun to lighten our moods. This is the time when the extra book in the briefcase is the last straw, and writing another hall pass breaks the camel's back.

This ambivalence about teaching, however, is not caused by my students. As a matter of fact, even when things are not going right, I still enjoy teaching. But what contributes to my premature burn-out (I've been a teacher for only 10 years), in my estimation, is the politics that surround the act of teaching. And the act of teaching brings a lot of extra responsibilities that many times put teachers in direct conflict with the powers that be. Because I'm constantly reflecting on my teaching, sometimes I feel that I fall short. Many times I've wondered if I have the personality to be a teacher. Why can't I smile more? Why can't I be more of a "buddy" to my students the way other teachers are? How can I shed the persona of a "mean teacher"? Why can't I be quiet in meetings and just do what administrators ask? Why am I even teaching?

Other times I feel powerless. I use this term because teaching is about power. But it is also about morality and ethics. While the system entrusts me with the responsibility of protecting these children's freedom to learn, it seems that every time I attempt to advocate for them, I lock horns with the powers that be. Is it morally right for me, as a teacher, to witness injustice toward students and remain quiet? Perhaps I sound sanctimonious when I mention the word *moral*, but I merely wish to convey the notion that since

I have children—our children, our future—in my care, I should use my authority and my power in a way that benefits them.

By now, you may be asking why I teach at all since it seems so painful. Teaching for me is a combination of joy, sadness, elation, and helplessness. But it is also a mission with a tangible goal: I teach because teaching transforms my students, and it transforms me. I teach because the act of teaching touches many facets of my psyche and my soul. Teaching keeps me in check with my conscience and constantly pushes me toward *conscientização,* Paulo Freire's term for a heightened consciousness that comes from deep reflection that leads to praxis.[3]

Teaching also unsettles me. I'm continuously vigilant, constantly policing myself. I can let go of other things: I can pay my mortgage late, or let my car insurance expire by forgetting to pay the premium, but teaching is different. It has insinuated itself into my very being. It is a spiritual experience that brings peace to my life when I do it right, and I know I have done it right when I have exhausted all possibilities to make learning wonderful for my students and for me.

Teaching is also a revolutionary act for me because, depending on how it is done, it can determine whether a young person will have a chance at a good life or not. It has lifelong implications: If a child has access to a good education, she or he may go to college, get a good job, and live a good life. Advocating for children's education means advocating for a generation of young people who can become either casualties of instructional and social neglect, or citizens who promote economic and social stability in their communities.

I teach because teaching brings me hope. I see so many young Cape Verdeans becoming involved with the law, being incarcerated and deported to Cape Verde. I call them "fading rainbows" because in Cape Verde, where rain is so scarce, every time we see a rainbow, it's a sign of bounty, of hope. But these young Cape Verdeans, especially the boys, seem to look at the future and see only the desolation, racism, and xenophobia that surround their lives. Education for them no longer means a promising future. It appears they give up on themselves before society has a chance to reject them. As a result, many of these young people are headed for a life of poverty, isolation, and incarceration.

I teach because our only hope as a community is to make certain that our children acquire the tools to be able to face the racism, despair, and poverty that assail their young lives. Many times, immigrant parents come face to face with overt racism for the first time when they enter the United States. Consequently, they do not know what they must teach their children, especially their boys; how to diffuse situations with the police; or how to resist the allure of fast money. As Janie Ward, an educator who has written widely on racism and resistance, puts it, we must raise "resisters" who have the knowledge and strategies to survive racism in this society.[4] I teach so that my classroom can be what Ward terms a "homespace," where our children are nurtured and equipped with tools to gain access to higher education, regardless of obstacles put in their way. I teach because to survive as a community, our boys must remain the rainbows that bring us hope in the midst of the tempest. At this point you may be wondering why I mention boys only: About 95% of those who are incarcerated and subsequently deported to Cape Verde are male. This tells me that girls are faring much better in terms of social well-being in the United States. It is for this reason that I mention the boys most often.

I also teach because of young teachers who inspire me with their eagerness to try new things in their classrooms and their passion for social justice and social change. They inspire me because they are not jaded like me; they still believe. And because I see that they believe, I in turn am renewed in my faith that teaching has the potential and the power to bring academic and economic hope to people who are marginalized in this society.

I am inspired by teachers like Antonio, whose history class I once observed. What stands out in my mind is the fact that he encouraged his students to question historical facts. For example, he introduced the topic of "discovery" of America and, through his questions, made his students realize the injustice done to Native Americans. Afterwards, when I spoke to him, he told me that he felt compelled to teach his students to question their history books because the books did not tell the whole truth. He showed me a copy of his book, *Lies My Teacher Told Me*, by James W. Loewen.[5] But more than the facts about curriculum, what inspired me in this young teacher was his passion for justice and fairness as they related to his students.

Antonio told me about an incident in his school that illustrates this point. He told me that during an assembly for seniors, a teacher went on stage and told the students that they could not submit to the yearbook anything written in a foreign language. This was in a school with students from five or more ethnic and linguistic backgrounds. The students were very upset when they left that meeting, and they went straight to Antonio. He told them, "Well, we discussed organizing in our class. What do you think you should do?" The students proceeded to get signatures from other students of different ethnic groups who wanted their language and culture represented in the yearbook. Afterward, they met and drew up a plan of action. They did research to find out which companies actually could print the yearbook with different languages. They did this because one of the excuses that the school had used was that they could not find a printing company to print languages other than English. They then contacted the American Civil Liberties Union, which responded readily and made itself available to defend the interests of the students. Next, the students met with the principal and presented their plan of action should the school not change its plans concerning the representation of other languages in the yearbook. To make a long story short, the principal backed down and the students had their languages and cultures represented in the yearbook.

I believe that pedagogy, especially affective pedagogy, can be symbolized by a smile. It may seem simplistic, but because of my experience as a teacher and as a student, I know that affective pedagogy is extremely important in a classroom. According to Paulo Freire, we teach with our emotions as well as with our words. We teach because we love. We teach with our being. This kind of teaching is not coddling because, as Freire explains, we also teach with reasoning.

I know that in some schools, children feel alienated: There is no sense of family, of community, of camaraderie. I have seen examples of alienation, but I have also seen wonderful examples of affective pedagogy where children feel included and supported. I once did a pilot study at a school with Cape Verdean students in two general education classrooms. I noticed that in one classroom, the Cape Verdean students sat in a corner of the room and hardly volunteered answers when the teacher spoke to them. When I interviewed the students, I was shocked at the level of anger they felt toward the school, their American classmates, and the teacher. When I asked them why they were so angry, they said that it was because they felt humiliated in their classes. Their peers laughed at them when they spoke English, and many of them felt that the teacher did little to stop it. When I interviewed the teacher, he had a dramatically different explanation: He said that the students had not assimilated sufficiently into the American culture and that was why they were isolated in the classroom.

I then interviewed students in the other teacher's classroom and I engaged them on the subject of language. I asked them how they communicated with the teacher. One student responded, "Oh, I speak to him in Creole." I was very surprised because I knew for a fact that the teacher did not speak Cape Verdean Creole. I figured the kid was making up stories. When I mentioned that Mr. D. did not speak Creole, the student looked at me and answered in no uncertain terms, "Well, he understands what I tell him. He just . . . knows."

Needless to say, I could not wait to visit the classroom and see what was going on. What I saw was amazing. That teacher epitomized what I call a smile: He emotionally embraced all his students in a way that made them feel united in that classroom. The Cape Verdean students would sit together explaining concepts to their Cape Verdean peers, but they also would get information from native English-speaking students. They sometimes would physically lean on each other as they spoke to the teacher. When I interviewed the teacher, I told him what the student had said about his speaking Creole. He laughed and his answer said it all: "These students bring so much in terms of language and culture. I want them to use these resources. When I think that many of them will not go to college, *my heart hurts.*" The students in Mr. D's class felt such deep connection with him and their classmates that a different language and culture ceased to be a barrier. It is for reasons such as these that I continue to try to learn to smile. And it is because of teachers like Mr. D. that I teach.

Teaching unsettles me because it is such an overwhelming responsibility. It is not only an emotional responsibility. It is not just because I want the students to feel good and feel comfortable. Part of learning is to question things that we take for granted, to discover issues that need to be debated, to uncover hidden realities that need to be transformed. The more we learn, the more burdened we are because it becomes our responsibility to bring that knowledge to others, to make it explicit, and to do something with it.

Teaching for me then becomes connected to the reality that I live, that my students experience within their reality. Right now, for many Cape Verdean youth, this reality is fraught with poverty, urban isolation, violence, and deportation. Teaching these students becomes an urgent responsibility. The teaching must be explicit in terms of the kind of opportunity it may give them for a good life. They must acquire the tools to change the course of their lives. Truth telling in the classroom becomes a matter of a stable future or a life of incarceration and subsequent deportation. I teach because of what teaching means for our children, and for our community. These children are our rainbows in the midst of the storm. They must not fade away.

When I face this awesome responsibility, I am encouraged by my colleagues, both novices and veterans, who through their teaching, their support, and their passion for social justice give me hope every day. They do not give up, and they do not let me give up.

I teach also because I believe that young people have rights, including the right to their identities and their languages. This has meant that I've had to engage in many struggles to retain bilingual education (a right that was eradicated in 2002 when the voters of Massachusetts supported the elimination of bilingual education through a ballot initiative). I vividly remember one particular experience a number of years ago. The State House that day was crowded with students, parents, and teachers who were there to advocate for bilingual education in Massachusetts. Many of the spectators in the audience held signs that proclaimed the advantages of learning in one's own language. Opponents of bilingual education were also present, intent on convincing the legislators that immigrant children needed only to learn to speak English and that bilingual education was a hindrance.

This was probably my 8th year attending a hearing in which legislators decided the fate of bilingual education and immigrant children. I was very happy to see so many students, parents, teachers, and administrators who had taken time to make a statement with their presence and their testimonies. I felt that our presence as a collective body was symbolic because we were in this stately room, with powerful people who were making decisions about immigrant children's lives. The decisions they made about bilingual education might well determine the children's educational trajectory in this country. They would be deciding whether immigrant students would learn academic content and ultimately make it to college, and even perhaps what kind of lives they would have. These legislators also would be deciding whether the children would be able to fulfill the dreams that drove their parents to cross continents and oceans to reach the United States.

That morning, I saw about 20 of my students in the second row. I was very happy for a few minutes and then realized that something was amiss: The day before, the school administration had refused to let the students attend the hearing because, according to the administration, their time was better served in the classroom. I knew that I most likely would be blamed for the fact that the students were at the State House.

Next morning, I experienced one of the most defeating moments of my career as a teacher and as a human being. In a meeting with the headmaster, whom I admired and still admire greatly, I was accused of indoctrinating my students to the point that they felt compelled to go to this hearing without permission from the school. For my part, I believed I was teaching my students exactly what schools want us to teach: critical thinking skills.

The walkout and the suspension were connected to a unit from the Massachusetts curriculum standards entitled "Dreams" that I had taught that term. When I looked at the book, I saw that it included the speech by Dr. Martin Luther King, Jr. and the poem "A Dream Deferred" by Langston Hughes. Since the students were Cape Verdean, I decided to include an excerpt from an essay by Amilcar Cabral, the leader of Cape Verde's independence. We also discussed the civil rights movement so that students would understand the role of African American leaders in the lives of immigrants of color in this country. I figured that they needed to know who paved the way for them in Cape Verde (Amilcar Cabral) and the United States (Martin Luther King, Jr.). But in order for it to make sense to them, I related the dreams to bilingual education. The point was that if they were able to learn their subject matter in their native language as they learned English, they would be better prepared for high-level courses in college, and a college education might allow them to fulfill their dreams. In addition to the texts, we watched the speech by Dr. King and zeroed in on the concept of civil disobedience.

The students were having difficulty understanding some high-level concepts; they were stuck on just comprehending the text and they were not really relating the concepts of freedom and dreams to their own lives. So I showed them Bloom's Taxonomy and explained the different levels of understanding so they could see clearly where they were.

When we got to the step in Bloom's Taxonomy that calls for application of what the students had learned, I thought I would take them to the State House where the aforementioned bilingual hearing was taking place. In that hearing, the representatives were going to discuss a bill that would either cut bilingual programs or limit them to certain grades. What better opportunity to see the people who actually made decisions about their lives and their future? I asked them to ask their parents to attend the hearing as well. I appealed to their sense of civic responsibility and urged them to take hold of their dreams and make them a reality.

When I asked permission to take the students to the State House, I was shocked that the administration's answer was no. I was very upset because I felt that I had done everything I could to teach the curriculum, to help students to think at an abstract level and connect the concepts to their lives. When it came to seeing who in this society made decisions about their future and their dreams, they were barred from going.

When I told the students they could not go, they were very upset. I told them, however, that I had decided to take a day off and go. Imagine my surprise when I saw them at the State House the next morning. These were children who rarely ventured outside their neighborhoods because they did not speak English well and they were afraid of getting lost. Later, I came to learn that they had gone to school for homeroom and had left the school grounds to go to the State House. The administrators were up in arms because the students passed by them and told them they were going to fight for their right to an education. As they walked out of the school, I was told they shouted, "I have a dream too!"

I had to examine my teaching, to retrace my steps to make sure I had not indoctrinated or brainwashed my students. I had to make it clear that what I taught my students persuaded them that they had to take an active role in deciding their future and participating in the democratic process. What truly broke my heart, however, was the manner in which my students were taken from my classroom, one by one, to be suspended from school for 3 days. As they were escorted out, they looked at me as if asking for help, and there was nothing I could do. I have never felt so powerless in my entire life as I felt at that moment. After they came back from suspension and we were processing what had happened, one of them said, "It was worth it. I'd do the same thing again if I had to. If I don't fight for my future, who will?" That day, the roles were reversed and my students embraced me and surrounded me with love. They restored my spirit when I felt totally defeated in a system that I felt had betrayed us. That day they rekindled hope in me and I vowed that someday I would tell their story.

My students taught me that sometimes we do things that bring us so much pain, so many disillusions, that we do not see victory at that moment. I do not know what ramifications this episode had on their lives. I hope that they will look back and realize that they stood up for themselves, although they paid a price. That is the lesson they taught me. Because of them, I teach.

Chapter 11

Being on a Moving Train

AYLA GAVINS

A yla Gavins considers herself lucky: Not only does she work with colleagues whom she deeply values, she also taught for 6 years at Mission Hill School, where renowned educator Deborah Meier is the principal and guiding force. At this school, Ayla taught grades 2 through 7. Several months after writing this essay, she began a new job as academy director at an urban K–8 pilot school with a diverse student population. Always on the go, Ayla serves as a senior member of her staff, and she is responsible for teaching, learning, organizing and community outreach for one of the three academies in her school. Moreover, she frequently presents at education conferences, most notably at the national Spring and Fall Forums sponsored by the Coalition of Essential Schools, of which her school is a member.

Ayla knew she wanted to be a teacher early on, and this is what she studied at Boston University. Although when she wrote this essay she had already taught for 12 years, Ayla finds teaching always new and intriguing. She is fascinated by the insights and humor of children as well as by her colleagues' intelligence and commitment. She also is energized by involvement in other activities outside of school, especially the arts, and she is a member of the New England Women of Color Artists Association.

Teaching helps Ayla understand the world a little more clearly. But teaching is also ephemeral and hard to get hold of. In her essay, Ayla speaks about this aspect of teaching, comparing it to being on a moving train.

Ever since I was a kid, I have been touched by the power of my teachers. In hindsight, I don't think most of them were especially good teachers, but in small ways they still had a memorable influence on me. Their comments about my handwriting, my pleasant demeanor, or my talent as an artist stuck with me. As a high school senior on the college path in a school that tracked students, I was able to spend a semester trying out different careers. I decided to try teaching and was paired with a teacher in a nearby school. I remember being assigned to a male teacher who sometimes fell asleep at his desk. I can't recall a single interaction he ever had with children. I only remember one piece of advice he gave me: "Don't cross your legs or wear knee highs. They both will give you spider veins." It was during that internship that I first saw teachers as ordinary people and experienced being on the other side of the desk.

When I think back about what school was like for me, I think about how much smarter I could be now if I had had a different kind of schooling, or teachers who tried to get to know me. I went to a series of traditional schools in a suburban town outside Pittsburgh, Pennsylvania. I don't remember ever sharing my voice in a powerful way publicly. I coasted through school. One of my few elementary school memories is of a Black boy named Jack. He used to crawl under a desk and was regularly yelled at by our teacher. That boy was the only other Black student in my class. Skin color was our only connection, but it was strong enough to make me feel both empathy and a private embarrassment for him. I wonder what ever happened to Jack? Did he ever recover from those incidents?

I remember sitting in my high school English class when my teacher announced that there was only one student who had a perfect paper. It was mine. I sat in the front row and tried to suppress my uncontainable laughter. I laughed out of nervousness and partly out of surprise because I put little effort into following writing rules and also because the class clowns who sat in the back of the room had a field day at my expense. I became new raw material for the rest of the year.

Those school memories are part of why I teach now. As a teacher, I've begun to understand, question, and change many things that are part of my education biography. I'd like the experience of students I teach to be richer and more meaningful than mine.

I began to teach full-time 12 years ago. I was hired by the Wayland, Massachusetts Public School System before I had even completed my senior year in college. One of my professors had children in the Wayland public schools and she was excited about my educational outlook and the possibility of diversifying the teaching staff. I became the youngest and the only Black teacher in the school.

Unlike many beginning teachers, I had a wonderful first year. The staff I joined was older and excited by my youth. I soon learned who my allies were and I developed informal mentoring relationships with them. Those mentors turned into friends I still have today. Feeling I had so many things to prove that first year fueled my fire and creativity to meet the needs of my students, eight of whom were on special education plans. For 11 years, I kept the photo of my first class for good luck. At the beginning of each school year I'd look at that picture as a reminder of my beginnings. There's a lot about teaching that first class that I want to keep in my practice now, 11 years later. I still have a letter that Joseph, one of the students from my first year, wrote to me several years after he had been in my class. He had Down's Syndrome and wrote me a letter asking me how I was doing. It felt great to know that he was still thinking of me too.

Through teaching, I have met many people whom I admire and who have contributed to my life and character. Most of them, like Joseph, just happen to be under the age of 13. Another is Becky, an 8-year-old girl I've had the pleasure of teaching for 2 years. She has many behaviors that set her apart from other children, including an obsession with imaginative and dramatic play. She craftily continues to play dramatic roles all day long. During class meetings she often has a scarf wrapped around her head, possibly representing a fancy hat, long hair, a mask, or a veil. Accompanying her headdress is some new creation constructed with glue and paper or anything sparkly she can find. Some days she carries her mom's old pocketbook, digging through it as though searching for important documents. Inside the purse are incomplete workbooks that she's had since 1st grade. Becky is the color of milk chocolate, a beautiful girl with large and expressive dark brown eyes. "I don't want to crush her spirit, but . . . " her mother said to me as we shared our joys and frustrations regarding Becky's progress and performance at school. Becky's mother did not want to stop the creativity in her daughter or want her to feel that fun was no longer a part of their lives together. At the same time, she wanted Becky to see that it was time to become more responsible for her learning.

Becky is constantly creating something new and often unrelated to schoolwork, and she is sometimes defiant. One afternoon as she was working on a drawing, she ignored the clean-up warning and refused to stop working even though it was time to go home. I took the drawing away from her. Upset, she covered her face with her hands and stormed off into the coatroom to get her things and go home. She grabbed her coat and dragged her school bag on the floor as she clumsily tried to catch up with the rest of the children taking the school bus. I moved as quickly as she did, pulling her coat up on her shoulders with a backpack to follow. As she went down the stairs I continued walking down the hall. A tapping noise caught my attention. I turned back and saw Becky excitedly waving good-bye to me. I waved back and she scurried off to catch up with the other children taking the school bus. Tomorrow would be a new day. I was looking forward to seeing her.

Lance is a 7-year-old boy more excited about learning and life than anyone else I have ever known. He religiously says hello every morning and has his learning plan for the day on his mind. His goals are to become a better reader and speak more articulately, a challenge as a result of cleft palate repair surgery. His aggressiveness to learn as much as possible could create an unfair playing or learning ground for others in the classroom if he was given the teacher time he seeks. At the same time, it's difficult to resist a child who follows your every move, just waiting for a chance to read a book to you or practice the "th" sound.

What is so appealing to me about being in the company of Becky and Lance and other children like them is that their approach to life is different from mine or anyone else's I know. They are so truly themselves. That's hard to find in adult circles. They are also young and need the kind of adult guidance that does not crush their spirits. On any given day teachers make hundreds, if not thousands, of decisions to keep a balance of fairness and equity with regard to learning and social policy. I learn more and more each day that every decision and action I make is rooted in a belief or experience I've had. My decisions might be based on my sense of morality. They also might be based on how I view best educational practice. Over time and repeated experiences, I have developed a style and philosophy that are progressive and democratic.

I love to laugh. To be a good teacher, you have to have a good sense of humor. As a student teacher years ago, I remember how the daily laughter influenced my decision to become a teacher. Few days have gone by since then that I have not laughed. Even on the toughest days, I can chuckle. What makes me laugh? Kids are naturally humorous in the ways they discover and make sense of the world. Their literal interpretations of adult sayings and figurative language are funny, as are the behaviors they model and adopt from adults. The questions children ask about what things adults do and how they do them also can be hilarious. The way children share their special passions and take interest in one another's special collections and hobbies makes me smile. Also comical are the individual quirks they reveal without regard to how others might perceive them. With older children, these things still happen, despite their effort to suppress most things that make them unique.

The other day a little girl named Judy attempted to walk out of the classroom with bulging pockets. She was questioned by my student teacher about her destination and the contents of her pockets. Judy feigned a bathroom emergency and scurried off to the girls' room. Watching from afar, I was amused by her zest to accomplish her mission of getting to the girls' room. When Judy came back, her head was draped with plastic beaded necklaces. My assistant described her as looking like a lamp. I laughed so hard inside at the sight of the green, blue, and red acrylic beads wrapped around her plats and dangling in her face with her eyes peeping in between the strands. Of course, you can fully appreciate children's humor only if you allow space for that kind of sharing and familiarity in yourself and in your classroom. I chuckle to myself when I watch students construct, create, and debate their best next moves.

One part of teaching that has always appealed to me is that it gives me time to paint. The time I spend as a painter has contributed greatly to my effectiveness as a teacher. I know of several teachers who garden, play a drum, or travel for pleasure and rejuvenation. Those are the kinds of people that I would want teaching my child. I'd like my daughter to be in the company of interesting, well-rounded adults just as I like to be in the company of interesting, well-rounded adults. The long days spent with children and colleagues deepen my character and intellectual capacity. The time I spend away allows me to grow and return to work with new experiences and perspectives to offer.

Another reason I teach is because feeling smart and being in the company of smart people feels good. It provides a rich combination of experience and theory that keeps me questioning, thinking, and coming to my own conclusions. I feel smarter at the end of every year. Every day presents a case study, a child, or an interaction worthy of reflection or closer examination. I am fortunate to work in a school where intellectual stimulation is a way of life. In fact, at Mission Hill, the school where I teach, the basis for teaching and learning are the five habits of mind created by our principal, Deborah Meier, that encourage critical thought and responsible action. Teaching keeps my intellectual life alive.

There is perpetual conflict among educators about whether it is best, or possible, to educate the whole child when society's ills are so strong. Of course, all the societal dilemmas that impact school life, such as violence, poverty, and racism, are real. As disheartening as some of the circumstances are, they fuel my work and they are the reason why some schools exist at all. Every teacher and school has a position on those questions. When I am in the company of my brilliant and interesting peers, I am always changed by our conversations about these topics.

Twice a week, the Mission Hill School staff meets for professional development. During our 1½-hour meetings, we take time to look at the work we have done, question it, and plan for research, improvement, or additional learning. The teachers I work with largely plan our own professional development. In the school's beginning years, the staff sought out experts on a variety of topics to lead our growth. Before long, Deborah Meier reminded us that we are all experts in different areas. At one of our retreats, we took some time to think about this. In what ways were we experts? What did each one of us have to offer our colleagues and the school community? As I began to plan and facilitate professional development sessions with the staff, I saw myself changing as a teacher, more able and comfortable with adults as learners. This is important because I believe in teachers as spokespeople for the work we do. Sharing daily challenges and triumphs with the public is not exactly a strength we have as a collective group. My vision of myself and other teachers as scholars includes believing that we know something and sharing it with others through writing, lectures, or workshops.

When people come together to do a job as complex and rewarding as teaching, bonds form. I have worked in three very different schools. In each school, I have met people I don't think I could have met anywhere else. They are brilliant, creative, hardworking, loving people who often have passed up a higher salary to do this difficult job that has mostly nonmonetary rewards. My relationships have lasted with a few people in each school. They are a group of people that I would forever like to be a part of.

I teach as a way to bring the world in, but also to be able to speak to the world from the position of a teacher. It is not often that I hear the teacher's voice, especially one that I respect, in the media. During every election, education is in the news. Yet, I can't think of one teacher who has spoken during one of these addresses to the nation or election debates. I try to keep this in mind when speaking or writing opportunities arise.

There will always be a platform for my voice as a teacher because the educational forefront is always changing. As a teacher, I am on a moving train. I am a part of something—globally, nationally, and locally. That is an empowering thought and it gives me a choice of contexts where I can make changes. If I thought I could go into my classroom and shut the door, letting others fuss and fight over the next curricular mandate or policy as I remain untouched, I would be wrong. I cannot remain untouched and neither can my students. I understand that many people don't want to—or cannot—put time and effort into political action or publicly sharing their viewpoints. For some, that would be risking the loss of a job. I'd just like teachers, including those considering joining the profession, to think about what is right. Shutting the classroom door does not stop the larger world from influencing our classrooms.

There is something very self-reflective about teaching. Every day that I teach, I learn something new about myself. I am slightly changed every time I get to know a student. As a teacher I exude my values and what is important to me. My sense of right and wrong filters through the rules, the standard of good work, and how we treat each other in my classroom. What is important to me is out there for everyone to see. Daily I am questioned and must reaffirm what I see as important. The Mission Hill School makes that work easier because what is important there is in line with my thoughts: *Work hard and be kind,* our school motto.

Chapter 12

Teaching Outside the Lines

E LAINE S TINSON

B y the end of 4th grade, my granddaughter Jazmyne confessed that, although she had cared for all her teachers up to that point, it was Ms. Stinson whom she most loved. Relationships have always been important to Jazmyne, and in Ms. Stinson's class all relationships—student to student, student to teacher, student to family, and teacher to family—were nurtured and valued. This aspect of teaching is often taken for granted or even neglected, but for many children it is relationships with teachers and peers that can make or break their schooling experience.

It is not just social goals that are central to Elaine Stinson's curriculum. She wants students to get along and care about one another, of course, but she also wants them to learn to think critically and to act honorably in the world. Her curriculum reflects these values, as will be clear in her essay. Elaine reasons that if students are comfortable in their identities and in the world, there's a good chance that they also will do well in school.

A 4th-grade teacher for 15 years, Elaine takes the profession very seriously and several years ago went through the rigorous National Board Certification process. In all the years she's been teaching, she has loved her job. In spite of this, she came to the profession not because of positive experiences, but mostly because of negative ones.

"I hate school!" I often would lament as a student. I had yet to develop an interest in learning. I found reading boring, and the social aspect of school didn't come into play until 9th grade. I realize that school lacked relationship for me, personal relationships with teachers and peers, as well as an overall sense of community and acceptance. In many ways, it lacked purpose. High school was a social event, middle school, a dreaded obligation. And in elementary school, I felt like an outsider.

I remember my early years in school as painfully difficult. Leaving the warmth and love of my mother and my home and embarking on the strange, new world of 1st grade was scary and unfriendly. The adults in this new environment did not seem to provide the kind of security and nurturing that I needed as a little girl or as a learner in their classroom. The divide between my home life and my experiences at school was made wider because I was too shy to initiate friendships. My teachers did not come to my aid, and I can only conclude that they were unaware of the social challenges I encountered as a 6-year-old. They lacked knowledge about my home life and how it contributed to my experience as a learner. I do not believe they took the time to understand me as a whole child from an emotional, psychological, or familial perspective.

Teachers seemed focused on my academic aptitude to the exclusion of my need to feel included, cared for, and appreciated as a valuable member of the class. I do not recall a feeling of community, or the sense of a school family that is so important to me as a teacher. Many of my teachers seemed to be more concerned with *what* they were charged to teach rather than with *whom* they were teaching.

Throughout my life as a student, the curriculum was flat and uninspiring. Sadly, my earliest reading experience was limited to "Dick and Jane." Using segments of isolated material, reading was taught in groups of children who were separated according to those who could sound out letter combinations and those who could not. I remember group names like the "bluebirds" and the "robins." Surprisingly, I remember how we all seemed to know which group was the "smartest." It was apparent that I did not comprehend the subtleties of "Dick and Jane." Teachers suggested that I read more at home, but unfortunately my family did not have their own books, nor was there a public library to visit even if we were able to find the transportation. Later, I repeatedly learned about Columbus and his perilous journey to discover a "new world." I was not taught to question these things; they were presented as fact. Thinking outside the lines was not part of the plan. Quite the contrary, it was discouraged. History was presented with all the answers in place. There were no mysteries to solve, no lessons to learn. They were all learned long ago, well before I began attending school.

A lot has changed since I was a student, but sadly some things have not. Shallow frameworks and curriculum guides, mandated high-stakes testing, and memorization of the "facts" still play a role in education. Not unlike my experience as a student, many kids today are bored and uninspired, leaving school passionless about global justice, with little sense of personal agency, and less able or likely to critique those in power.

Given my experiences as a student, why did I choose to become a teacher? When I began to contemplate this question, one thing became clear: I love the relationships I build with my students and their families. This is one of the jewels of teaching and what I have learned is that it is the most effective way to inspire learning. It is by building deep relationships with my children that I come to understand who they are, what they are interested in, what they know and are passionate about, what they are curious about, and their individual ways of learning. It seems natural to me that children learn best when they are appreciated as whole and unique individuals.

Perhaps teaching is my way of providing something that was missing in my own experience as a student. I've found that meaningful learning happens through meaningful interaction, whether it's with peers, teachers, music, authors, or poets, or through nature. When children feel liked and accepted for who they are, they are more willing to open up and share their ideas and, in turn, to make connections with other ideas.

As a teacher I have learned that unpacking the "facts" with a community of unique and critical eyes is essential to engaging learners and allowing learning to unfold. I am also aware that this kind of teaching leaves me feeling vulnerable because the lesson plan is never finalized. The direction and depth of the learning are as diverse as each of my students. True to life, there is no manual with all the answers. The "answers" are shaped by the direction we take as a learning community. Most important, we come to realize that the answers are not as important as the process we take to discover them. Providing the kind of education that promotes these values requires that I "know" my students from every vantage point, that I be with them in their world. In that way, I feel more prepared to share the experience, and less vulnerable to its varied direction. Not only is this experience challenging, but it is also meaningful—for everyone. When I nurture positive relationships with my kids and their families, students blossom as learners and I inevitably improve as a teacher.

I have learned that my students need to know that I care about them; they need to know that their peers do, too. They need to believe that their opinions are respected and important to the overall learning experience of everyone in the classroom community. They need to be included in the process of developing the space, the curriculum, and the overall learning experience through sharing personal stories, feelings, questions, history, and understanding. I have discovered that this process is rich with energy, creativity, and challenge.

Through the years, I also have found that creating a community can take place only when the risk is minimized and when everyone, even the "problem child," is included and respected for his or her unique contribution to the class. Building this kind of community requires that everyone be onboard. It means nurturing a deep and significant relationship with each child and creating a mutual understanding that promotes caring for all members of the community. As a result, the community is a living ideal that grows as the year progresses. It becomes part of recess, and it extends outside of "best friends." When members of the community are hurting, whether it happens on the bus, the playground, or the local ice cream shop, others in the group come to their aid because they know them, feel for them, and care. I know we have a caring community when something like this happens: Last year, a group of children at the beginning of the year were apt to tease a young boy for his impulsive behavior. One day, they came to tell me that other students outside of our class were taunting him and that he was terribly hurt by it. They wanted some advice on how to help him.

Within the classroom, this kind of caring occurs when one student wants to help another understand something that seems difficult by putting it in "kid-friendly" language. This is reflected in the kind of listening and questioning that my students do when others are talking. Or it's apparent when we cry when we've read a very sad story, or when we laugh because someone has "broken wind" during our math circle. Our community became evident to me last year: Armed with a new strategy for teaching the children how to follow directions, I began asking them to "watch and follow!" They did exactly that, all too well! They kept following me, mimicking my every movement and sound for what seemed like a very long time, much longer than I wanted them to. Together, we couldn't stop giggling. My cheeks and sides were hurting from so much belly laughter.

Being aware of the tenor of the community is vital to its success. Building meaningful relationships means becoming vulnerable to the silliness of 9-year-olds, being open to them, and allowing them insight to your sense of humor and humility. It means sharing yourself in a way that makes the teacher a real person, with deep feelings about life and humanity. It means laughing so hard I cry or tearing up because one of my kids says something so incredibly sweet and profound. The more *real* I am to my students, the more open they are to me. When I nurture this kind of relationship it carries over into the kind of learning that blossoms into life-changing moments and revolutionary thinking. When children learn to care about one another and to show empathy, they also learn to extend this way of being to those outside the classroom. They begin the practice of appreciating the "others" in the world.

I know this way of teaching is more challenging than following a core curriculum that is bottled up in neatly stacked chunks of time: a 40-minute block to read textbook pages, 20 minutes to impart strategies to master homonyms, and so on. I have found that my students are more open to understanding these ideas when I have built strong relationships with them and when a sense of community is in place. Building a community that is home to all the unique personalities, feelings, and commentary is essential for engaging learners with any curriculum.

A fortunate thing happened when I began my teaching, although I may not have felt that way at the time. The formal curriculum was broad, allowing me some liberty in the choice of specific content. Although this was incredibly stressful at the time, it also offered me the opportunity to weave a social justice perspective into most of the guidelines provided by the administration.

Through continued practice as a teacher, I encourage my students to participate in developing our course of study. As an example, most recently, my students researched and wrote biographies about historical characters. To include a social justice perspective into the language requirement of writing biographies, I developed a list of social activists from which the children could choose and research. After they made their choice, students developed key questions about their person's life, and in particular about the person's activism. I asked my kids to get inside the character and learn about his or her life and passion for justice and how it compared with social issues of today. I asked them to learn their character's message: "What would your person want to share with people today?" In essence, I asked the children to understand and empathize with an injustice of the past, and to critically examine the social inequities that exist today. To share their knowledge, each student created a quilt square about his or her person's life message, which we combined to make a "Justice for All" quilt. The quilt is now showcased in the school for the extended community to view.

As an example of how children lead the way, when we discuss a topic or a question that is unique to a particular child and we explore it together, it becomes a pathway to deepen everyone's understanding of that topic. When studying maps of the world, one student wanted to know why each of the four maps in our classroom was so different from the others. This prompted us to compare the accuracy of the projections, asking why Europe and North America are much larger than Africa on two of the maps. A second student, Jeremy, wanted to know why "north" was on top and who made that decision. These kinds of questions led the study, and the experience became deeper and more consequential than the mandated curriculum of learning lines of latitude and longitude. These kinds of questions are far better than my "teacher questions" because they allow students to easily connect with their prior knowledge.

My experience has taught me that children possess an amazing sense of fairness. When Jeremy's question was posed and explored, it became a pathway for us to understand something about our own assumptions of the world. Why *do* we think the north is so much larger than the south, or why is it that where we live happens to be on the top? Is this a fair or an accurate representation? Is it fair to kids who live in South America? I have found this method of teaching rewarding as both a teacher and a learner. The students are invested, challenged, and involved because they are exploring topics they find moving and meaningful to their lives. And so am I.

As the teacher, I know that I must be willing to allow the content of the day to unfold. This is necessary if I truly want to "step-in" where the students are. I need to acknowledge that I don't have all the answers, or even all the *questions*. I also have learned that it takes courage to relinquish total control of what gets said or thought and discussed, courage to make mistakes and to own up to those mistakes. It takes courage to broach unpopular or controversial subjects with my students, their families, the administration, and most important, myself. This way of teaching inevitably exposes some of my own vulnerabilities, but the trade-off is a rich and rewarding experience for my students and for me.

An activity that I love to use year after year is to ask students to examine the perspective of an author whose book they are reading. During this activity, the students pose questions that perhaps reflect their opposing opinion about the topic, or that point out what they perceive as a weakness in logic or historical relevance. Essentially, the students are asking the author to support what he or she wrote with stronger reasoning. This activity becomes the stimulus for discussion and study, as the other students respond by sharing their interpretation of the reading.

For instance, during a Thanksgiving study about the Wampanoag people, students questioned various authors about some of the "facts" asserted in their text. The children found contradictory information and critically analyzed the material I had provided. My students wanted to research all the picture books in the school's library to learn about opposing opinions, and in some cases to locate nontruths. One book portrayed the Wampanoag nation more as a Plains people in dress and lifestyle, while quite a few neglected to mention how the Pilgrims stole food and provisions from the Wampanoags. Students created charts to analyze the various texts, and they graded books for their accuracy and depth of truth. I added to their pile of books by bringing in books from three public libraries and more from my own collection. In all, the students examined some 16 books as well as original documents I provided from the text

Rethinking Columbus.[1] After completing their work, they presented their findings to the school librarian along with a list of recommended books. She not only appreciated their research, hard work, and honest comments, but she also ordered several of their recommended books for our school library. This project was rich and rewarding because I gave my students the room they needed to direct it. They were eager to learn as much as they could about the Wampanoag people because their knowledge had a purpose. They knew they were working to make positive change in their world.

In my classroom I ask students to join me as we become more thoughtful about our assumptions, as we practice using our voices respectfully to question, to become better listeners, and to make informed decisions. I have learned that when I give students the opportunity to practice critical thinking, they blossom as thinkers. When they are encouraged to find ways to promote social change, they do and they begin to see themselves as people who can make a positive difference.

Another reason I chose to be an educator was tied to my deep passion for justice. When I was a teenager in the 1970s, my sense of fair and unfair and the beginnings of my understanding of social justice were shaped by the many different social movements of the day. I was deeply moved by the struggle for civil rights and gender equity. I believe I would have made a significant connection with high school had these events been discussed in class. Discussing events that are close to my students' lives inevitably becomes part of a curriculum that takes its direction from the learners. Exposing my students to a variety of viewpoints gives them the opportunity to form educated opinions about their world. Exploring voices outside of the dominant voice often found in textbooks emphasizes the many sides to a story.

Diversity as an asset is played out regularly in my classroom, whether we are exploring various ways to solve a math problem, or sharing our own stories in class meetings. During class meetings my students shine because it is here that they show their feelings, vulnerabilities, and desires to their classmates. As a class family, we discuss personal problems. My students listen, ask questions to better understand, empathize, and brainstorm possible solutions to a problem that is not theirs. They practice this throughout the year and learn they are capable of solving their own problems and helping their friends solve theirs too. They learn that it is definitely better to have many different perspectives and, therefore, possible solutions. The children experience problem solving within a caring and respectful environment, while learning that problems happen to everyone. The remarkable thing about class meetings is that they extend beyond the social sphere into every aspect of the classroom experience. Students work together throughout the year with a deeper understanding and respect for one another, and as a result they are more open to learning from one another.

If children are to help create a society that is more socially responsible than that of their parents' generation, I believe it must begin with quality classroom experiences. By allowing the class to be a forum for open discussion and respectful listening about meaningful "stuff," by grounding the subject matter in the lives of my students, and by trusting them to evaluate their own sense of fairness and justice, I have discovered that students are better able to critique the real world. They are better prepared to make positive change in a world that desperately needs it.

When writing this essay, it became quite evident to me why I became a teacher. I work in a place where the students always seem glad to see me, where I feel cared for and respected, where discussions are rich and learning is inspired, and where I laugh each and every day. I know I am building deep, lasting, and caring relationships. I know I am providing a venue for children to talk about real-life matters, and share real feelings, where children learn to appreciate the diversity of people in their world and where they can practice caring for others. I believe I am helping to inspire thoughtful activists with strong voices. Perhaps it is my small way of teaching outside the lines.

PART IV

To Help Students Name and Claim the World

S everal decades ago, Brazilian educator Paulo Freire linked the ability to "read the word" with the necessity to "read the world."[1] That is, simply knowing how to decode and decipher words is not enough. In Freire's judgment, teachers must teach students to read both the word *and* the world because helping students understand, navigate, and change the world takes a more critical approach to education than is generally the case.

The essays in this part exemplify what it means to teach to help students name and claim the world. In the case of Kristen French, her own struggles as a student, as well as the power of significant relationships with family members and mentors over the years, led her to become a teacher. She wanted to help other students facing similar challenges, and this explains her decision to include in her essay poetry written by three of her students. Sometimes teachers simply recognize that a good education is the only hope some young people might have for a full, productive, and meaningful life. This is the case with Melinda Pellerin-Duck, a high school teacher who writes about the colors and strands of a Kente cloth as a metaphor for teaching. Other teachers enter the profession because they want to help open students' eyes to possibilities they might never have even dreamt about. This is the case with Yahaira Marquez, a young Puerto Rican woman who had just completed her first year of teaching when she wrote her essay. She writes that her early decision to become a teacher was motivated by a desire to let other young people like herself know that they had other options in life.

Hence, sometimes it is teachers' identities that help them be courageous in ways that also help their students claim their piece of the world. This is one reason that Beth Wohlleb Adel, who was inadvertently "outted" by a student, came to make the decision to be honest and open with them not only about her identity but also about other controversial topics. In the process, this experience taught her how to encourage her students to also "read the world." Nina Tepper, an urban teacher for over 2 decades, also wanted her students to learn to discuss difficult issues. This desire was what led her to develop a unit with a colleague that, unfortunately, did not end as happily as Beth's. Through this experience, however, Nina came to the conclusion that teaching is inevitably about taking risks. This part concludes with an essay by Seth Peterson, a young man who writes movingly about the power of language, his subject matter, and the students in his Boston classroom—"the corner room facing the alley and the church"—and how they challenge conventional knowledge while also learning to master it.

Chapter 13

Teaching for Empowerment, Love, and Mentorship

Kristen B. French

With help from Jennifer Leonor, Anissa Little, and Shatara Smith

Kristen French returned to teaching last year after a 3-year leave to work on her master's and then doctoral degrees. Although she has not yet completed the latter, she missed the pace and energy of classroom life and decided to go back to work with children, this time as a literacy teacher of 4- to 12-year-olds in a public urban Montessori school. But whether working with children or adults, Kristen is a gifted teacher. While a doctoral student, she supervised student teachers and also taught several courses, including curriculum development and multicultural education. Very beloved by her students, she was nominated for the Distinguished Teaching Award at the University of Massachusetts, a distinct honor that few graduate students receive.

Teaching young people also has been a joy for Kristen although, as she explains in her essay, as a child she herself often felt invisible and unvalued in school. A number of teachers made a difference in her life, a difference that opened her eyes to the power of teachers. Her drama teacher in middle school helped her get through those years, but it was not until she was in community college, barely fitting in the chairs because she was pregnant, that she met the teacher who would be her inspiration for many years to come.

In her essay, Kristen ponders the many ways her mentor changed her life, and as a result her responsibility to others. Drawing on her own identity as a Native American, she writes about the power of connection with students of diverse backgrounds who often feel marginalized in school. Including poems by three of her young students, Kristen's essay reveals how she tries to fulfill her mentor's advice that she do for others what he did for her.

How do empowerment, love, and mentorship translate into everyday teaching practices, especially during a time when testing and prescribed learning standards are such a strong presence in our schools? In my own case, how can I maintain the connection to my dreams of empowerment and activism for both my own practice and for the children I work with?

For starters, I should define what empowerment means to me. Empowerment encompasses most of what I hold dear in my teaching philosophy: It is the process of collective collaboration where multiple voices of students and teachers are shared, heard, and acted upon. Empowerment can be a loaded word, as if one person can empower another. I don't want to presume that I have the ability or power to empower anyone other than myself, but the possibilities for empowerment *can* be created when a foundation is provided. And hopefully, within the process of dreaming and imagining a just community, students will take an active role to become agents for change in their own lives.

I come from a large and close family. I was raised by a mother who supported and loved me through many tough years. When we lived in the midwest, she worked two jobs to make ends meet, and we survived. When we moved back home to the Pacific northwest, I lived with my aunt while my mom took care of my grandparents.

I wasn't much of a student. When I was little, I was quiet and invisible. I didn't speak; I just tried to blend into the background. I liked it there because no one picked on me and I could daydream for hours. Later, when I moved from my Pacific northwest home to a midwestern city, I was finally noticed—but only as a student who couldn't read. I began to see myself as different, a struggling student, first invisible, then dumb.

It wasn't until I got into middle school that I found a teacher who inspired some sense of academic pride in my education. She was my drama teacher and she encouraged me to focus my rebellious and often troublemaking energy into theater and writing. Again in high school, I didn't see myself as an intellectually competent student and I wasn't recognized as one either. I barely made it out of high school when I became pregnant at 18. Frightened that I was going to be another statistic—an uneducated pregnant teenage mother—I nevertheless was determined to create a better life for me and my unborn child. I registered to attend the local community college.

I could barely fit into the short desks. I wanted an education but I was terrified. Am I smart enough? Can I do this? My mom was the first in the family to go to college. School wasn't easy for her either. I wanted to do the same. I wanted to make my family proud.

At the community college, I stuck out almost as much as my belly as I started to attend a physical anthropology class. I read and studied and worked really hard. One day we had a guest speaker, Dale McGinnis. He was like no man or teacher I had ever seen. He was earthy and majestic with his grey and white beard, a beaded glasses chain around his neck that fell onto his trademark vest, and faded blue jeans. As he confidently began his guest lecture, I was mesmerized by his dynamic teaching style. I was on the edge of my seat as he moved around the room explaining concepts by telling stories. He then jumped up on the table to physically and vocally demonstrate the mating call of a gibbon. I almost fell over! He was hilarious, and at the same time, I learned so much in just one lecture. I really wanted to meet him but I was afraid to introduce myself.

Somehow, after class when I walked by him, even though he was surrounded by other students, I found the courage to say hello and how much I appreciated his lecture. Immediately he asked me what nation I was from. (How did he know I was Native, I wondered?) I said, "Blackfoot and Gros Ventre." He began teasing me that the Crow, his nation, always beat us in basketball. We laughed and joked a bit. He asked me to come visit him sometime to figure out my academic coursework.

It wasn't long after our meeting that I decided to major in anthropology and I became the teacher's assistant for the anthropology department. Dale pushed me to work hard and to let go of my fear of failure. One day he was running late so he asked me to introduce one of the films and lectures for an introduction to anthropology class. I was petrified but I would do anything for this man who had supported and encouraged me. This was my first experience teaching. I was scared out of my mind, but I loved it. Then he encouraged me to speak at local elementary schools on American Indian issues and to tutor foreign students in anthropology. In the meantime, he worked with a small group of students on anthropological theory, a seminar open usually only to master's students or students in upper-level courses at 4-year universities. He invited me to spend time with his amazing family and he became a grandfather to my daughter. Dale provided me with an academic home.

I graduated with honors in anthropology with a minor in Native American studies and double majored, receiving my degree in elementary education. When I finished my associate's degree and was nervously preparing to leave my supportive environment, I discovered that Dale had nominated me for the Student of the Year Award. When I received this award, I was deeply moved and surprised. I had never been recognized for anything before. Most important, this recognition was for academic achievement. With Dale's assistance, I received a scholarship to a 4-year university. I went from being a scared, invisible, pregnant teenage student to being a young woman with an endless future of possibilities.

I did not know how to thank Dale for the tremendous gifts he gave me, the gift of believing in myself, of seeing myself as academically capable, of seeing my future as a teacher. One day, I asked him why he had done all of this for me. He told me that he had been a lot like me, a young person who wanted so much more out of life, to contribute, to learn—but who as a nontraditional student was a bit rough around the edges. He too had a mentor who could see through the tough exterior and who encouraged, prodded, and believed in him. His mentor told him that it was his responsibility to share these gifts with his students. He then turned to me and said, "It is now your turn to do this for your students."

I wish Dale could see today the seeds he planted in me. He passed away before he was able to see me as a teacher working with students who are like us both. But I hear his voice everyday, especially on those tough days when it would be easy to forget my calling. He challenges me to stay strong and pass on to my students the courage to succeed.

After graduating from the university, I taught for several years in a rural setting working with Native, Mexican American, and poor White working-class students. I loved teaching. In that school, I found a community of educators dedicated to the universal and cultural needs of children, unified in the struggle against the oppression of our students. We were a family.

Although I was deeply satisfied with my career decision, I became frustrated with the nature of impoverished schools, particularly those directly connected to communities of color. I yearned for the opportunity to become actively involved in a strong culturally diverse community and to work with dedicated educators to change the systemic issues that especially plagued our second-language parents and students.

During this time, I had the opportunity to attend a multicultural education conference and see one of the academics whose work had inspired me during my undergraduate and teaching years. As a result, a year later, my daughter and I packed up our bags, loaded the U-Haul, and moved from Washington State to Massachusetts. Two years later, I received my master's degree in bilingual, ESL, and multicultural education, and I am currently a doctoral student in the language, literacy, and culture program.

I spent the next 4 years working in teacher education at the University of Massachusetts at Amherst. Working with teachers and future teachers was inspiring, particularly on an institutional level, but I longed for the connection with children. I was also 4 years out of the classroom and felt the need to reconnect with my teaching roots and go back into the public educational system. So last year, I became the writing specialist in an inner-city school in western Massachusetts, and I began to re-evaluate and document why I teach.

This year I have put my beliefs of empowerment, love, and mentoring into action through a student/teacher critical literacy collaborative. This dream was realized through an amazing group of students who reminded me why I teach. As a writing specialist, I saw each class in the preK–7th-grade school for 40 minutes a week. Once a week, I had an Open Publishing Center that students could attend to finish work or receive writing support. Shortly after the beginning of the school year, students wanted more space to connect with each other, the assignments, and me. So I offered students and teachers a short prep time that I had from 2:40 until the end of the day at 3:05. Students began joining me at this time to discuss the writing class, finish work, or share stories. This eventually became our Open Publishing Center research group. An average of 25 to 30 students from different 3rd- through 6th-grade classrooms began participating in our group.

During open publishing, students began sharing their lives through the classwork. We also used the work of Patty Bode (see pp. 49–57), an Amherst art educator and scholar, whose students create hand portraits with symbols that reflect their personal images. Throughout the year, the students who took part in the Open Publishing Center began to share joys, including their love of contemporary culture and leisure activities, but also their fears, disappointments, concerns, and the events that took place in their communities. At first we spent time getting to know and trust one another but then, over time, students became focused on issues they felt needed to be addressed, particularly the homeless issue in the city. This issue arose after a man froze to death on the steps of the symphony building on a cold January night, two blocks away from the school. Many of the student researchers couldn't understand how someone could be without family or support.

The students decided that they wanted to do something about it. The three young women who contributed their poetry to this essay were among the students who initiated the discussion on taking action in their community to do something about homelessness. After a long discussion, they decided to make a quilt for the local shelter. As we began making decisions about the quilt, many students became involved on a deeper level and started to consider other ways they could assist. They thought of food and clothing drives, and they considered fund raisers to collect money to donate to the shelter. One student invited his mother, who works at a local family shelter, to inform students about what it means to be homeless and who homeless people are. This motivated us to move from stereotypes of homeless people to the reality that families are homeless, too. They were bonding together for a common goal that would improve their community. It was magical.

Over the course of the year, students took on more responsibilities for leading meetings and keeping themselves on task. They became reflective of their process and wanted to continue the group for the next school year. The possibilities for this kind of work are endless.

I invited three of my students to share what teacher Linda Christensen calls "I Am From Poems," which we had worked on this year in writing class.[1] These young women have ignited in me an even stronger love for teaching than before. Their poems symbolize why I teach, and it was through their poems that I was inspired to consider the events that led to my becoming a teacher and why I remain in the teaching profession.

These young women and the other students who participated in the group have reminded me how important it is for teachers to share their power, creating a space where students have a voice that can lead to empowerment. My students' "I Am From" poems speak to their strength and to the power they have had in my learning and teaching process.

I AM FROM

by Shatara Smith, age 10

I am from Mississippi
And that's where my family is from.
I am from Baby Back ribs on the grill
And peach cobbler in the sun.

I am from every Sunday at church
And dinner on the run. I am from
Hand clappin' and toe tappin'.
I am from "Honey, eat, eat, eat!
There's good fish on the table."

I am from my funny aunt Jonnymea
I am from charades, mimicking,
big smiles and loud laughs.
I am from a big family.
I am from people celebrating,
dancing and cooking at the same time.

I am from running
and playing in the park
under shady trees with my sister.

I am from playing where
the grass is always greener
and the sun is shining all day.

That is where I am from.

Shatara's poem is a celebration of life, a reflection of love and joy. Like Shatara's poem, this essay is also for me a way to honor those who have made it possible for me to teach and share my experiences in writing, as well as provide opportunities to collaborate with my students and mentors.

Anissa's poem, which follows, symbolizes a sense of familial history, a snapshot of what she has learned over time that has formed who she is and how she sees herself.

I Am From

by Anissa Little, age 10

I am from fist fights, pulling out knives
with silent cries. A fighting family is
where I'm from.

I am from a mixed family.
Some are sick and some are dying.
I am from different cultures.
A different family is where I'm from.

I am from sometimes feeling
Nervous, sad, scared and lonely.
I am from "I want my mommy".
But, I am sometimes from being mad at my mommy, too.
I am from "stop crying you're acting like such a baby."
A loving family is where I am from.

I am of dancing from the heart,
Letting my heart take over my dance moves.
I am from ballet, jazz, hip-hop and drill team.
A talented family is where I'm from.

I am from spending quality time with my family
Having good laughs.

I am from Twister and Monopoly.
I am from "say you're sorry".
A fun family is where I'm from.

I am from everybody cooks in our family.
I am from macaroni and cheese,
chicken and peas.
A well fed family is
where I'm from.

I am from Mom and Step Dad,
aunts and uncles, brothers and cousins,
grandmothers, grandfathers and godmothers.
A humongous family is
where I'm from.

I feel a strong connection with Anissa's words in terms of my thoughts on the importance of community, collaboration, and mentorship. Finally, there is Jennifer's poem.

I Am From

by Jennifer Leonor, age 10

I am from the Dominican Republic,
where it is always hot.
I am from a place where waves
took the lives of many people in Himany.

I am from proudly speaking Spanish.
I am from being called Orgullosa,
by my Grandpa and cousins.
It makes me believe that I am
beautiful and pretty.

I am from pool parties and cooking.
I am from Plaintains and Rice and
Beans with chicken.
I am from Marco Polo with my cousins.
I am from BBQ's on Sundays and
Resting on Mondays.

I am from loving parents.
I am from different generations from
both my mom and my dad.

I am from many cultures and
crazy family stories.

I am from good relationships
with friends. I am from friends who
help me survive school and keep my secrets.
I am from friends who help me with school work
And keep me out of trouble. I am from supporting
my best friends too.

I am from everyone and
everything I want to be.
That is who I really am.

Jennifer's poem recalls the power of believing in yourself, having pride in your heritage, and the dreams associated with these beliefs that can empower us to visualize and create a bright future.

Why do I teach? When I began to ponder this question, I found that my reasons for teaching reach far beyond my educational training in public institutions over the past 10 years. Writing this essay has become a process of self-reflection that has taken me back through my own journey of how I became a teacher, how I teach, and finally, of what the gift of teaching has given me. I have been reminded of the power of community among my family, mentors, and students. Throughout my educational history and my professional life, empowerment and social justice have galvanized me in my desire to remain teaching, even in tough times. But overall, I have come to the conclusion that love is at the center of everything, especially why I teach. It is through collaborative and open-ended relationships with my family, mentors, and students that I receive and share this love. It is love that provides me with the ability to give back. In turn, I hope these young ladies, and other students that I have had in the past and those I will have in the future, will share their gifts with others like themselves so that future generations will continue the chain of community, social action, empowerment, and love.

Chapter 14

The Colors and Strands of Teaching

MELINDA PELLERIN-DUCK

Even as a young child, Melinda Pellerin-Duck knew she wanted to be a teacher. She credits the Sisters of St. Joseph at Holy Name Elementary School in Springfield, Massachusetts, with influencing her teaching. Currently a high school teacher of social studies and technology, she works at the High School of Commerce in Springfield, the only school in the state approved to offer the International Baccalaureate Program. The program provides young people between the ages of 11 and 16 with a rigorous curriculum that focuses on academic achievement and intercultural awareness.

I came across Melinda's name when I read about her in the local newspaper after she was selected the 2003–04 Massachusetts Teacher of the Year. She was recognized for her creative approaches to curriculum and her unyielding belief that all children are capable of great things. She also believes that children need to be actively involved in their own learning if they are to get something from it. As a result, she works hard to create an appealing and challenging learning environment for her urban students. According to Linda Tammi, who coordinates the program where she teaches, "Melinda absolutely lives to teach. It is what animates her and her great satisfaction and joy in her life."[1]

In spite of the great honor she received in 2003, the past few years have been difficult for Melinda. Her husband, Philip Duck, died of lung cancer 3 years ago. Her grandmother and father were both diagnosed with cancer the following year, and her grandmother died a year later. Melinda's father died shortly after she was honored with the Teacher of the Year award. Although he was able to attend school only until 8th grade, he encouraged her to learn as much as she could and to put it to good use in the world. In her essay, drawn from her submission for the Teacher of the Year award, Melinda reflects on how her father, grandmother, other family members, and mentors influenced her life, which she compares to a Kente cloth.

My early teachers were family members: my great-grandmother, my grandparents, my father. I have had many influential teachers in my lifetime. Their lessons have been woven lovingly into the fabric that makes me a teacher and a person. Like Kente fabric, the multicolored African cloth, their lessons emerge in many different colors and strands. No two pieces of string are exactly alike, yet together they form the person I am and the person I am always striving to be.

My family's rich history of storytelling will always be our most treasured heirloom, passed from one generation to the next. Like an African griot, my great-grandmother Virginia and my father would tell of our family's triumphs and tragedies in a segregated South. Their stories taught me to understand the tremendous power of history.

One of their stories that made history come alive for me was that of my great-great-grandmother, a slave in Louisiana whose master beat his slaves relentlessly for even minor offenses. She worked in the big house cleaning and polishing, always watchful, trying to be careful. As the story was told by my great-grandmother and my father, she made a fatal mistake one day when she broke the delicate handle off a piece of the master's china. My great-great-grandmother knew the consequences of her actions. She had been beaten unmercifully in the past and was tired. Instead of reporting the offense or letting her master find the broken china, she tied a rope around her neck and hanged herself. Angered by her crime, the master instructed his son, whom my great-great-grandmother raised, to leave her hanging so that the buzzards could eat her. The son refused.

The first time I heard the story it seemed to hold no lesson. Both my father and great-grandmother insisted that with this simple act, a woman with no education and no freedom took a stand and fought back in the only way she knew how. With this act of defiance she created a story of courage, an attitude of, "I'm not going to take this anymore." I once asked why this story was important, and my father's reply was, "She was someone who lived, took a stand, and this is who you are."

My father and great-grandmother were right. I am descended from a slave who withstood tremendous odds, lived and raised her family, and gave her family heirlooms not of material wealth but of the wealth of words, stories, prayers, and love. This woman, my great-great-grandmother, who had no formal education, was my first teacher, one who helped me understand the power of love, sacrifice, and vocation that teaching truly is. This is who I am!

Later in my life, Richard T. became my teacher, and taught me lessons I will never forget. Richard T. was a student I met when I began student teaching. His class was the class from Hades, and Richard was the principal antagonist. I was convinced that he and his classmates, on a daily basis, planned to make my teaching experience less than rewarding. They did not succeed! I took on their challenge because I loved teaching. One day while I was correcting papers in the school's library, Richard T. walked up to my table and asked to sit down. This student, this incorrigible young man, sat down next to me and told me that he thought I was a very good history teacher. He went on to explain that he was really a very nice guy. He must have seen the sheer look of shock on my face, so he insisted that he was a good kid and that he was an expert on the constellations. I made an agreement with Richard: He would try to tone down his negative behavior in class and I would become his student at every lunch period to learn about the stars. He taught me not only about stars, but also to be consistent, to be firm, and never to judge a book by its cover.

Another teacher was José, a former student with a speech impediment and hearing impairment. He helped me to understand that the words "I can't" have no place in the classroom. With his own hard work, combined with my positive reinforcement, his project on Hyper Studio became a monumental success. The thoughts of failure were replaced with a winning presentation that proved an enriching personal experience and an easily transferable lesson to his classmates. I hope my enthusiasm for the lesson helped foster his success.

I repay these early teachers each and every time I watch a student soar in my classroom or in the computer lab. I try to be true to José by banishing the words "I can't" from my classroom. If my ancestor could fight back, if Richard T. could teach me to reach for the stars, then I can help students replace "I can't" with "Look what I have accomplished!"

I was meant to be a teacher. It has not been one experience, but many that have taught me this. Life's lessons have made me the person I am, and continue to transform me into the teacher I am becoming. Lessons from students, family, and friends have taught me that patience is a virtue to be embraced in my classroom every day. I've learned perseverance, even when the struggle seems insurmountable. I've learned love, and I've had this love reinforced by the gifts each child brings to my classroom experiences. I've learned about hope, and I know not to judge a person by outside distractions because it is inner beauty that counts. As a teacher, I continue to search for it in each student. These are the lessons I try to instill in each miracle that walks across the threshold of my classroom.

I have always believed that classrooms must transcend traditional convention. Students should participate actively in their own learning; they cannot just sit passively while knowledge is being poured into them. Instruction must be well planned, relevant, interesting, and exciting. To be an outstanding teacher you must see your students as fellow travelers and learners. In my classroom, we are all "in this together."

A successful teacher understands there is always room for improvement. I am never satisfied with the notion that the longer I teach, the more expert I become. I am not an expert, but I am striving to learn more and to become experienced. I live in the "learning mode." I am motivated to learn more because I am a teacher reaching for higher standards for myself and for my students. There is nothing more rewarding than helping to transform students who thought they could never create anything meaningful into confident and excited historians. A lesson in world history on the art of Michelangelo finds me jumping on a desk, lying face up, showing students how Michelangelo created his masterpiece. Students are engaged, excited, answering difficult questions about art, style, and form. The students add their own critical analysis to the work and I, as their teacher, am in awe of them. This is a gift, a miracle.

The rewards of teaching are many. Watching our school's mock trial team, a team that was never supposed to win or achieve, compete against suburban school systems with many more advantages and economic resources makes my heart skip a beat. I have watched the team transform into a confident, well-prepared legal team. It has become a formidable adversary. As the team members advance to the final round of statewide competition, I am inspired by their dedication, their spirit, and their performance. I am like a proud parent watching them soar. In 1995, the team placed second for the Commonwealth of Massachusetts!

Activism has always been an integral part of my teaching. In 1993 one of my colleagues and I created a curriculum unit that used technology to foster greater understanding between students enrolled in African American history and French classes at the Springfield High School of Commerce and students from College Catholique, a secondary school in the Ivory Coast. The unit asked students to use electronic mail and video to practice speaking, writing, and translating English and French while learning about student life in another country. Charged with documenting "Life for a Typical American Student" and sharing it with their Ivorian counterparts, our students acted as tour guides for the city of Springfield, Massachusetts, learning about the history and culture of their city and using a video camera to create a virtual tour. Students in the Ivory Coast used video to share their "Trials and Tribulations as Typical Ivorian Teenagers." Senator Edward Kennedy sent representatives from his office to watch the students and their cultural exchange. The project culminated in a teacher exchange when a teacher at College Catholique came to visit and teach in Springfield, and my colleague and I traveled 4,300 miles to teach in Africa.

While I was teaching at Duggan Middle School in Springfield, students enrolled in my law related education class became actively involved in a campaign to reopen our local public library branches. Budget cuts had prompted the city to close the libraries in some neighborhoods, and my students believed this would deny them a powerful learning tool while denying the community a central gathering place and resource. Working with the Pioneer Valley Project, a voluntary social activist organization, my students and I campaigned before, during, and after school as well as on weekends to share our message about the importance of neighborhood libraries to community leaders. Students produced a multimedia display on the role libraries play in their lives. They learned civil rights strategies for nonviolent confrontation and participated in demonstrations, speaking at rallies and labor meetings. They wrote to the mayor and city council, and addressed parent groups and the superintendent. Our commitment to this effort, and the students' hard work, have resulted in a new library system and longer branch hours. Even more important, this collaboration has forged lifelong relationships and a sense of activism in my students.

Whether it is a technology class or a class studying the effects of crucifixion on Judea and the Roman Empire, an after-school mock trial team, or an art lesson, teachers must understand and help students understand how the curriculum they share relates to the world into which the students will enter. Our classrooms are windows into the world and our students must learn that they are part of an ever-changing global family. I strive to make lessons memorable for all students so they will learn not only the curriculum, but that they are valued members of the global family.

Some may question why I continue teaching. My answer is that I teach because I see extraordinary possibilities in students. I could not see myself doing anything else but teaching; it is my vocation. It is part of my life, my soul, and my heart. It is challenging, at times difficult, but the rewards are overwhelming. As a teacher I have the most fortunate experience of nurturing our future. If we do it well, combining unforgettable and meaningful instruction with a sense of community, our students will become not only stewards of their destiny, but productive citizens of our nation and the world.

Too often, I hear that old quotation, "Those who can't, teach." It has been used in popular film and culture to poke fun at and criticize our profession. Yet ours is a vocation, a vocation of love; true teachers know this. Those who instruct, who nurture, who hope patiently and lovingly each and every day understand the quotation is really, "Those who *can*, teach." Those who can, find joy in walking into a room with open minds. They teach. Those who can, take students from "I can't" to "I can." They teach. Those who can, counsel and dispense positive discipline, while staying well after school hours with students. They teach. Those who can, struggle with self-doubt but endure. Those who can, worry about their lesson plans and whether a particular student will have enough clothing to wear, or whether there will be heat in that student's home. Those who can, teach and they do it everyday. I am lucky enough to be one of those who "can."

My greatest contributions in the classroom are displayed proudly and lovingly as threads woven into my brightly colored Kente cloth. The strands are as unique as those I have learned from, and as those I am fortunate enough to instruct. These threads have been given life through the lessons I have learned. The fabric grows each and every day. It has become my greatest contribution and accomplishment. It is forever who I am, a teacher.

Chapter 15

Opening Their Eyes to a New and Bigger World

YAHAIRA D. MARQUEZ

When she wrote this essay, Yahaira Marquez had just completed her first year of teaching and it hadn't been easy. In spite of her enthusiasm for her chosen career, the reality of working in an inner-city high school was far more challenging than she had imagined. Undaunted by the challenges, Yahaira is determined to be a great teacher, one who makes a difference in the lives of her students.

Born to Puerto Rican parents and raised in New York City, from the beginning Yahaira was an excellent student. She attended public schools and graduated as valedictorian of her class. She decided at an early age that she wanted to be a teacher. This decision was put to the test when, during her teenage years, she volunteered during school hours to help her peers. She was also a Sunday school teacher for 4 years. Despite the occasional negative comments she heard about the profession, Yahaira says it was the look on the faces of students, when she taught them something they hadn't understood before, that helped to solidify her decision to be a teacher. Enamored of English literature, English became her major at Boston University, where she received a scholarship that covered nearly all her tuition and expenses. She is, as her Uncle Roberto says, "the star of the family."

But Yahaira is no stranger to adversity. Not only have she and her family had to struggle financially for years, but even more tragically, her father was killed while she was still a young child. The blow left a deep imprint on her, her mother, and her two siblings. It was, however, also one of the things that motivated her to excel and to help students who, much like her, have had a difficult time in life.

It was the first day of school and I was standing at the front of the room with 28 pairs of eyes staring right at me. Their unspoken fear and the questions they had (*"what will it be like?" "I wonder if high school will be hard"; "I hope I don't fail"*) were clearly evident on most of their 9th-grade faces. Little did they know that, as I stood there, I too was trying to conceal the same fear and questions from them. After years of working up to that moment, I was now the teacher, the authority, the decision maker, the role model. Almost daily, I think of all the responsibility and work associated with the title *teacher* and I can't help but sometimes wonder why I chose to be a teacher.

Let's face it, a public high school teacher in Brooklyn, New York, doesn't exactly make a six figure salary, so it would be safe to say that money was not a deciding factor in my decision to become a teacher. And yet, I usually meet with the same response, as if money should be the only basis and incentive in choosing a career: "A teacher?? Why *teaching*? Teachers don't make much money." It is at that moment that I immediately flash back to that time when the idea first crossed my mind, a time when I didn't fully understand the importance or concept of money, so it couldn't have been a reason. Not many people plan out their goals at age 3 or 4, but there I was in preschool, looking up at my teacher and thinking, "I want to be like her and do what she does . . . I want to have my own class one day." Perhaps it was the seemingly effortless control she had over us, the creativity she had in the classroom, or maybe it was that sense of happiness and satisfaction she seemed to exude every day. Whatever it was, it was then that I set my goal of becoming a teacher and my response to the "what-do-you-want-to-be-when-you-grow-up?" question remained the same as the years passed.

Now, looking back, I realize that my first teacher was more than a teacher. She was proof that there was something more to life, that

I didn't have to be stuck, unhappy, and struggling like so many of the Latin women I saw daily with tired and longing faces, walking up and down the streets of Brooklyn, New York. I was becoming aware of what I wanted to avoid and of all that I could achieve. With that in mind, as I got older, although my dream remained the same, the reason changed a bit: Not only did I not want to find myself in a dispiriting situation where life itself would become a burden filled with seemingly impossible dreams, but I also felt that, rather than just leave them behind, I should do something to help others escape from that lifestyle. I don't mean to sound like I was a full-fledged philanthropist at the age of 15, but it was around that time that I began to think of teaching as a career where I could work in a field in which I am interested, try to get others excited about my subject area (which happens to be English), and gain a sense of personal fulfillment and success. I basically want my students, who remind me so much of myself and where I come from, to think that *they* can do it as well.

In order for children to feel that they are capable of achieving great things, it is important for them to have positive role models whom they can look up to as they come of age. That is exactly what I feel students in my school and community lack. This is why I appreciate the fact that, as a young Latin woman, I work at a school of predominately minority students. There are also a good number of minority staff members. Learning in such an environment allows the students, who do not usually experience positive representations of their race and ethnicity, to be taught by adults who as young people were similar to them in terms of living environments and experiences. However, this situation is important not only because the teachers are able to impart academic knowledge, but also because they can serve as positive examples of success and deliver important lessons of life.

As a student, I always had secretly enjoyed having teachers who I felt were "more like me," teachers with whom I felt a certain and sometimes immediate connection despite the fact that we had never had a conversation outside of the classroom. It was always an added bonus when those teachers would step out of "teacher mode" for a few minutes and speak to us as more of mentors and guides. Those were the teachers who genuinely gained the most respect from the students and whom we looked up to with admiration; they were the ones who *truly* made a difference for me and my peers.

The experiences I had as a student guide my teaching and the approach I use with my students. There is a thin line between getting too personally involved with your students (where they no longer may see you as an authority) and being mutually comfortable around each other so that, when necessary, you are able to speak about issues and decisions outside of the subject-area realm while still maintaining their respect. Because I have found a good balance, I appreciate the relationships I've developed with many of my students. Having students look up to me as not only their English teacher, but as a mentor when they need one, has allowed me to see them as *whole* people. I understand them better when they are in my English class because of what I have gotten to know of them *outside* of class. In my opinion, wearing—and switching between—these hats of "teacher," "advisor," and "confidante," and striking a balance between these identities, is important in order to actually make a significant difference in the lives of our students. By doing so, I have gained a lot more in personal terms than I expected when I first entered this profession.

Students, especially those I teach at my school in Brooklyn, aren't usually interested in anything "different" or unfamiliar, anything that is not popular with their peers and age group. That's where I come in. I want my students to realize that it can be interesting to read and be pulled into a time and place we may not be familiar with, while also noticing that many of the problems, issues, and ideas that we deal with today were areas of concern decades and even centuries ago as well. Making such comparisons between time periods and cultures, as well as noting the portrayal of emotions and ideas in various genres, allows students to think differently. I constantly challenge my students to "think deeper and harder" with the questions and discussion topics I pose. And trust me, in my classroom, there is no easy way out! Since I want my students to gain confidence in themselves and realize that they are just as important in my classroom as I am, I don't ever conduct a class in which I'm the only person speaking, or in which students don't work equally as hard as I do. I'd like my students to learn to see the world differently, with a new set of eyes, and to leave my classroom conscious of the fact that not everything is clear-cut and fixed, and knowing that their voices are just as important as anyone else's.

With that said, I feel that it is my responsibility to teach students how to positively represent themselves with language, both written and spoken. At times I feel that if I don't do it, *who* else will help them understand the importance of a first impression and the value of representing oneself favorably to others when there's no time for "getting to know you"? Many of my students come from broken homes or homes in which the parents are not much older than the children. Lots of them may not have much support coming from home, and they know only what they have grown up seeing around them. It is because of this that I tend to find myself teaching my students a lot of the "basics" and trying to undo lots of the mistakes they have learned over the years. Because I think that being able to use language well and properly is extremely important in one's ability to succeed, I have no problem spending extra time with students who desire and need the extra help. What I do is picture my students in my mind as they are now, then try to place them in society about 5 to 10 years from now based on what I know of them. Using that image, I try to help them in the area I feel would have the greatest impact on their success in the future.

But can I help *everyone?* How much is *too* much? These are questions I often ask myself, especially when I start to feel overwhelmed by many of the "unexpecteds" (as I like to call them) associated with teaching. These so-called unexpecteds are the demands I did not anticipate before entering the teaching profession, and they fall into various categories. An example is the seemingly never-ending days where I feel I am spreading myself too thin after teaching a full day of classes, giving up my lunch and prep periods to meet with students to clarify ideas and projects, and holding extended after-school sessions with students who need extra help—all of which tend to make my 1½-hour commute home (where I will continue to work on lessons and/or grades) unbearable. I also have to successfully manage the classroom and meet the expectations and demands of the administration, while at the same time coming up with innovative ways of getting David, who has been out of my class for well over a month, to understand the purpose of the current unit and to get involved in that particular day's lesson.

The latter is one of the greatest challenges I face, one that completely blind-sided me. What *do* I do with a student who is chronically absent from my class and gives sporadic "guest appearances"? I see David, who is only one of a group of these long-term absent students, open the door and walk into my class after not being there for at least 4 weeks (he's either been in jail, been in a detention center, or earning money for the family), and my initial reaction is to run over to him and help him "catch up." But how feasible is that? As I sit next to him to discuss the work we've been doing in class, I continue to note many of the other connecting lessons that he has missed, and all I get back from him are blank stares. It is at that point that I begin to feel disillusioned and start to question whether this conference with David is in vain since he'll sooner or later miss yet another few weeks of instruction. So do I just give up on him and let him sit there, let him slip through the cracks because there's "no point in trying to teach him" (as other teachers sometimes phrase it)? Unfortunately, the answer is not that simple for me since it's not in my nature to ignore students or deny them access to knowledge. This is definitely one scenario I was never presented with in my education courses, and one that I never expected to face in the classroom. It is the combination of all these unexpecteds that force me to question my ability—or perhaps just realize my limits—as a teacher.

What I feel is a sense of frustration. The frustration I'm referring to stems from recognizing the lack of interest and effort students have in their own education. It's frustrating to think that, as the teacher, sometimes I care more about the students' education and future than they do. I am not exaggerating when I say that I've had students who have straightforwardly told me that they "don't care about school," that "school is stupid," and that they "don't need this." There are even some students whose goal is to flunk out of school so they can just get a GED and start working. It honestly breaks my heart to hear them speak in such a way. In high school, I had friends who said the same things and I see what has happened to them as a result of their decisions.

I try to help my students comprehend how succeeding in school *now* will only benefit them and place them at a higher level later on in life. This is why I frequently can be heard telling them that "everything good comes with time, patience, and hard work." I've already had three repeating 9th-grade students with whom I have had numerous conversations and "pep talks" and who have made a complete turnaround since September and are now working harder than other students in their class. That may sound like a small achievement, but it is an accomplishment of which I am extremely proud.

Being such a young teacher, at 23 years of age, I understand how much can be accomplished when you are determined and when you keep the ultimate goal in mind at all times. I only hope that all my students leave my classroom knowing this and that they never give up on themselves. Whether I'm able to make a difference in the lives of 3, 30, or 300 students, I will feel that I've succeeded in what I wanted to do. I keep that in mind whenever I feel that I'm being pushed to my limits.

In addition, there are the issues and struggles one may need to face with the "powers that be." It can get pretty aggravating when the teacher, who knows her students best and knows what methods will be most successful in her classroom, is told about methods that supposedly will work for everyone and yield the best results. Sometimes ideas and strategies that look good on paper do *not* work when put to the test. I'm a firm believer in first knowing one's audience and then approaching that particular audience with the techniques that will keep them engaged and benefit them. I always thought that teachers would get full support from everyone who mattered when it came to helping students in what they thought would be the best way possible. Unfortunately, my experience has proven that this is not always the case. The field of education turns out to be more political than I would ever have expected, but instead of getting disillusioned when I find myself standing alone with an idea, I keep focused on what is truly important—the success of the students—and I try not to let such experiences bring me down or make me forget why I became a teacher in the first place.

What I feel tests me the most in this occupation are the sacrifices one must make constantly as an educator. This is not the kind of profession that ends when you leave the building; it carries over into what is supposed to be your personal time. You work just as hard when you're at home alone as when you're in school with the students. There are hours upon hours that go into lesson and unit planning and grading, in addition to workshops and professional development. Hours that, I must admit, I'm not always too thrilled to give up. There are many nights when I wish I could just come home and relax, that is, until I see a stack of papers I must work through.

Teaching is a career in which you constantly try to improve. It's like you're learning along with your students, day after day and year after year. The idea of teaching as becoming part of who you are and what you do on a daily basis definitely can—and *does*—take some getting used to.

I teach because I want to help others succeed and expand their minds and knowledge. I also love the fact that I can never predict what will happen from day to day. Teaching is anything but a monotonous job; there is always something different and new, and something unexpected may throw your entire plan out the window. I go into class every morning not knowing what kind of day it will be, not knowing whether I'll have to change an aspect of my plan because it doesn't work, not knowing how my students will react to my lesson that day, and not knowing the kind of mood the students will be in or kind of mood I will leave in. It is that uncertainty, that element of surprise, that I think drives me even harder. Being a teacher tests me as a person, and I leave every day knowing a little bit more about my ability to adapt to and control unforeseen situations, even when at times I may not think I can handle them.

As a teacher I'm able to help others better themselves, share one of the subjects I'm passionate about, interact with and learn more about others, establish different kinds of relationships, and learn more about myself while making myself stronger. All that with one job and at the age of 23! So next time I'm asked, "Why *teaching*?" I think I'll answer clearly and simply: *because there is more to it than meets the eye, and because it makes me a better person.*

Chapter 16

Teaching to Engage

B̲ETH W̲OHLLEB A̲DEL

E xtensive world travel, beginning as an undergraduate, helped develop the international perspective that is evident in Beth Wohlleb Adel's middle school social studies classes. Her curriculum also focuses on presenting history as a collective experience, one in which all voices are heard. Beth believes that social justice is an important consideration in teaching. She wants students to understand that some individuals and groups, because of their very identities, have been victimized and

exploited. She also wants them to know that, in a democracy, oppression of all kinds needs to be confronted, resisted, and transformed. As an example, she was one of the core teachers in a team that developed an innovative integrated unit on family diversity sponsored by the Family Diversity Project (the organization that developed and distributes a number of photography exhibits of multiracial, gay and lesbian, and all sorts of families). In that curriculum, all families are presented as valid and valuable.

Beth has been a leader in her school community in promoting awareness and advocacy for GLBT rights. She brings this same attention to students who have not done as well academically as they could. As the co-parent of a 3-year-old adopted African American daughter, Beth wants to make sure that her children, and all children, have an equal right to an excellent education, and she works hard to make this happen in her own classroom.

That first year of teaching was rough. I worked 80 hours a week to create active lessons, encouraging critical thinking, employing multiple intelligences and cooperative learning. But my students didn't respond with excitement. My classroom wasn't alive. I tried more active lessons, harder work, higher standards, but it wasn't until a shy boy, Tom, took a risk one day that my classroom started to change.

One Monday morning about halfway through the school year, Tom had a smile on his face before class began. "How was the movie on Saturday night, Ms. Wohlleb?" he asked, loud enough for the class to hear and perk up their attention.

"Uh, it was good. . . . How did you know I went to the movies?" My nervous first-year teaching self was caught off guard, but Tom was a sweet kid just being playful before class started, no harm intended.

"I saw you with your boyfriend there." Now everyone in the class was definitely listening.

"I don't have a boyfriend." This was going too fast, and I didn't know how to get out of this conversation.

"Then who were you snuggling up to in the movie theater then?" And now the whole class joined in—"Ooooooooooo . . . Ms. Wohlleb!" and lots of eager faces. I hadn't had their full attention like this all year.

"Well, I have a girlfriend. Her name is Vanessa. She was wearing a baseball cap, so you couldn't tell she's a woman." I had come out of the closet to my students—ak! That was *not* part of the lesson plan for today. But I had no other choice—except to lie. And in that moment something told me not to lie and to trust what would happen. I was lucky to be in a progressive school with a supportive principal. I probably wouldn't get fired, and I decided to risk the possible repercussions from students and their families.

Tom's face grew red and he slunk down in his seat. He was as surprised as I was that I had been that honest. "I'm sorry," he stammered, "I didn't know . . . I just assumed . . . "

"It's okay, it was a perfectly understandable assumption to make."

It took about 15 seconds for the rest of the class to recover from their shock. "We sure are getting to know more about you, Miss," was the first comment from a student. I smiled, and confirmed that they were. This was the turning point in that class. I had been courageous and honest, allowing students to see a part of me that I had kept hidden.

I went home exhilarated that day. I was also scared to death about what would happen next. I waited for the negative repercussions from families. But instead, I noticed my classroom worked better. My students started being more honest and open with me. A student who hadn't turned in a single essay started coming in after school to talk about her deep fears about writing. I listened, confirmed her fears, and noticed that she began to make first attempts at writing. When a soft-spoken boy started raising his hand to ask critical questions, I could hear, "Go, Jim!" from classmates. The class felt more like a community. And the change in me was equally rewarding. I felt more whole, more real, more alive, more excited about teaching.

Real teaching and real learning both require great acts of courage. As teachers, we constantly ask students to take big risks: to try a new way of thinking, to answer a question without being sure of the answer, to reveal their true opinions. If I wanted to be a teacher who taught students to truly engage, I had better model courage, continue to be open and honest about myself, and take the same risks that I am asking them to take. When I do take these risks, my life becomes richer, more exciting, and more exhilarating than I ever thought middle school teaching could be.

Of course, "coming out of the closet" did not end in one moment. I found ways to answer students' questions and dispel stereotypes both in informal conversations with students after class and through including gay people in my history classes. When a student complained several months later about students in class using the word "gay" as a derogatory term, I wasn't afraid to take the time in class to do an exercise to develop sensitivity toward different sexual identities, and to make it clear that derogatory terms are not allowed in the classroom. Students saw me as a resource, and they respected me for my courage.

Engaging honestly and courageously does not come naturally to me. I grew up in a White middle-class Protestant community where I learned that lying was a normal part of life. We call them "white lies" or we call it "being professional." I learned to avoid open conflict, even if it meant lying about who I was or how I felt. I was taught that my arguments would be invalid if I was too angry, that I needed to be "objective" in order to be successful, and that honesty was often a liability. Unaware of the distance that was growing between my own heart and other people's hearts, I continued being "polite" and "successful" in my White world.

I went into the teaching profession in order to make a difference in students' lives. I wanted to help students develop analytical skills to become better able to make informed decisions as active players in a democracy. I set about learning how to teach critical thinking skills and in-depth historical fact, as if no one in the classroom had hearts. It wasn't until I started teaching that I began to realize that in order to be a truly effective teacher, I needed to unlearn some of these cultural messages. Only by my courageously being myself would students allow themselves to open up and learn unhindered. In the act of being courageous, I found the reason that I continue to teach: I become a fuller human being.

It's risky for students in middle school to be themselves; they are bombarded with messages from their peers and the media to be something other than who they are. They spend an enormous amount of energy trying to keep up with the latest fashions, look older, be more athletic or sexy. Being "cool" means being distant, having a thick skin. If they resist these messages, they are teased for being a "nerd" or, worse, a "fag." When I honestly describe my family to my classes, I demonstrate the respect and trust I have in my students. They understand that it's a risk for me to be open with them about my life, and they begin to take similar risks with me. One student revealed to the rest of the class her frustration with people ignoring her just because she was in a wheelchair. Another student wrote in a journal about how her brother's violent anger was taking over the whole family. After each of these moments, students are more connected, more open to being alive and to engaged learning.

Once my students start to practice being open and honest, they don't let me get away with any less. I continue to live in a White cultural space with messages to value efficiency and commodities over people. Sometimes I find myself focusing on "covering the curriculum," trying to rush students through a lesson instead of really listening to them, worried that we will "get behind." I get stressed, and I grow impatient with my students. But my students remind me that I am not connecting to their hearts, I am not being my whole self. They don't remind me directly, but I get the message. They participate less, do their homework less often, and write dry papers. Students drag in and my classroom loses vitality. I would not last long as a teacher in a classroom like this. So I remember to resist the rush, and I thank them for the reminder.

After several years of teaching, I am beginning to learn how to invite students to speak courageously from the heart, instead of hoping this will just happen by itself in the midst of a middle school culture that encourages the opposite. I still focus on critical thinking skills, but I teach to full human beings instead of "objective" minds, and I value courage and honesty over "covering the curriculum." When I sit down on a Sunday afternoon to plan my next unit, I consciously resist the urge to cover the most information in the least amount of time. Now I start with opening, listening, connecting. I start with asking what questions the students might have about the topic. I teach them to research the answers to their questions independently, using multiple sources and viewpoints, and to share the information with others.

When I began to plan my unit on cultural change in Latin America, I looked for ways to teach history and also connect to students' hearts. I decided to focus on the Mexican holiday *Los Días de los Muertos*, the Days of the Dead, a holiday starting the night of October 31 and lasting through November 2. After teaching the history of Mexico, the students analyze this holiday for the unique contributions of the Aztec, Spanish, and Yoruba to present-day Mexican culture. In addition, I challenge myself and my students to take courageous steps to participate with their hearts, not merely as passive bystanders. We talk about how Mexican people who celebrate *Los Días de los Muertos* are staying connected to those who have passed away by honoring and remembering them. Each family creates an *ofrenda*, or offering, on an altar onto which they place favorite items of the departed. But we don't just talk about it; we experience a piece of it. We collaboratively plan to honor those who are important to us who have passed away. I write a letter to the students' families describing our unit and our plans to create an *ofrenda*, inviting families to participate, or to call me with any concerns. I drape a table with brightly colored cloth and invite students to think about someone in their lives who has passed away—an ancestor, or a neighbor, or a grandparent—and bring an object in to honor them.

This kind of lesson may be disorienting to students, many of whom have been socialized away from revealing feelings as personal as sadness and deep loss in the context of a classroom. Students cross their arms and legs, shielding themselves from possible ridicule from their peers. I model what to do by describing my friend Suzanne who died of cancer. I tell the class how she loved to laugh, and I place a picture of her laughing on the table to remember her. I gently invite other students to come when they are ready, and remind the class about the importance of quiet respect. One student blurts out, "I bet no one is going to do it," giving voice to the trepidation everyone feels. But students rise to the challenge. Thirteen-year-olds open their lives for the rest of the class: an apple for a mother who passed away when her kids were very young, a doll for a neighbor's child, a fireman's hat for an uncle who lost his life in the Twin Towers. The previously skeptical students who did not bring in an object to share, scramble over to the construction paper to honor a relative through a drawing, and they find themselves going to the table too. They are taking a risk by opening their hearts among peers who can be cruel as soon as class ends and they step into the hallway. But they are not cruel this time. The next day, students linger by the *ofrenda* for a few minutes before class begins. They take their seats, now a bit closer to becoming a vibrant community of learning, where they are willing to take other risks too. They are willing to let other students critique their writing, they challenge me to be more clear in my instructions, and they root for one another.

I encourage my students and their families to find issues that are meaningful to them. I take time to talk to individual students and their families, and I keep their interests and identities in mind when I plan lessons. When I had several students with family in Puerto Rico, for example, I chose to focus on the U.S. Navy bombing practice on the island of Vieques in Puerto Rico in order to build critical thinking skills. Instead of encouraging students to "stay objective," we talk about how we feel, the biases we have, as well as the biases of the authors we read. Students get involved through writing and role playing, and they are not distanced.

Students use their hearts by role playing different agents in each event. When we studied the civil war in Colombia, students role played characters in the conflict. In each of the small groups, one student represented the President of Colombia, another represented a Colombian farmer, another represented a guerrilla fighter, and still another represented a diplomat from the United States. I encouraged students to be accurate, but also passionate. One student expressed dismay at the complexity of motives in real life: "But no one here is the bad guy; everyone has their reasons for what they're doing."

We end the unit by writing letters to businesses or elected officials to persuade them to do something that matters to us. Every year students resist this. "This is so pointless, it won't do anything"; "They don't really read these letters"; "They don't care about what we think"; "Do we really have to mail them?" I think, "How have 13-year-olds become so cynical already? How have we shut down their hope and faith?" I push them forward, and we really do mail the letters, and the students really do get responses. One student researched the type of paper the school uses and wrote to the paper company asking that they use environmentally sound papermaking practices to preserve the rainforests and other old-growth forests. She came running into class clutching the letter from a public relations officer who assured her that they will respect the environment, and we excitedly shared it with the whole class. We then talked about whether these letters can make a difference, and I cite the recent news that McDonald's started to change its environmentally destructive practices because enough people wrote to them, and now many other restaurants may follow their lead.

Teaching to actively engage all students requires constant reflection, creativity, courage, and humility. Each season I have new students who disengage. Malcolm, a quiet, slightly overweight boy, used to spend more time looking at his shoes than his classmates. I tried to gently ask him what was going on, but he only shrugged his shoulders. I tried to observe the classroom dynamics, and even asked a friend to observe my classroom because I know that I am too busy moving around the room to see everything. After talking with him, it became clear to me that his classmates were excluding him, in what can be typical 7th-grade social torture. I remembered the agony of my own 7th grade and how impossible it was for students to be open and courageous in a hostile social atmosphere. I assigned new seats, separating an exclusive pair and ensuring that

Malcolm was surrounded by friends. Without mentioning names, I led a small activity meant for the entire class to reflect on inclusion and exclusion in their multiple circles of friends. I shared some of my struggles: times when I have not been inclusive, and times when I have been left out. Students wrote in their journals about inclusion in their lives. Malcolm did not write much, but I did notice that his eyes left his shoes and he was talking more with his classmates. He even smiled a little.

Sometimes I fail students. Sometimes they remain disengaged despite my efforts. Sometimes I am not my most courageous or insightful self, and I find myself angry at my students for not being easier to teach, and angry at the profession for not allowing enough reflection time, or rest. But anger is an essential part of any meaningful relationship. I apologize to my students for my frustration, I take a personal day, and I learn more about being a whole human being. I learn my own limits.

I teach because it requires that I become my most courageous self, and I am constantly inspired by students who learn the power of being whole people along with me. This kind of learning is life-giving and hope-filling. Creating communities of learning that engage the heart, breaks down the cynicism and passivity that threaten all of us in this culture. If I forget to value people over efficiency, my students remind me of the importance of connecting to one another and resisting the messages to play it safe. The reminder to be courageous and open filters into the rest of my life, too. I have dared to risk open conflict with my family when I point out the racism that we all still carry with us, and when I came out of the closet to my religious grandparents. We have grown closer, more honest, and more alive. And I have my students to thank for continuing to push me to courageously engage with life.

Chapter 17

Teaching Means Taking Risks

NINA TEPPER

W hat is it that brings Nina Tepper back to the classroom year after year? Although she has been honored for her teaching over the years—most recently as a semifinalist for the 2000 Massachusetts Teacher of the Year—this is not what defines why she teaches. Her story is above all about commitment to social justice, a commitment she developed early in life and that still keeps her going strong. An innovative and caring teacher, Nina can't see  herself anywhere but in an urban school with the children she has served for so many years. Besides teaching ESL, Nina has been active in teacher union activities and in professional organizations, and she is known for the workshops on creative writing that she gives for other teachers.

In spite of her enormous enthusiasm for teaching, however, Nina went through a very painful time as a teacher, a time when she began to question whether this was the profession for her. She decided to leave the school system in the city in which she also lived and begin anew in another urban district. The adjustment was a difficult one, but fortunately for the children in her care, she continues to find joy in teaching. In her essay, Nina describes the situation that led to her decision to move, and she explains why she continues to teach.

After more than 20 years as an inner-city public school teacher, I still identify with the initial motivation to teach I had in my youth.

As a college dropout in Boston at the height of the anti-Vietnam War movement, I had been reading books by Jonathan Kozol, William Ryan, and Paulo Freire that reinforced my belief that there were important changes that needed to be made in education and in society as a whole. I developed with the idealism that people united could make a difference and that we each have a personal responsibility to make the world a better place. I felt passionately that I could make the greatest contribution by working in schools.

My commitment to education began when a friend gave me the book *Death at an Early Age* by Jonathan Kozol,[1] a first-year Boston schoolteacher who documented the deteriorated conditions and lack of compassion for minority and poor students in the public schools. The injustice moved me to think about going back to college as an education major. William Ryan's book, *Blaming the Victim*,[2] highlighted how teacher expectations have an important impact on student success. This message complemented Kozol's book and strengthened my growing awareness of the role that racism plays in society. But it wasn't until I read Paulo Freire's *Pedagogy of the Oppressed*[3] that I understood that educators must truly believe in their students' ability to learn and must present curriculum that motivates and respects each individual's culture, experience, and developmental learning needs. If Paulo Freire could define education as a force for radical social change, then I could be a "revolutionary."

When a group of progressive educators in the city where I was teaching came together to design a public "magnet" middle school for the arts, the idealism of my alternative school training, combined with my growing experience as a teacher, made participating in this project a natural. Everything about the school was innovative, from the interdisciplinary curriculum to the school-based government and leadership. It felt like an opportunity of a lifetime to work with other professionals to bring together all the most promising practices in education and create from scratch the necessary conditions for learning. All that I stood for felt validated by the honor of being chosen to teach in this school.

The first year of the Magnet Middle School for the Arts opened uncharted territory for all who participated. Amid community doubt and criticism, we struggled through our first year under the microscope. Through it all, the school continued to grow and had one of the most exciting arts programs in the area. Curriculum was designed to integrate the arts in all content areas and to create an atmosphere sensitive to adolescent development. Gradually, some of the original vision began to dilute due to slow administrative and staff changes. However, a small core group of teachers stayed on to keep the dream alive.

Statistics showed our city to have the highest teen pregnancy rate in the state, the second highest rate for infant mortality and sexually transmitted diseases, and the third highest rate of AIDS. These statistics did not surprise many of us who saw these realities daily in our classrooms. Even in middle school, each year we would see a small number of pregnant 12- and 13-year-old girls. It was not uncommon to discover students using drugs in school. One of my 15-year-old students confided that she had been diagnosed with HIV. Another spoke of her as a runaway engaged in risky behavior while living on the streets of New York. Clergy and city officials had held meetings looking for ways to work together on issues affecting the city youth. In this context, a teaching colleague and I never questioned the appropriateness of allowing students to design a bilingual teen video project addressing issues of importance to young people.

The video project was designed for an experimental two-way bilingual classroom team taught in English and Spanish to foster language development in a natural setting. Our curriculum objective was to provide opportunities for listening, speaking, reading, and writing in two languages, using video as a motivating, artistic medium for learning. Who would have anticipated the overwhelmingly negative reaction of administrators when they discovered the nature of this project and the topics chosen by the students? All the wind left my sails as I found myself in conflict with the school system, a situation that left me questioning all that I stood for and wondering how I could survive in the profession.

It was a crisp October morning in 1994 when I was called into the principal's office. Sitting on a couch and clutching a Bible was the mother of one of the 8th-grade students participating in the video project. Without warning, the principal said, "This mother wants to know what you are doing teaching sex in a language arts classroom." He handed me a list of questions our students had brainstormed the day before focusing on the dangers of engaging in sex at a young age. As is the nature of brainstorming, not all the questions the students suggested were relevant or plausible, but we had chosen not to censor their ideas at such an early stage. The list was intended as a tool to determine what questions would be most effective for a 30-minute TV show featuring peers talking to peers in a moderator-and-audience-participation format. Although there were 42 questions on this brainstorm worksheet, only 14 had been circled by the students and teachers as relevant to the topic. This final list of questions was well thought out and never deemed inappropriate for classroom discussion, even by the administration. Students were each assigned one question to respond to, using an index card as a cue while taping the show. But because the original brainstorm list unintentionally made its way home to this mother, the principal panicked and threatened to have us fired.

This was the beginning of a long process that took my colleague and me through investigative meetings with the superintendent of schools and school committee, union grievance hearings, and ultimately a legal arbitration. The process left me depressed, fearful, full of self-doubt, feeling betrayed and with a deep loss of optimism. It didn't matter that both my colleague and I were well-respected veterans in the school system. My colleague is an accomplished author of children's books. I had received commendations from the state Board of Education for initiatives taken in the development of a "Family Folklore" writing project. These facts did not alter the attack on our character and professionalism. Ultimately, we were suspended without pay for 5 days.

The incident had a chilling effect on the staff. As the arbitration hearings slowly unfolded, my colleague decided to resign from the school system. A personal issue had made leaving necessary, but he also was tired of living with the stress of working in a school in which a principal showed little respect while teachers withdrew from fear of association that this could happen to them as well.

I stayed on a while longer, believing I could work through this period and overcome the stress that I too felt. When I bid for a different teaching position, in an attempt to change my surroundings, I was overlooked even though I was the most qualified candidate. It became evident that I was being targeted and denied full professional consideration in the school system. When I was offered a position in an inner-city school system nearby, I felt I had to take the risk of losing my 13 years' seniority and accumulated sick time to regain a sense of well-being. Leaving the children I saw outside of school, in the community in which I live, was like losing a family.

More than 2 years passed before an independent arbitrator made a final decision on our case. It was decided that my colleague and I had acted responsibly when handling the sensitive content of the teen discussions, that brainstorming was a legitimate teaching technique, and that the school system did not have any written curriculum or documents specifying what content we could or could not cover with students. The 5-day suspension was deemed inappropriate. The school system had to pay us our lost wages, with interest, and remove any reference to this case from our professional files.

It sounds like a happy ending, but the consequences were so great, the suffering so intense. Even vindication could not erase the impact this ordeal had on our personal and professional lives. Holding onto the idealism and optimism with which I entered the profession was more about principle than confidence. Most people who enter the profession of teaching do so because we care about youth, learning, and the future. We are aware of the many issues that make it difficult to teach. Many children come to school not prepared to learn due to neglect, poverty, abuse, illness, family stress, learning difficulties, and more. Knowing the limitations of the school environment to meet the needs of our students, we often take heroic steps to find the help a child needs. Rarely do we question our responsibility to confront the issues affecting our students. Everything that affects them is our responsibility. Standing up for what I believe has always been a part of my being. This meant that I would have to muster up the courage to continue to take risks for the benefit of my students.

How have I managed to survive as an inner-city public schoolteacher 10 years after that ordeal? What is the key to longevity in the field of education? Although it was not my original intention, change provides an opportunity for growth that stimulates and energizes teaching. Moving to a different school system, participating in a variety of professional development courses, and challenging myself as a consultant with the Western Massachusetts Writing Project have kept me motivated and current. Working with the teachers' union provides the unity of numbers that makes reform possible. Stagnation and isolation lead to teacher "burnout" as they would in any profession. Mentoring new student teachers working toward certification also has allowed me to believe that I am leaving a legacy beyond my own career.

Teaching has remained as challenging today as it was when I first started. I have lived through three cycles of teacher layoffs and underfunding of public education. Students continue to cross the school threshold with many of the same issues that have plagued society throughout my career, making my commitment as important now as it was 30 years before. The greatest gift I receive as a teacher is being recognized by a former student who might have had difficulty learning to read, became a parent too young, or was involved in gang activity. More times than not, these students tell me of their latest accomplishments. One might be attending community college, another has a good job, and another might recall a literature project that made it possible for her to enjoy reading. Those cherished exchanges fuel my commitment and motivation to teach.

Life as a teacher has never been easy. My family has seen my ups and downs, the hours I plan at home, and the financial struggles to make ends meet. It was never my intention to model teaching as a profession for my own children but perhaps my passion and commitment rubbed off in ways I never intended. Recently, my three daughters, although so different from one another (one has a master's in early childhood education, another is an athletic trainer, and the third an art student in college) have all indicated an interest in teaching. They see working in public schools as a way to contribute to the future by using their individual talents. Their decisions are the ultimate source of pride and a validation that my life's work and values are being passed on by my own children.

I teach for the youth and the future. No more do I believe as I did when I first entered the teaching profession that I can "change the world" or the public schools, for that matter. There are so many factors involved in true institutional change, from administration, finances, staff changes, ideologies, and more. What I do believe is that, as a teacher, I can affect the future, one child at a time.

Chapter 18

Always Another Beginning

SETH PETERSON

He looks like a college student, so it's hard to believe that Seth Peterson has already been teaching for 9 years. It was a decade ago that he began student teaching in a Boston public high school, specifically in Stephen Gordon's English classroom. The combination was prodigious: Stephen, whose essay also appears in this book, is an exceptional teacher, one described by Seth as "a master craftsman who would help shape me as a teacher and a person." Seth, in turn, brought to the work an enthusiasm and freshness that inspired Stephen.

Outside of school, Seth plays in two bands and goes bird-watching with his fiancée. He reads and loves spending time with his family. But it is school that he thinks about most. He is driven to do this work, he says, by "the twin sisters of joy and anger," joy from the hours in class with dynamic students, and anger at the bureaucracy and lack of respect for teachers. In spite of it all, he loves going to school and hasn't missed a day in years.

As an English teacher, Seth is especially concerned with making words matter in the lives of the young people he teaches. During the summer of 2004, he was engaged with 14 other Snowden High School teachers as a Calderwood Writing Fellow. And even though he is both a gifted teacher and a gifted writer, it was harder for him to write this essay than he thought it would be. In an email, he wrote, "Capturing why we do what we do is almost as hard as doing it." In his essay, Seth reflects on change, and on how teaching is always a new beginning.

Change, forging a new beginning, is what makes a teaching life, my teaching life, rewarding. It's the little revolutions and the subtle surrenders to text that carve out futures and outlive the schedules, scanner sheets, and buzzwords. In the world of public schools, in the world of adolescents, in the fiat-producing district offices, things are constantly changing. While many of these shifts and permutations, these commands and acts of defiance, are the sources of frustration or agony, they ward off tedium (no small victory in a world wrought with boredom).

Valerie is tall. This is what I notice first. I am 5'7" on a good day. Valerie is tall, not for a girl, not for a 9th grader, not just compared with me, but in the absolute and permanent sense. It is not up for debate . . . like the rules of the class. "Valerie, this is writing time. You need to spin forward, stop talking to Renee, and get back to your short story."

"No. What I *need* to do is talk to Renee about what happened last night." She says it without contempt, but with brassy certainty. It is a statement of fact more than contradiction. Then, softening a little, she adds, "Besides, Mister, you know I'm not a creative person."

We both were wrong that day. Although she should have to (and eventually did) face forward in class and write, what she needed at that moment was reassurance and closure in the conversation with her best friend. Such are the priorities of adolescents and, really, the needs of human beings. Valerie knew what she needed, but she didn't know herself . . . not yet. She was dead wrong about what kind of person I knew her to be. Within the week, her own words would prove her to be an innovator, a creative force. With the same matter-of-fact certainty, she would respond to one of her peer editors, "I know it's not in the dictionary, but it *is* a word."

Along with several other small groups of conferring students, I was drawn over to this debate in the corner of the room. The thin-framed boy with her story in his slight hand sensed he was getting in over his head, but moved forward cautiously: "*Confuzzled* is not a word. You can't use it here."

Valerie was a confident, self-assured rebel. Knowing her audience had doubled, she spoke in a louder, triumphant tone. "It's my story and I know how I felt. I felt confused and puzzled . . . *confuzzled*. That's probably how you feel right now! You're confuzzled, too." And so he was. Valerie created a word that still lives in the vernacular of our classroom. In a miniscule way, the language had just grown. Valerie and the forces of change—and maybe even this teacher—won a tiny, unheralded victory that day, one more little revolution.

When I sit down to consider how I ended up in this profession and what it means to me, my wheels turn in the motions of a true Bostonian driver. I continuously circle back to where I started only to find a new on-ramp, a new traffic pattern, another beginning. Thus, it is through a network of unfinished tunnels, through unfolding narratives, that I find my truth and struggle to explain it.

It begins with Levi Grigsby. It's a great name, destined for paperback or box-office use, but it's not the name alone that comes to me. The truth is, the whole entity, the massive bulk of mannish-boy appears when I consider my path to teaching.

I see Levi, sitting hulk-like on a curb, convulsing with long-bottled tears, a mountain of teenage hurt shaking against the cruel, flat, grey Ohio afternoon. He was crying out all the things that made him hate school, hate our tutoring sessions, and hate himself. All the things that his teachers and classmates thought bounced off his tough, obnoxious, mile-thick skin, actually had been absorbed. Here on the corner of East Lorain Avenue, they were finally oozing back out.

"You're fat and ugly so no one wants to work with you."

"It's your fault your dad left."

"You won't learn if you're too lazy to try."

"Of course you failed, all you do is talk in the back of the room."

It was an awful, pitiful, private moment to witness, but there I was beside this defeated child, seeing what he would sooner die than have his mother, teachers, or classmates see. He sat there, his breath coming in fits and starts, heaving with the final passing sobs, tears dotting his grey T-shirt and glistening against his dark cheeks. At some point, his thoughts must have turned to me and to the worry of what I might do with this spectacle. Who would I tell and how soon? Like many kids on the wrong side of the poverty and race lines, Levi was used to people exploiting the power they wielded. "Don't tell no one about this, okay? Y'know, what I just said and all the crying." He said it halfheartedly, as if it was a foregone conclusion that people would still find out.

I was just a kid myself, a sophomore in college, earning a few class credits tutoring kids in the local high school. A psychologist would have known what to say, how to answer this fit of self-loathing. A closer companion might have won the day with a simple, reassuring arm around the shoulder. I, however, was none of these things to Levi. At the time, I wasn't sure whether it was incidental or intentional that I was the sole witness to his unraveling. It may well have been my utter insignificance to his world that allowed me the chance to see Levi so disheveled, allowed him to drain his misery before me. Yet, I cling to the hope that he saw something in me, some hint of sincerity or compassion, that at least opened the possibility I might not use a moment of weakness against him. In fact, believing it was a sign of trust and respect has fueled many subsequent decisions . . . so, I happily persist in this delusion regardless.

Levi's tears proved to be a turning point for him as well. What we said that day probably mattered much less than the bond that was formed by sharing so desperate a moment. Whether he trusted me before, he needed to trust me now since I had seen him at his most vulnerable. Even then, I recognized the sacred nature of that trust. My words of encouragement and my expectations of success, although much the same as they had been for months before, suddenly took on greater significance for Levi. He started doing his homework, albeit grudgingly. He sat closer to the front in French class and actually tried to answer questions "en francais." He would write a paragraph or two of his English essay before saying, "I can't do this." Levi taught me a great deal during those tutorials in my sophomore year of college. I learned that building trust across years and cultures is a slow business; that, however well-meaning and powerful they are, words hit their mark only when they are loosed by a trusted archer; and that I wanted the chance to earn that trust again. I learned that I wanted to be a teacher.

Now, as a teacher, I try to pay close attention to the ways I continue to change. I hope to become the kind of teacher whose trust and faith in his students translate into unwavering expectations. I used to believe it was enough for my students to discover and trust their own voice, to write at a level and style that pleased them. Then

I realized that being a teacher often means being the voice they *don't* want to hear, pushing, pressing, lobbying for the extra mile. Access to power in our society—the ability to change and be changed—is dependent on mastery of formal language. My students don't have to choose the conventional path to power, but I never want them to be denied that choice because of mechanics I chose not to teach them.

Learning is a voluntary act; it cannot be mandated. It is forever dependent on a human connection, person-to-person contact. It may occur across oceans, generations, even centuries through text, but learning is, ultimately, a willing exchange. Thus, I have come to believe that while the power dynamic in a classroom is too real, too reinforced to wish or pretend it away, it can and must be tempered with trust. Letting students know that I am sincere in my dedication to their success and have no interest in exploiting the power of my position is the first order of business in my classroom each year. On the occasions when I actually get that message through, learning becomes a much less daunting task for all involved.

I begin to see returns on my trust when a student marked absent appears in the doorway at 10:23 with a sheepish grin. In her hand, she carries a note from the hospital where she spent the night. She hands me the note and says, "I didn't want to miss my group's presentation." Sometimes trust means listening with extreme bias and positive partiality, as in the case of Jolene, who let my voice pull her off another girl, breaking up a fierce, crowded hallway fight: "Hey, it's me . . . Mr. P. Look at me. It's just me. Let's take a walk."

I feel trusted, and therefore validated, when, after 2 years of silence, Raoul writes me from prison asking for a character witness. He is still confident I will write about his charisma and concern for others, qualities we both know he possesses regardless of one bad decision made in anger one ill-fated night. When Ashanti whines rhetorically, "Mister, how come I feel so guilty when I don't do the homework for this class?" I know some level of trust, some connection between what we do and what she could become, has been formed. Some days, these signposts of trust, these affirmations are nowhere to be found. Those days are filled with deafening silences between bells, heavy eyelids, and endless train rides home, but they dissolve into others that hold another chance to earn trust and actually teach.

Since learning must begin with trust, I struggle to start the year with words that might promote its permeation. Each September, I begin my classes with a letter to my students explaining who I am and why I do what I do. Here's part of the letter I gave them last year:

To the Snowden Class of 2007:

My name is Seth Peterson and I would like to welcome you to Snowden International School. It's a pleasure and honor for me to call myself your teacher as I welcome you to this class, this cluster, this school, and this 4-year journey through time and knowledge. Though they will go by quickly, these years will help define you, contribute to your sense of self and place in this complicated world. I hope I can help you use your precious time wisely, make more meaning of the world around you. I hope you will leave here with the world at your fingertips and no regrets.

If we are going to succeed together, it is important that we begin by trusting and understanding each other. Writing to you about who I am, what I believe, and why I'm here is my way of asking you to understand me. Without understanding, there can be no honesty. Without honesty, there can be no trust. And, without trust, there can be no learning.

I teach because I believe that knowledge is power and I am committed to seeing each of you empowered in a society that far too often tries to limit your power or discredit your voice. Many adults quickly forget how much they learned as adolescents and how much they can still learn *from* adolescents. Teaching you keeps me very close to this reality, keeps me on my toes, and forever learning. Yet, being a teacher also comes with great responsibility. It is my job to make sure you leave here with the reading and writing skills necessary to succeed in whatever path you choose. I owe it to you, your family, and myself to ensure that no lack of knowledge, practice, or skill ever holds you back. This is a challenge I enjoy meeting, but I need your help in it.

This class and this school exist because of you. Without students, this place is nothing. Therefore, I insist that my students participate in their own education. It is only because I respect your intelligence, your dreams, and your mind, that I expect you to take responsibility for your own learning. That means you must be willing to express your ideas, ask questions, raise doubts, and challenge ideas that don't make sense to you. You must feel strong and comfortable enough to respond honestly and thoughtfully to questions about literature and life. Most of all, you must read and write with passion and a purpose. Here, we must pull together and support each other so that everyone feels comfortable taking that risk. Then, and only then, we get the best of everyone . . . and we all learn much, much more.

Each year, I take great pleasure in watching the ways my students take charge of their own learning and strive to make the hours we spend here meaningful ones. Our schoolwork should matter in the world beyond these four walls. . . . All over the state, and all over the nation, people are arguing about what we should teach and how you should learn. Publishers are getting rich pushing the latest curriculum model. Politicians are using your test scores, your successes and failures, to further their careers. Even in this corrupt environment, I still see tremendous potential in turning this classroom into a true workshop for our ideas and art. . . . We must have the strength, patience, and courage to make the reading and writing we do here mean something.

I try not to take myself too seriously, but as you can tell, I take my job and your learning very seriously. In turn, I expect you to be serious about your education and the work that comes with it. I can't promise to entertain you at all times, but I do believe that part of my job is making the hours we will spend together interesting and meaningful ones. I look forward to reading your thoughts and hearing your ideas . . . sooner than you might think!

For homework, please write a response letter to me explaining some of your own ideas about school and learning. How do you feel about being here? What do you think school is all about? What should happen in a high school English class? What can I expect from you (as a person and a student) and what do you expect from me (as a teacher and a person)? Remember that this is my first chance to get to know you as a writer and thinker . . . be yourself and make an impression that lasts.

Sincerely,
Seth Peterson

Patrick begins his response letter by saying he knows what school is all about: It starts at some God-awful hour so that the rest of society, the commuter culture, won't have to put up with teenagers on the bus. Kids go to school because their parents and the law make them go, at least until they're 16. In school, teachers tell you what to do. If you sit down and do it quietly, you pass; if not, you repeat the year. Once the parents, laws, and teachers have beaten you into submission, you're ready to pay more money than you have to go to college so you can make more money than all the kids who never got past the "sit down quietly" part. Patrick ends with some statement like, "Yeah, I know all about how the bullshit system works." He does. He knows a great deal. Later in the year he will publish controversial poems, earn honor roll grades in English, and win a writing award.

I feel lucky to work with the age group I do. Even when I am at the humbled, humiliated end of its blade, I admire adolescents' piercing candor. Teenagers have built-in lie detectors and sniff out insincerity like truth-hounds. Students coming from urban environments—the big, neglected, bustling underbellies of our society—have the best bullshit detectors of all. They have to because survival on the street means making quick, accurate judgments about who is fronting and who is for real. Safety lies in knowing who is fluff and who is follow-through, who makes threats to mask fear and who has no qualms about doing serious harm. Furthermore, people and communities that have been burned by empty promises and self-serving opportunists acquire skepticism and distrust rapidly. Truth and trust, therefore, are essential forms of currency in the urban classroom, precious for their scarcity, but easily distinguished from the cubit zirconium and pleather so readily offered in place of the genuine articles.

To trust other people, we must believe that we know them. Keeping our cards close to the chest serves no one's needs in the classroom. I must begin with what I value, empowering myself by making myself vulnerable. So I tell my students of my love for words. As perhaps our most intimate and indispensable invention, language, like people, must be allowed to grow, evolve, shift and lurch, change, regenerate, scar, and heal anew. In reading and writing literature, words are our medium. I teach my subject in the hope that my students might cultivate their own words, and then their own lives, with enough structure to support their ambitions and enough wiggle room to transform their tastes. I teach for the love of words; for the change, rebellion, and innovation we spawn in life and mark in language. Our understanding of who we are and how we relate to the world around us usually begins in adolescence and always begins with words.

My fellow teachers work in a system that trusts and expects them to know how to respond to a suicidal student, a bomb threat, or a hate-crime. Yet, this same system does not trust them to design the final exam for their own course. They teach the glory of this nation's struggle for freedom and defense of individual rights, and yet are asked to do so with a curriculum that is standardized so that government agencies can measure growth more efficiently.

The contradictions don't end with the policymakers and centralized offices. We, who do this work, are caught in a conundrum, working within the system to create change. We willingly hand over our careers, sometimes it seems like our lives, to a massive bureaucracy so that we can work hard to connect with one individual at a time, light a fire in just one mind. Our successes, the ones the "system" sees as such, usually go unnoticed or, worse, become institutionalized failures: mandates that crash and burn. Our failures—our frustrations and defeats in the classroom, where the work that matters actually is done—become our successes, our chances to rise from the ashes and become new again. Renewal is an oxymoron, another paradox we strive to attain. Perpetual proximity to youth, though, gives me courage or delusion enough to believe I can come in and try it again a different way, make the lesson, the text, or the class new again.

Is it duplicitous to live this contradiction? No, choosing sides is simple. Living with the consequences is the greater challenge. Life's beauty lies in its contrast and complications. We must teach our young to expect complications, to love the uncertainty and embrace the contradictions; such things are our mortal inheritance, the human condition. It might be courageous and perhaps radical to foster outright rebellion and ransack the rulebook, to give up any notion of education beyond the moment of creation. It might be radical, but selfish. For, in the process, our students would be forfeiting their options, their own power to choose success as defined by our society. That choice is not mine to make for them. My role, my responsibility, is to expose students to the complications, the choices and consequences that await them.

The challenge of living in the cracks of pure logic, the spaces in between, exhilarates me and keeps me teaching.

I have made my choice and live happily with the consequences. My job now is to empower others to make their own choices: to rebel or conform, or, as most of us do, live complicated lives between the two. Language, like those who create and amend it, is resilient enough to exist in that "confuzzled" state and endure the problems that stem from so paradoxical a life.

I sense another possible beginning coming on. Maybe the one that keeps me here in the classroom, keeps me looking forward to another day of students, questions, books, and pens. It starts with the blaring sound of the alarm. A quick shower and a hot cup of coffee, a yawning train ride, the familiar trudge up three flights of stairs to the corner room facing the alley and the church, and then it begins again. The first student pokes his head in the door, "Good morning, Mr. P." And, the odds are, it will be. It certainly won't be the same one we had yesterday. Each one begins anew.

PART V

To Become More Fully Human

G iven the precarious situation of public education today—a largely unsupportive public, unresponsive bureaucracies, and seemingly unending mandates—it is hard to romanticize teaching these days. Yet in spite of difficult conditions, people continue to choose teaching for what may appear to be idealistic, even romantic and naive, reasons: They love working with young people; they consider teaching a mission and a calling; they see it as an opportunity to share their enthusiasm about learning and to leave their imprint on the future. These, among others, are some of the reasons articulated in this book.

But something besides romantic notions of teaching is also at work here. Teachers enter the profession because they *also* benefit from teaching. Forget conventional notions of teachers as saviors or miracle workers: If it were not also deeply rewarding, if it were only hard work and sacrifice and selflessness—at times, even agonizingly difficult work–if they did not *get something back* from teaching, people would not teach. It is as simple as that.

One way to look at this, is to understand that teaching helps make people more human. Much in the way that becoming a parent may help make one less self-centered, more responsive to others, more aware of one's obligations beyond oneself, teaching too has this kind of effect. In this part, you will read several essays that illustrate how teaching helps teachers themselves become more fully human. In the case of Mary Ginley, a teacher for 35 years, she makes it clear that teaching is about many things that help make her more fully human, including "saving the world one child at a time." For Bill Dunn, becoming more fully human means developing a profound empathy for his students and what they go through to navigate not only their education, but also the world. Kerri Warfield, a relatively new-comer to teaching, sees herself as a "life-toucher," someone who will leave a mark on students' futures, and this is all it takes to make her want to continue teaching for a long time. The chapter concludes with an essay by Mary Cowhey, a 1st- and 2nd-grade teacher who calls her classroom the "Peace Classroom," and who views education as a force to help everyone in the class become more fully human, including herself.

Chapter *19*

Saving the World One Child at a Time

M ARY G INLEY

M ary Ginley confesses that she
has spent her entire life unsure
and unsettled, never quite feel-
ing as if she was getting it "right," always
worried about whether she was doing
kids a disservice by not following the party
line. She remembers, for example, when
she taught whole language at an urban
early childhood center with a primarily
Puerto Rican student body. Although she
believed it was the right thing to do, she
also worried that the kids might go to 1st
grade not able to circle everything that
began with "B" or sound out three-letter words the way other kids could. She
also was concerned that other teachers would not notice the children's wonderful invented spelling but instead complain that they couldn't print on the lines.

Nonetheless, feeling unsure and unsettled is something Mary had not
experienced in quite the same way as she did 2 years ago. A kindergarten,
1st- and 2nd-grade teacher for 33 years, Mary started teaching 5th grade
2 years ago. She thought she would always be a 2nd-grade teacher. She
was certainly good at it: Mary was selected Massachusetts Teacher of the
Year in 1997, and even before then, she was widely recognized throughout
the state as an excellent and inspiring teacher. Because one of the 2nd-grade
classes in her school was to be eliminated, she volunteered to teach 5th grade

169

instead. It was a challenge teaching a new grade after so many years: It meant creating a whole new curriculum, becoming familiar with a different discourse, and even immersing herself in reading large amounts of 5th-grade children's literature the entire summer before she began teaching this new grade.

Mary is passionate about what she believes, but she says that there will always be this little voice that tells her, "You're not good enough," and that the kids won't be ready for what's coming next year. Last year the voice probably shouted rather than whispered, but it's always there. In spite of this, Mary is not afraid of new challenges. In her long career as a teacher, she has taken many risks: She has taught her students to question what they learn and to be critical of conventional wisdom; she also has been an outspoken critic of the high-stakes test in Massachusetts, even appearing on *60 Minutes* to speak against it; and she has taken other actions that have done little to endear her to some administrators or even to some of her colleagues. But because she views teaching as more than simply transmitting a prepackaged curriculum to her students, she has been willing to take these risks. Mary feels that she becomes more fully human by taking risks in teaching, as well as by "saving the world one child at a time."

About 3 years ago I came home from school to find a letter from Florida. It read:

> Dear Mrs. Ginley,
>   I don't know if you remember me. I was in your kindergarten and 1st-grade class at the Early Childhood Center in Holyoke. I don't remember a lot about kindergarten but I remember I was scared and you were nice to me.
>   Recently, I was accepted to a specialized high school nearby and my mom and I were celebrating. Remember my mom? She's a recovered alcoholic and she wasn't in good shape back then. Anyway, my mom told me that I owed everything to you, that you were the one who got me headed in the right direction. So she told me I should try to find you and thank you and I did find you and want to thank you for all you did.
>   I am enclosing a picture of me in my kindergarten class. I put an arrow in case you didn't recognize me. I'm sending you one of me at the 8th-grade dance we had a few weeks ago too.
>   I hope you are well. Thank you very much for all you did.
>
>   Your former student,
>   Steven Jackson

I looked at the pictures, at the frightened little boy in the front row (with an arrow pointing to him in case I really forgot him) and at the young man dressed up for the 8th-grade formal. Oh, Steven, I thought, how on earth could you ever think I'd forget you?

Steven arrived one day in mid-October. I was teaching 20-something kindergarten kids in Holyoke in a tiny classroom on the second floor of a renovated junior college. Steven had a rough start that day. While his mom was filling out the paperwork and chatting with the principal, Steve escaped and ran out the front door. He hid behind the bushes and came out only when our secretary coaxed him with the promise of a cherry lollipop. So, it was a tear-streaked, sticky-fingered little kid that appeared at my door around 9:30 that morning with the principal and his mom.

I knelt down to talk to him (he spit at me) and then I looked at my principal with a question in my eyes. "Why me"? I wanted to say but couldn't because Steven's mom was right there. "I have the most kids already. It's someone else's turn." Instead, I smiled at his mom, asked if she'd like to stay for a few minutes, and coaxed Steven onto the rug to listen to the story. The others watched wide-eyed as Steven scrambled up on his mom's lap and wrapped his arms and legs around her. I passed out lollipops to the gang, who were staring more at Steven's lollipop than they were at my book, and went on with the story. Slowly, very slowly, Steven unwrapped himself and moved to the rug. When the story and singing were over and we were moving to centers, I told his mom it was probably time for her to leave. She hesitated, kissed Steven good-bye, and headed for the door.

"No!" he shrieked and started after her. I blocked the door and sent her on her way. He kicked me and threw his lollipop in my hair, screaming and sobbing and wailing. I scooped him up and rocked him for the next hour, watching the other 5-year-olds from the rocking chair in the front of the room and silently cursing my principal, who later told me the reason she put Steven in my room was that he needed me.

Steven had a rough year. He flew into a rage without warning, turning into a miniature tornado, throwing blocks and ripping papers off the wall as he catapulted around the room. He'd sit and sulk if he didn't get his way, describe in minute detail what AA meetings were like and why his mom went to them, refuse to join the circle, refuse to write his name, refuse to share a toy. The only time he seemed calm was when I was rocking him or he was off in a corner with a picture book. He taught himself to read that year but he never learned how to make a friend.

I kept those kids for a second year. I remember when I was discussing this with my principal. She knew how Steven wore me out. She knew that I walked in the room every day saying, "Dear God, help me love Steven a little more today."

"I could move him to another class," she offered. "You can't," I wailed. "He needs the stability more than anyone does and I can't let him think I don't want him." So 1st grade rolled around and Steven arrived the first day, grinning and glad to be back.

Steven still had his days that year but he had mellowed and as he began to feel safe, at school and even at home, we saw a very different little boy. Toward the end of that year, he and his mom moved and I never heard from him again. Until now.

Foolish child, to think I wouldn't remember him.

I suppose the reason I still teach, after 35 years, is because there are some Stevens every year who might need me. Most likely, they won't write me letters (a few do) and they may not even remember me, but I need to be there for them. School is supposed to be the great equalizer. That may be the American dream but I have never been in a school (other than the one I was in when I had Steven) where there was an active policy to make sure that every child had equal access to quality education, where every child was made to feel welcome, respected, valued, and safe. From the minute a child walks through the school doors in kindergarten, the rich get richer and the poor get poorer, and the smart get smarter too. It seems schools *say* that everyone is valued, but when you look closely, you'll find it isn't so.

Part of this isn't the teachers' fault. They are overworked and there are days when there are just so many demands being made on them that they feel as if they are more into "crowd control" than into quality education of the whole child. But if we really believe that it is our job to educate *all* the kids, not just the ones who come to school clean with their homework ready to be corrected, we have to keep on trying to find ways to move beyond crowd control to creating places where everyone can grow and learn and find out who they are and what they can be.

Throughout my career I've been asked why I became a teacher. Some teachers have very clear memories of the events or ideas that brought them to the teaching profession. I actually can't remember. I tell people that it seemed like a good idea at the time. It had to do with saving the world, making a difference, changing kids' lives. I graduated from high school in the middle of the 1960s, full of idealism and dreams and not a little arrogance.

It's been pretty humbling, I must say, to find out that perhaps I was the one who needed saving, that I had a lot to learn about what other people's children needed from me, that I didn't have all the answers, that I wasn't even asking the right questions.

Letters like the one from Steven are few and far between. And I was no miracle worker, not then, not now. I can only do what I can do. And there are days when I don't even do *that* particularly well.

Slowly but surely I learned and keep on learning. I learned that my first job was to learn from my students and their families, to listen carefully as they tried to tell me who they were and what they wanted from me. I learned that any saving of the world that I did was going to happen one child at a time. And that more than likely, I'd get it wrong as often as I got it right.

Thirty-five years later, I still get out of bed every day and head to school, try to figure out what I can do to connect kids with one another and with learning. I know I need to help them "make it" in today's world. I also know they need to know that things do not have to be the way they are. There may be better ways of doing things. There may be other ways of looking at things. If I just teach them how to survive in this inequitable society, how to get along, I am doing them a tremendous disservice. Teachers have enormous power and we must use it wisely. If we teach them to accept the status quo, most of them will do just that. If we teach them to ask questions, most of them will learn to think carefully before they accept things just because it's always been that way. I am always asking kids, "Are you sure that's true? How do you know? Where is your evidence? Could things be different? Do you think everyone sees this the way you do?"

At present, I am teaching children of privilege. They are mostly White, middle-class kids from two-parent families who love them, check their homework, take them skiing, and have read to them since they were 6 months old. That is not to say that *all* of them have easy lives. It is as much a mistake to stereotype suburban kids as it is to do so for urban kids. But, let's face it, in general, their lives are easier in many ways than those of their neighbors down the road, and their lives will continue to be easier as they grow older.

In 2003, when our President and his advisors decided we needed to go to war with Iraq, I tried to decide whether—or even how—I would address this in school. At the time, I was teaching 2nd graders and I had begun to wonder whether I laid too much on them too soon. Were they too young to talk about war? Should my anti-war activities spill over into school or not? I had been out of favor with school authorities for awhile because of a very public stand against the emphasis put on the state's high-stakes testing, and I was enjoying a respite from the subtle harassment of a conservative superintendent and school committee.

I needed to get clear on exactly what I wanted to do before I began and so I hit the library and Internet, first to learn as much as I could about the issue and about Iraq as fast as I could, and next to find out how other teachers were dealing with this. In general, the recommendation was to discuss it with older elementary kids but not the little ones.

"Good," I thought. "I'm off the hook." But I couldn't let go of the realization that even if I didn't mention the war, *the kids* knew we were at war and they were hearing all sorts of reasons why we needed to get rid of the "bad guys" in a faraway country, and why war was a good thing.

In the midst of my research, I came across only one book about children in Iraq that my 7-year-olds could understand. The book, *A Family from Iraq*, by John King from the Families Around the World series published by Raintree, was pretty innocuous.[1] It was a small book full of color photographs of a family in Baghdad and described in simple language the life of this family in modern-day Iraq.

We had read about families in other countries before—China because Alexa was adopted from China, Ecuador because Joey's dad went there on business, Puerto Rico because Ceci's grandmother lived there and her mom grew up there. I started the book about Iraq without comment. I often ask kids at the end of a book to tell me why they thought I chose the particular book I read to them. Usually someone can figure it out.

We read about a middle-class family in Baghdad. The dad was a plant manager in a factory and the mom was a kindergarten teacher. They had four kids. One was newly married and lived in an apartment down the hall from the family. One was in high school, another in 4th grade, and the baby was a year old. We read about the 4th grader and her dreams of being a great soccer player. We saw her team picture from that year. She worried about good grades and long division. We saw pictures of her playing with her baby brother and going to the local shops with her friends. She loved family gatherings on Sunday at her grandmother's out in the country. She hated homework and doing dishes. If you looked closely, you would see the picture of Saddam Hussein on the wall in their apartment.

I read the book without stopping for questions or comments and when I finished Matthew raised his hand.

"Did you read that to us because our country is fighting Iraq in a war?" he asked.

I nodded.

"Are they okay?" someone asked. "Where did you say they lived?" "Do you think they went to the grandma's in the country when the soldiers came into Baghdad?"

"What's the copyright date?" one of the kids asked. We'd been checking copyright dates in books about dinosaurs because in general books written before 1990 have so much misinformation they're hardly worth reading. Since then, these kids check copyright dates on everything.

"Why do you ask?" I questioned.

"Well," he said, "I want to know what grade she's in now." We checked. She was in 8th grade; the baby was in kindergarten. "They aren't going to school," I explained. "Schools are closed in Baghdad."

For days after that, the kids came in with news of bombings, food shortages, full hospitals, and deaths. A few wrote to the publisher asking for information about the family. We didn't receive an answer. We decided we could just hope for the best. I pointed out that this was just one family among thousands and thousands of families that were being affected by our efforts to "make the world safe for democracy."

Did I change minds in this mostly conservative, prowar town? I don't know. I just know I put a human face on the war and for a little while, at least, these kids could not just glibly recite the company line about why we needed to invade a country halfway across the world.

I am now teaching 5th graders. Unlike the little ones who looked at everything through wide-open eyes, my 10-year-olds have watched and listened for a few years now and they are sure that homeless people and people on welfare are too lazy to get jobs, that gay people are not "normal," that we need to go to war and kill people to make sure our country can stay free. I sit and listen and ask questions and I am amazed at how strong their opinions are by the time they are 10. What's that song? "You've Got to be Carefully Taught" from *South Pacific*:

> You've got to be taught before it's too late,
> Before you are six, or seven or eight,
> To hate all the people your relatives hate,
> You've got to be carefully taught!

So I keep on asking questions, make them think, make them ask questions. I wonder, though, whether it makes a difference. One third of my current students were in my 2nd-grade classroom. I remember our discussions 3 years ago about Christopher Columbus, racism, problems of the homeless, Native Peoples during the westward movement. They came up in social studies or when we were collecting canned goods at Thanksgiving or when we read legends in literature. And I actually thought they were beginning to understand.

It's a humbling experience to teach them again. They remember very little . . . not the discussions, not the stories, not even the role play of Rosa Parks on the bus. What did I teach them when they were 7? More important, what did they learn? How much can one teacher do in 1 year with one group of children? Is it really possible to change the world?

There's this cartoon I once saw that shows a father and son on a camel in the middle of the desert. The caption reads, "Stop asking me if we're there yet. We're nomads, son. We're nomads."

So whatever would make someone get on a camel and travel across the desert and keep on moving and never arrive? I can't even imagine. But I suppose people can't imagine why anyone would get into education, keep on moving, and never arrive. I keep trying to get it right . . . the education of our children, I mean. And every time I think I've figured something out (how to hook a kid on reading, how to help kids form some kind of community where everyone's safe, how to establish an environment where everyone's voice is heard, how to help kids understand that might does not make right), I find out I don't really know as much as I thought I did. And I continue to ask the same questions.

I began my teaching career in 1970 with lots of answers and a few questions. Here I am after 35 years of teaching—still trying to get it right, still trying to help kids make sense of it all while I'm still trying to make sense of it myself. And with far more questions than answers.

It's not comfortable, up here on that camel, trying to get it right and knowing you'll never be "there" because you've chosen to be a nomad. But I stay and keep plugging and have no real regrets. I have loved what I do (even on the days when I don't even *like* what I do) and will keep on trying to get it right because I know each year there is at least one Steven whose life is changed because I was there.

Chapter 20

Confessions of an Underperforming Teacher

BILL DUNN

"Underperforming" is the last word that comes to mind when describing Bill Dunn. A veteran teacher, Bill has been teaching social studies and English for over 25 years, most of them at Dean Vocational High School in Holyoke, Massachusetts. He is indefatigable, working two jobs for most of his career, serving as chairman of both the social studies and the English departments, raising three children, and completing a master's degree in the midst of it all.

When Bill started teaching, the student population in his town was overwhelmingly White, mostly children of working–class Irish, French, and immigrants of other European descent. Now, the student body is about 85% Puerto Rican and poor, a dramatic shift that has left many of the schools and teachers in this former mill town unprepared and confused.

Bill faced the challenge in characteristic style. A number of years ago, he decided, in his words, to "come out of the closet as a Spanish speaker" when he realized that he was understanding most of what his Puerto Rican students were saying to one another in Spanish. He had been in their midst for so long it seemed he was learning Spanish almost by osmosis. Thus began his odyssey to become fluent in Spanish, a journey he continues to this day.

He kept a journal of his experience and I was so moved by it that I asked him if I could publish it in one of my books.[1]

The urge to become fluent in Spanish is typical of Bill, who wants to understand who his students are and what their lives are like. His fierce defense of them, and his anger at the injustices they endure, is also clearly evident in the eloquent essay that follows.

I work in an urban vocational high school. Eighty-five percent of my students are Hispanic. Eighty-three percent qualify for free or reduced lunch, and 70% are native Spanish speakers. I wish I could tell you that I don't encounter gangs, weapons, poverty, high pregnancy rates, and the other social ills that plague city schools; but these problems are the realities of where I work. These things trouble me, but I understand them because I live with them daily, as do my students. I know the cause of these problems, and I also know that the majority of my students are the victims and not the perpetrators. Violence in schools is as real as metal detectors and police officers. The stresses that students and teachers encounter in schools today should evoke compassion and admiration from the public; unfortunately, quite the opposite occurs, and this troubles me even more. Test results are released and inner-city students and their teachers are ridiculed in bold headlines. My favorite label is "underperforming." I sincerely couldn't have come up with a word with nastier connotations to attach to schools and the human beings who inhabit them.

About a decade ago *Parade Magazine* ran an issue devoted to stress on the job. I was surprised to see teaching listed as the most stressful job in the nation, followed by such obvious careers as air traffic controller, police officer, fire fighter, and so on down the line. Our world has changed considerably in the past 10 years, and I doubt that teaching would still head the list. The irony for me is that the stress of the job 10 years ago seems laughable given the atmosphere and working conditions in schools today.

The simple truth about teaching, in my opinion, is that it is an inherently stressful profession. Most students do not want to do what their teachers want them to do. It takes a great deal of patience to spend 8 or more hours a day cajoling students who would prefer to socialize and not to be bothered. My strategy used to be to expose kids to interesting ideas that made them wonder about commonly held assumptions. Interested kids cause fewer problems. I used to console myself with the rationalization that I was doing the right thing for my students, but lately I'm not so sure.

Over the past 10 years my state has very rigidly defined what it means to be an educated student in a Massachusetts public school. There are clear winners and clear losers. Unfortunately, even the kids who pass the test in my school are considered losers because it usually takes them three or four tries to pass the test. Schools throughout the state have been forced to goose-step to the beat of mandated exams, and the result is continuous drill, and in urban schools that drill often goes on for 3 to 4 years. Gone are the interesting ideas and intellectual curiosity that made it a pleasure to teach. They have been replaced with the stress of doing the same thing over and over again. It's a lousy deal all the way around for students, teachers, and schools. Eventually it will be evident that it's a lousy deal for society as well because uninterested kids on the street often cross the line from victim to victimizer.

The major source of stress over the past 10 years has come from unexpected places, and the most insidious thing about the march to higher standards and "high-stakes" testing is that those leading the charge purport to be doing it on behalf of the students in "underperforming" schools like mine. No Child Left Behind translates into horrendous dropout rates between freshman and senior years; and in schools like mine 30 to 40% of the students who continue through senior year are still left behind through little fault of their own. The rhetoric of educational reform is in itself appalling. Headlines such as "State Threatens Takeover of Underperforming Districts" should insult everyone, not just those students, parents, and teachers in poor districts. If you're a fascist regime, you "take over" the states next to you. When you're a state and you "take over" schools, you're on the road to being a fascist regime. As I write, my school has just been threatened with a takeover, which means a visit from the "accountability and targeted assistance team." I am uncertain who constitute this group and what I am going to be held accountable for, but I am dead certain that they are not on my team. I am fairly certain that they have less classroom experience than I have. I am also fairly certain that they do not live in a community like mine, and that their children have not attended "underperforming" schools like my children have. I am also dead certain that they will not know the realities of living in a community like mine, which ranks among the highest in poverty, teen pregnancy, and drug and alcohol abuse in the state. In fact, as a community, we are first in the state in just about all the bad things, and I am certain that they will not see me or my students. They will see only artificial scores that have little to do with anybody's accountability, intelligence, or effort except those who made up the test in the first place. Finally, I'm a bit queasy about the oxymoron "targeted assistance."

Often when I rant about testing and the MCAS (the high-stakes test in Massachusetts) in particular, I am accused of making excuses for my students. I refuse to make excuses; I think they're doing fine. Fifty-four percent of our students are passing the English language arts part of the test and approximately 30% miss by a few points. I have an acute knowledge of the test because I have spent most of the past 4 years going over the questions again and again and again. The vocabulary on the test is just plain nasty. Recently I was doing an item analysis of last year's test, and to my surprise there was a question that limited English proficient (LEP) kids got right at a much higher rate than regular education students. It was a multiple-choice question based on an excerpt from *The Scarlet Letter*. Most students across the state had trouble with the dense, archaic text. Students had to pick the correct synonym for the word *edifice* from the context of the passage. This was difficult because the usage of the words in the passage was buried with Nathaniel Hawthorne. The correct answer was *building*. Obviously, Spanish speakers knew the correct answer because the Spanish word for building is *edificio*. Did the test makers put in that question as a concession to LEP students? I'd bet the ranch against it. In fact, I think they screwed up. The rest of the test plays with bizarre word connotations that are simply beyond the reach of second-language learners. My point is that one question out of 40 favored LEP students, and it was an accident. The other 39 questions favor middle-class kids who are native English speakers, who also tend to have educated parents, and who tend to live in relatively affluent communities. Now there is nothing wrong with any of those things, but there is something very wrong with labeling kids "failing" because they were born short on cultural capital and on the wrong side of the language tracks.

So why do I teach? I teach because someone has to tell my students that they are not the ones who are dumb. They need to know that only the blissfully ignorant and profoundly evil make up tests to prove that they and people like them are smart. I teach because my students need to know that poverty does not equal stupidity, and that surviving a bleak, dismal childhood makes you strong and tough and beautiful in ways that only survivors of similar environments can appreciate and understand. I teach because my students need to know that in their struggle to acquire a second language, they participate in one of the most difficult of human feats. My students also need to know that 4 days of reading in a second language under high-stakes testing conditions would shut down even Einstein's brain. I teach because my students need to know that right and wrong are relative to one's culture, and that even these definitions become laughable over time. I teach because the people who make up these tests don't know these things or, worse, they do.

Chapter 21

Becoming a Life-Toucher

KERRI WARFIELD

The first thing you notice about Kerri Warfield is her smile: It is big, all-encompassing, and contagious. It is, above all, enthusiastic. Kerri brings this same enthusiasm to everything she does, including teaching. An art teacher for 5 years, Kerri is convinced that she made the right choice all those years ago when she decided that teaching was what she wanted to do with her life.

The other passion in Kerri's life is art. As a child, she found great joy in art and she wanted to share that joy with others. That was one of her motivations for becoming an art teacher. However, she doesn't think of her responsibility as teaching only art, but also as exposing students to different views of the world. Her medium for doing this happens to be art. When she talks about her students and their art projects, Kerri's eyes light up. In her essay, she reflects on why she became a teacher, and on her curiosity about why others have made this decision.

Recently, I attended a retirement party for an assistant principal at my school. His career spanned an impressive 35 years, 30 years as a physical education teacher and 5 years as an assistant principal. In the weeks before his retirement, I had the opportunity to talk with him about his experiences as an educator. For the previous month,

I had been thinking about this job we call teaching, and I came to the conclusion that I needed other perspectives besides my own. The main question I wanted to answer was, "Why become a teacher?" I thought this question would be an easy one to answer because I became a teacher only 5 years ago and my intentions are still fresh in my mind. But in reality, it is a complicated and challenging question.

Since the assistant principal was at the end of his career, I thought he would have more insight than I into this central question. His response to my question was in fact helpful and inspiring, but it didn't hit home until the night I attended his retirement party. In a crowded room filled with co-workers, former students, and family, his eyes welled up with tears as individuals shared stories about how his work had touched their lives. It made me realize that, although each educator has his or her own set of personal stories and reasons for teaching, there is one reason that all educators share: We have the desire to touch lives. I have come to believe that this is a core value that connects educators.

This realization does not mean that we can't have other ambitions when it comes to teaching, or that our individual approaches and perspectives are not important. What it does mean is that we want to be *life-touchers*.

My own story starts in the little town of Sutton, Massachusetts. I loved going to school. School meant seeing friends, learning new things, and interacting with teachers. My classes were small, so this gave me the opportunity to get to know teachers, and for them to know me. I wanted my teachers to like me and, in return, I wanted to impress them. This was most true in my art class. I can remember as far back as 1st and 2nd grade what my elementary school's art room looked like and, of course, I remember the teacher. She was thrilled with my enthusiasm for art and with the effort I put into my work. During an Open House, I recall her delightedly informing my mother that I was very gifted in art. I can still remember where I was sitting in the room when she said that.

As I went through grade school, my passion for art kept growing, partly because of the positive encouragement I got along the way. In high school, I met an art teacher who was fun, talented, and a great motivator. She was the first person to tell me that I would make a great art teacher. I don't know exactly why she thought this;

she may have seen something in my creativity, my enthusiasm for art, or the way I interacted with other students, or maybe it was a combination of all three. All I know is that she saw potential in me to be an artist and an art educator. If she had not come into my life, I wonder whether I would have reached this conclusion on my own?

After high school, I was accepted into the art program at the University of Massachusetts, Amherst. The first year or two in college, I tried to keep an open mind about possible careers in art, but in the back of my mind I could hear my high school art teacher saying, "You'll make a great art teacher someday!" When I took my first art education course during sophomore year, I knew she was right in pointing me in this direction.

The summer after I graduated from college, I was offered a teaching job in Westfield, Massachusetts. It was a part-time teaching position in the high school art department. I was petrified! Looking back at those first days of teaching, I think what scared me the most was the thought that I wouldn't have any impact on the students. I wanted to share my love of art and learning with them, and in return I wanted them to love learning and art. It took awhile for me to realize that teaching does not always get instant results, and sometimes we don't ever get to see the fruits of our labor.

When I asked other teachers why they got into teaching, most of their replies started with, "I had a teacher in school who . . ." Along with this initial reply—very much like my own—they went on to tell me their individual stories. One came from my assistant principal, Ron, whom I mentioned earlier. After completing high school, Ron had taken a job delivering mail and hadn't applied to college. He assumed his grades from high school weren't good enough to get into a decent school. One day, his high school physical education teacher spotted him on his mail route and yelled, "Why aren't you in school? I thought you wanted to become a phys. ed. teacher?" Ron explained his situation and his teacher told him that if he wanted to go to school for physical education, he would make a couple of calls. The next day, Ron got a call from the physical education director at the University of Massachusetts inviting him to join the program. Just as in my case, a teacher intervened because he saw potential where others had not. Ron knew that he wanted to become a teacher, but he just didn't know how to make that dream a reality. Luckily, he knew someone who did.

Another teacher I spoke with didn't start her teaching career until later in life. Jan, who is now a family and consumer science teacher, raised her children while working in various jobs that supported education, including library work and a teacher's aide position, before becoming a teacher herself. She always respected teachers and envied the courage it took to get in front of a class. Jan's friends who were teachers constantly told her that she could be an excellent teacher. At a crossroads in her life, she finally realized that she needed to face up to her fears and accept this challenge.

When I asked colleagues about hardships they had faced as teachers, their responses all centered around the dream of a perfect classroom and work setting. Lack of time, support, space, and materials, along with rising class numbers and behavioral problems, are common obstacles teachers face and complain about inside school. Outside the classroom, they are confronted with low salaries, lack of job security, and public scrutiny. All these things can wear teachers down if their passion for teaching diminishes or if they lose sight of the value of teaching, of being a life-toucher.

It is the utopian dream of teachers to see all their students succeed. Currently, I am a full-time middle school art teacher in Westfield. The utopian dream both motivates and plagues me. It is still hard to see some students succeeding while others seem unreachable. I'm always asking myself why some classes do so well and others feel like disasters. I continue to question and to search for strategies that will help my students, whom I genuinely care about. It is hard to accept failure, especially when it concerns children.

Not only do I believe in my role as a teacher, but I also believe in the power and importance of my subject area. Art is a unique subject to teach because it can incorporate many other disciplines. For example, within the context of art, students can learn math skills, gain new perspectives on history, examine social issues, use the laws of science in their artwork, and reflect on it all through writing. I don't think many people realize that an art program can be as valuable to learning as a "core subject," and that art education greatly enhances the educational experience. If more people did realize this, then music and art wouldn't be the first things to go when budgets are tight.

I recently asked a group of students to comment on their experiences in my art class. Specifically, I asked them to write about what they liked and disliked, and what they would change in order to improve the course. This type of assignment serves two purposes: It helps me assess my teaching and it gives students the chance to reflect on the work they've done in the course.

After going through their responses, I was pleased that a large number of the students enjoyed the atmosphere of the class and the projects in which they participated. One girl shared that I was the only teacher who always smiled and never yelled. In addition, art was the highlight of her school day (Wow, that made me feel good!). In the dislike category, a majority of the group did not like writing art essays (a requirement of my class) but many added that they understood it was important. I thought their responses were honest and I was pleased at the number of students who chose to see the value of these assignments. Lastly, in response to what they would change, the answers were mixed, but generally positive. For example, some students wanted to have the option to take art for a full school year rather than a quarter. Others gave me ideas for lessons or stated that they wanted the opportunity to create more projects.

Whenever I design an art project, I think about what my students will gain from it. Will it be a new skill? An exploration of personal creativity? A chance to ponder a social issue relevant to their lives? Or will it be all of these? I enjoy the challenge of creating art projects and I believe there is always room for improvement.

The question of why we teach could be answered with, "Why not?" In what other job can we help improve the future, share our knowledge, and learn every day? One thing I love about my job is that every morning when I enter school, I know that it is going to be a different day than the day before. Of course, you can't teach if you don't have a desire to work with others, in this case, with children. That has to be your foundation. What you teach and how you teach comes with experience and is done on different levels depending on the ambition of the teacher.

I got into teaching because I wanted to give kids an educational experience that would make them feel good about themselves and their future, like my teachers gave me. I keep teaching because every day I feel that I get a little bit closer to becoming that teacher I envisioned.

As a teacher, I want children to leave school with a social conscience, an appreciation for diversity and life, a thirst for learning, and an understanding of how knowledge can allow them to achieve their dreams. I also want them to leave the classroom with good memories because, since teachers are life-touchers, we want to be a part of students' childhood memories. Other teachers might not admit this, but I will: Even if I might never hear it from their lips, I want my former students to recall their time in my class. I want them to remember something worthwhile, great or small, that happened there. I hope that my students will remember my class not because it was perfect, but because of its unique flaws. Hopefully, they also will remember that I was a teacher who truly cared and strived to reach them. This is my definition of a *life-toucher*.

Chapter 22

" . . . We Shall Have to Begin with the Children"

MARY COWHEY

Mary Cowhey was a community organizer for 14 years. It was a life of commitment, hard work, and unending struggle. Mary was used to these things, and she valued them. But after many years of fighting all the time, 7 days a week, 365 days a year, she felt she was losing her humanity. She decided she needed to do something more hopeful with her life, something less combative, and more constructive. She became a teacher.

Going back to finish college as an adult, first as a single parent and then married with children, was not easy, but Mary excelled. She became an Ada Comstock Scholar at Smith College and graduated with honors, receiving numerous awards before moving on to graduate school at the University of Massachusetts, where she received a Master's Degree with a specialization in bilingual/ESL and multicultural education. Currently a 1st- and 2nd-grade teacher in the Northampton, Massachusetts, public schools, Mary has kept up the pace with breakneck speed: Besides a full-time teaching job, which she does with great talent and dedication, Mary facilitates workshops, gives guest lectures, and collaborates with her colleagues to help create a learning environment that is joyful, nurturing, and demanding. She also has written an innovative curriculum on teaching philosophy to young children, was filmed teaching lessons challenging gender stereotyping for the documentary "Oliver Button Is a Star," and served as a consultant for the project, among other activities. Mary is particularly proud of having been a delegate to the United Nations World Conference Against Racism in 2001 in South Africa, where she visited and established contact with four schools. Her young students maintain pen pal relationships with the students in those schools.

In 2002, after having been a teacher for just 6 years, Mary was presented with the Milken National Education Award, one of only 100 teachers nationwide so honored. At the awards ceremony at the Massachusetts State House, she explained what she hopes her students learn in her classroom: "I think it is essential for all students to connect with what they're reading, write persuasively, question authority, think critically about history and current events, and consider issues from multiple perspectives. I want my students to speak well, to listen to and hear other voices. I want them to take risks to learn and be problem solvers." In her essay, she describes why she is guided by the words of Gandhi, also the title of her essay.

Sometimes I hear teachers say, "I just love children!" More power to them. Honestly, I do not love all children. (Doesn't that sound awful for a teacher to say?) Surely, I do not love all *people*. Perhaps because I have witnessed and survived much violence, I guard my vulnerability a bit. I am not mean, but I believe in being honest, being clear about one's biases. I can say honestly that I am *intrigued* by all people. Many people are interesting, friendly, and helpful, and they share common interests and other things that help us connect and grow to like one another. Some people are less appealing, because they are depressed or self-centered, cranky or angry. While I may not like them, I am intrigued by them, wondering what would make them happy. What else might they care about? Are they in pain now? Did someone hurt them before? If this person is unstable or sometimes violent, how can I develop a relationship while keeping myself safe?

Needless to say, I am not automatically in love with my students when they walk in the door on the first day of school. My goal is to love them and nurture them all, so I give myself a head start. I visit all of them at home before the first day of school. I spend some time just visiting, listening, getting to know the parents and guardians who love them, the siblings, grandparents, and others who live with or near them. Often the children show me something important, like a pet or a fort, a special picture, toy, or book. Sometimes they tell me something they really think I should know. One little girl told me, "I can read one word, 'the.' I think I'm ready for 1st grade."

I visited one of my new students, Ahmed, this morning. He said, "Would you like to see my room?" He led the way and then hopped up on the very tall bed. "This is my favorite," he said, and showed me a baby boy doll, with brown skin and thick black hair like his.

"What's his name?" I asked.

"I call him Baby Daniel, because Daniel sounds like the end of my name," he answered.

Puzzled, I asked, "How is Daniel like Ahmed?"

"I have another name, a middle name," he explained. "My family calls me Samuel."

We went into the kitchen to visit with his mother, grandmother, and aunt. Sure enough, I heard each of them call or refer to him as Samuel. I asked his mother why everyone at school calls him Ahmed, when they call him Samuel at home. She shrugged and said, "He has two names."

I asked him, "What name would you like me to call you?"

"Samuel," he answered without hesitation. He had gone through 2 years, politely allowing himself to be called a name he didn't use, unable or unwilling to challenge kind teachers and administrators who called him the name that came on the computer printout. Yet in the first 5 minutes of having me on his turf, having come to learn about him, he was able to use his precious doll to subtly teach me this very important lesson.

By the first day of school, I know where my students live, with whom, and how they get to and from school. I know the names they call themselves. Most important, I know who loves them. If on that first day of school, a new student bites someone else on the face, or throws a chair or refuses to leave the building for a fire alarm, I take a deep breath. I picture that child at home with the parents or guardians who love him or her. I remember that they have entrusted me to teach and guide their child, and to keep her safe. I probably do not love that child yet, especially if she is hurting or scaring other children and disrupting my teaching, but until I grow to love that child, I borrow the family's love for her. I dip into the well that I have visited, without hesitation. In those sad cases where there is no one loving a certain child, I must find a way to start loving that child more quickly.

I teach because teaching is a job where you get paid to learn with other people. How cool is that? There are so many things I would love to learn more about, from astronomy to history, physics to geometry, statistics to botany, agriculture to ornithology, anthropology to geography. I could read books every day until I die and still not be done learning. I could read many more books at home than I can going to school every day, but it would be less exciting. There would be no one to share with, no opportunity to engage experts, no one with whom I could experiment and observe. If I read a book alone, without sharing or using the idea, I will forget it quickly. When I learn something with my students and in communication with their families, I know we will revisit the topic many times over the coming months and years as news articles, magazine photos, poems, songs, treasures, books, visitors, names of experts, and field trip opportunities keep flowing in.

When you are passionate about learning yourself, it is contagious. The learners around you do not necessarily become passionate about all that you are passionate about, but they learn to value learning with a passion. My third year of teaching I decided that it didn't make sense to start talking about civil rights history with Rosa Parks and the Montgomery bus boycott. That story really begs the question, "Wait a minute: Why did they have segregation? Who made up this idea that Whites were better than Blacks and why did anyone believe it?" So we started to investigate the history of racism in this country. We went all the way back to Columbus and learned how he brought hundreds of Tainos to Europe as slaves, and how the Spanish plantation owners in the Caribbean began importing African slaves after their Taino slaves essentially were worked to death. We had read about the Middle Passage and looked at a painting by Rod Brown in *From Slave Ship to Freedom Road* by Julius Lester.[1] It showed rows of heads stacked above rows of shackled feet above rows of heads, slaves stacked in the hold of a ship.

I had one student, Jimmy, who was very taken with this story of early slavery. Jimmy had a learning disability that made reading and writing very difficult for him, but he was a bright boy with a curious mind. He developed an effective strategy to help him learn. He would approach strong readers and ask them if they wanted to help him with his research. He would point out certain pictures and ask them to read the captions. Jimmy loved science and had volunteered for the job of keeping our beloved science encyclopedias in good order. One rainy afternoon during an indoor recess, I saw him excitedly talking to a student who recently had joined our class. Next I saw him very purposely scoop all of the science encyclopedias off the shelf onto the floor. As I approached to ask what he was doing, I heard him say, "They did the slaves like this!" He curled himself up and squeezed his body onto the bookshelf. "Can you believe it?" he continued, "They did them like they was books!" Jimmy grasped, and was outraged by, this essential idea, that for slavery to work, it had to dehumanize the slaves, that it treated people like objects. Jimmy understood that the institution of slavery required racism in order to function.

On the first day of school the next year, Jimmy approached me excitedly. "Ms. Cowhey, I went to Puerto Rico to see my cousins and look at what I got!" He opened up a carefully folded piece of tissue paper to show me an old-looking silver coin. "I got this where Spanish ships used to come in and sell slaves." He looked at me solemnly. "I think this coin might've been used to buy slaves." This was a boy fiercely captivated by history, a boy full of stories hundreds of years old that were as real and as wrong as if they had happened to him.

Of course, we move on to magnetism or static electricity or the life cycles of plants or whatever, but we are always ready to revisit and keep learning. A parent of a student I had 3 years ago continues to rearrange her work schedule to come on each of the five seasonal field trips I make to a nearby marsh each year, helping us identify birds. My students call her "Mary, Our Bird Lady" and they write her notes whenever they have questions or observations about birds. They like her and some of them want to be scientists in general or ornithologists in specific when they grow up, because she is passionate about birds and that part of our class. You just cannot beat being part of a learning community. I hope as my students grow up they will be lifelong learners and surround themselves with people who keep asking and learning, inspiring others to do the same.

Last spring, my good friend in New York, Joanne, was dying. We had been pen pals for nearly 10 years. About a month before she died, I visited her again. She had just begun to take morphine for the pain, which had become unbearable. She had always been the better correspondent. She apologized that she could not write me letters anymore, because the morphine clouded her mind too much. I said that I would write to her more often and she said no, that she couldn't read for any length of time anymore either. She said she was so bored, lying on the couch, just staring at the walls all day. I had read her a couple of poems that I had in my pocket and asked her if she would like me to send her a short poem on a postcard each day I wasn't there. She said she'd like that. While driving to and from New York each weekend, I would compose poems. I also started walking more often, as a way to fend off depression and sort out my feelings.

I composed poems as I walked. I kept my promise, writing poems every day and mailing them faithfully, even after Joanne was unable to speak, even after she seemed comatose. Her sister, who was her primary caregiver, told me how much she liked the poems. I couldn't help asking, "How can you tell?" She said, "Oh, I can see it in her eyes. And you know that one you wrote about spring snow, the two different ways? I liked the first way better." I kept writing the poems and driving down to visit every weekend.

At first, I didn't tell my students that my friend was dying, but I started to bring in the little poems. I wrote them on the easel and would read them with the children. They were so interested in the poems, sitting on the rug, closing their eyes as they listened, then sharing the images they saw in their minds. Inevitably, one would raise his hand and then rise, speaking with the urgency of a child needing to use the toilet, saying, "Can I go write a poem now?"

When the call finally came that Joanne had died, her sister said that she had just read her one of my poems that had come in the mail and looked up to show her an enclosed drawing from my daughter when she saw that Joanne was dead. I gathered the children together on the rug around the easel, on which I had written a short poem by Langston Hughes.

POEM

I loved my friend.
He went away from me.
There's nothing more to say.

> This poem ends
> soft as it began
> I loved my friend.

I told them about my friend, and thanked them for their patience with my cranky weariness and sadness of the previous few weeks. The poem gave us a way to talk about friends and loss. I told them Joanne had asked me to read "Blue Jay Valentine," one of their favorites, at her funeral. The whole experience gave me a way to teach the children about reading and writing poetry as a way to cope with and communicate about some of life's harder moments.

I teach because teaching lets me think critically about everything, starting with the things I thought I knew. While I have heard of teachers who teach the same exact thing the same way every year, I take advantage of the cyclical nature of the school year to rethink as I revisit. Since I teach 1st and/or 2nd grade and loop with my students whenever I can, I like to build on student interests and class history from one year to the next. For the past 2 years I taught 1st grade, but now I am returning to 2nd grade again, so I can revisit simple machines, states of matter, insect life cycles, early colonies, explorers, and so forth, considering what worked last time and focus on aspects of those units I would like to improve and learn more about.

I teach because I was a kid once, and my mother was a kid once, and everyone who makes it to adulthood was a kid once. When my son was about 2 years old, my father's house was scheduled for demolition. I went there and found an old portrait photograph of myself as a little girl, about 2 years old. I showed it to my mother and asked if she wanted it. She said, "No, I think you should keep it. This way, whenever you start to lose patience with your son, you can look at it and remember you were a child once." It seems like such a simple pearl of wisdom, but as a 43-year-old in a moment of frustration, one can lose sight of why a 6-year-old simply has not done the required task. Patience, however, is only a little part of it.

When I was a little girl, I had a life rich with mud pies, climbing trees, digging holes, making forts, and trying to catch fairies. My teachers throughout elementary school knew none of this. Between paychecks we were short on food. Our house was often without heat or hot water in winter. This made it difficult to wash myself and very difficult to wash my long hair. I worried that my clothing smelled of mildew and was ashamed that my face would get flushed in the heat of the classroom. I wondered whether my teachers noticed and worried what they thought of me. What I remember about elementary school was mostly being silent.

I remember that my teachers talked about the Mets winning the World Series and about astronauts going to the moon, but we never talked about why there was fighting in Vietnam and Northern Ireland, why there were riots in American cities, why Martin Luther King was killed, what possible reason there could have been for inventing napalm, why the National Guard shot the students at Kent State, why Patty Hearst decided to join the Symbionese Liberation Army. I wondered terribly about all these things by myself. Finally in 7th grade I had a teacher, Rita Rappaport Rowan, who was willing to talk about the world and who asked me to write about my life, from mud pies to mildew to napalm. She read what I wrote, and wrote back, asking me to write more and more. She was the teacher I needed. She helped me find ways to make sense of the world and encouraged me to question everything, not just so that I could learn the 7th-grade English curriculum, but so that I could learn and learn and learn. I know I am not Rita to all of my students, but I know that I am Rita to some of my students. That alone is reason enough to teach.

My mother often tells a story about herself as a 5½-year-old in 1st grade. She was very skinny, painfully shy, with crossed eyes and thick glasses. Her 1st-grade class had 86 students. One day, early in the school year, her teacher thought she heard my mother using swear words. My mother did not know any swear words and never spoke in class at all. The teacher told her to stand up, marched her over to the coat closet, and shut her inside, saying, "That will teach you to use swear words in my class!" With 85 other students to think about, the teacher forgot about my mother in the coat closet, and she stayed in there, terrified, all day. Not surprisingly, my mother did not learn to read in 1st grade. She thought she was stupid. Only later, after eye surgery, when she was 9 years old, when her aunt asked her mother if she could teach her to read, did my mother succeed. Every Friday night, she went to Aunt Mixie's house for a sleepover. Each week, they made a cake together. Aunt Mixie taught my mother fractions by having her measure ingredients and cut gum drops in small equal pieces to decorate those cakes. Then they had a reading lesson, and ate some cake. My mother did learn to read and loved it, and at 75 she still reads more books in a week than I read in 2 months.

One day I brought my mother to visit her friend, Betty, who is 84. My mother was telling Betty what it was like to visit my classroom. Mom said, "I just wanted to stay. I wished that could have been my 1st-grade classroom. She asked the children what they thought about things and then listened to what they said. Just imagine if we had teachers like that!" Betty shook her head and said, "I can't imagine that. All I remember of school was wanting to be invisible. All I wanted was to be unnoticed. I hardly listened because I was so busy praying that the teacher would not call on me." As Betty told her story, I thought of what it must have been like to be her, abandoned and abused, raised between an orphanage and her alcoholic father's place, not knowing what a sofa or a birthday party was, a girl without a doll or a sweater or a book of her own, with teachers who never noticed she was there. How I wish their teachers had noticed those little wanting-to-be-invisible girls, had made them feel happy, smart, listened to, appreciated, capable, and loved. Now I pretend that my mother and her friend, as 6-year-olds, are in my class.

In honor of Aunt Mixie too, we bake in my class. When I went on maternity leave, one student in particular was having a very hard time with the transition. A family trauma and placement in a foster home the summer before had caused his reading to regress from 2nd-grade to preprimer level at the start of the year. Eventually I had earned his trust and developed a good relationship with him, and he was making good progress. Although my substitute teacher was warm, wonderful, understanding, and familiar, he was angry at her because she was not me. He began a campaign to dispose of her, by taking her coat off the hook where I used to hang mine, taking her lunch bag off my desk, and so forth. One day, he disrupted her lesson, shouting, "I don't want you to be our teacher. You are not like Ms. Cowhey!" She sighed and said, "You're right. I miss her too. Let's all take a minute to think about Ms. Cowhey." She began writing a list of the characteristics the children suggested. This boy looked over the list and cried, "Yeah, and she baked with us . . . every day!" I laughed when my friend told me the story, how in my absence my baking exploits had multiplied and become so memorable.

I teach because teaching lets me fully be the person I am: a poet, a storyteller, an activist, a gardener, a baker, a naturalist, an amateur astronomer, a scientist, a historian, a philosophical thinker. Not only can I pursue all these passions, but I can work in the company of others who share their passions through their teaching: dancing, singing, language, traveling, music, raising animals, racing pigeons.

Last February, I got the flu and was out sick for a week. I was still sick on Valentine's Day, but I got up early and typed a poem I'd just written, "Blue Jay Valentine," on the computer, printing it out on a little card for each student.

BLUE JAY VALENTINE

Because you remind me
to slow down and just breathe
I am stopped short
by the fluttering blue
in the bare branches
of a small tree
between snowy ground
and looming hemlocks.
Then falling like blue meteors
more jays streak down
from the hemlocks
to fill the fragile branches
like animated ornaments.
Above
the sky aches
to be as blue
as just one feather.

I went to school to deliver the cards, and wrote the poem on the easel for the children. I was moving slowly, and they came in while I was still there. The substitute teacher asked me to stay while we read the poem together. As I watched and listened to my students pointing out their favorite phrases, describing the images they pictured, just loving up this poem they'd been given like it was better than chocolate, I felt much better. This is better than any award, I thought. This is why I come into school on my sick day to tell my students how much I love them. This is why I teach.

I teach because it is a positive way to make change in the world, starting in my community, but reaching around the globe as well. I teach the children how and why to compost and recycle, and then we practice it daily. On every nature walk we carry rubber gloves and shopping bags to collect trash. Writing to students in South Africa, they learn to accept boys or girls whom they don't know as their friends. They cannot tell from the unfamiliar names they struggle to pronounce whether their pen pals are male or female. They begin to rethink American consumption when they measure out a 5 × 12-foot house on the floor and imagine living in that space with a mother, sister, aunt, and two cousins, with all of the family's clothing in two small gym bags.

My students learn where to go for help and how to find out ways they can best assist, like meeting with the director of a local food bank, coordinating a drive to collect most-needed items, and pushing and pulling hundreds of pounds of food and supplies in wagons, carts, and old baby strollers in cold weather to deliver the items to the food bank themselves. They learn about keeping promises, even if that means delivering pies on a snow day for a community Thanksgiving dinner and volunteering to set up the tables and chairs in the hall. I remember Jack, carrying a pumpkin pie through the snow, saying, "You know what the Dalai Lama says, 'It is not enough to be compassionate. You must act,'" and skinny little Sadie showing her muscles to the volunteer coordinator, saying, "We can set this place up so fast because we are powerful!" I teach because children can learn to recognize and help solve problems, to care, to act, to protest, to be truthful and reliable, to take responsibility. Then, no matter how much is wrong and broken in the world, there is hope in these children.

I teach for all these reasons: so that I can make positive change in the world, so that I can live and work fully as the whole person that I am, because I can think critically and keep learning, and so that I can be there for a child who needs me to notice, to listen, to care.

I teach because I would be foolish to think I am done learning, or that I could learn more by myself than with others. I teach because I would be selfish not to share what I have had the privilege to learn from elders, from books, from teachers, from nature, from experience. I teach because I am part of a community, a country, and a world that could be better. I teach because I agree with Gandhi, "If we are to reach real peace in this world, we shall have to begin with the children."

PART VI

Conclusion

Teachers teach for many and varied reasons, too many to capture in a list or inventory. The teachers whose voices you have read in this book, in spite of their various motivations to teach, hold important lessons for all of us. In the final chapter, I explore what it means to be a caring and committed teacher of all students, and especially students of diverse backgrounds who attend schools in poor communities, that is, students who are most in jeopardy in our nation's schools. Not only new teachers, but also veteran teachers, teacher educators, families, policymakers, and the general public can learn from the reflections of these teachers.

I have chosen to focus in the final chapter on the qualities that bring teachers to the work they do. In order to capture the essence of why people teach, and what it means to teach well and with heart, I describe some of the qualities that the teachers themselves defined through their essays.

First, however, I offer a word of caution: I believe that one of the main problems in education is our tendency to jump on the bandwagon of the latest quick fix. Often, novel ideas that come attractively packaged are spoon-fed to teachers and administrators—through articles, programs, kits, checklists, university courses, or inservice workshops—as if they were the answer we'd all been waiting for. Some of these ideas may have merit; they often do. But quick fixes never work. All of us in education should know by now that it is only through critical reflection, the ethical use of power, collaborative and meaningful relationships, and hard work that any idea really works.

Hence, any attempt to capture something as dynamic and intangible as teaching, is fraught with difficulties. This problem concerns me because the last thing I want to do is suggest an inventory of qualities that can be used as gatekeepers for the profession, as if these qualities could be so easily determined ("loves students: check; demonstrates passion for teaching: check," and so forth). The danger of using inventories or check-lists is that they inevitably lead to rigid conceptions of good pedagogy, as if there were just one way to do things right. This is also the problem with the idea of "best practices." A more humble, and in the long run probably more helpful, way to think about pedagogy is as a set of "good practices" or "promising practices," or even "interesting practices."

It is, then, with some trepidation that, based on the essays in this book, I suggest a few of the qualities that seem to character-ize teachers who are caring and committed. In spite of the mis-givings I have about describing these qualities, I believe that the teachers in this book *do* share common values from which others can benefit. This is particularly true at a time when teachers are being described in the official discourse primarily in terms of certification and test scores. I begin, then, with the recognition that no set of qualities of caring and committed teachers is comprehensive enough, or true for all teachers in all contexts and all time.

Chapter 23

Qualities of Caring and Committed Teachers

W
hat can be learned from teachers who are committed to their profession, their students, their subject matter, and their craft? It is curious—although not surprising—that none of the teachers whose essays are included in this book mentioned passing a certification test, knowing a set of "best practices," implementing a prescribed curriculum, or teaching students to pass high-stakes tests, as being of primary importance to them. This is not to deny that these things might be necessary, but it is to say that they do not in and of themselves constitute what it means to be a caring and committed teacher.[1] On the other hand, teachers described their relationships with students, issues of social justice, and their own continuing professional development as most significant to them.

The thoughts of the teachers in many ways contradict the current official discourse about "highly qualified teachers." The teachers in this book are, of course, highly qualified, even in the traditional sense: Most have master's degrees, they write well and communicate effectively, they know how to develop curriculum, they are adept at many pedagogical practices, they keep up with their subject matter, many are active in professional organizations, and all consider themselves lifelong learners. But through their essays, they help redefine the core qualities of caring and committed teachers.

It goes without saying that some of the qualities of effective teachers are both well known and widely agreed upon. Countless books and research projects have examined this issue. Some of the broadly acknowledged qualities of effective teachers include the following: a solid general education background, a deep knowledge of their subject matter, familiarity with numerous pedagogical approaches, strong communication skills, and effective organizational skills. I will not go over this ground, as some of these qualities were discussed in Chapter 1. Instead, I want to propose a set of attitudes and sensibilities, apparent in the essays, that can help expand the rather limited qualities described above.

Through an analysis of their essays, I will suggest five core qualities shared by the teachers. In doing so, I realize that I may highlight some qualities over others. Where, for instance, is *patience*, something that almost anybody would argue is absolutely essential in teaching? What about *resourcefulness* and *collegiality*? Where are *open-mindedness* and *sense of humor*? I agree that all of these are vital qualities for teachers to have, but we could end up with an endless list. I am suggesting instead that the five core qualities below encompass all of these. Patience, for instance, is embodied within *solidarity and empathy*, and I could include all of these qualities within others. The point is not to come up with an exhaustive list, but to suggest key attitudes and sensibilities that define the teachers in this book and, by extension, many others who serve young people.

The five qualities that I am suggesting are: *a sense of mission; solidarity with, and empathy for, students; the courage to challenge mainstream knowledge; improvisation;* and *a passion for social justice*. In the remainder of this chapter, I briefly describe each of these qualities by providing a few examples from the essays, and I conclude with final thoughts on the future of public education and the significance of teachers.

A SENSE OF MISSION

In every case, the teachers in this book write about the sense of mission that is deeply embedded in their reasons for teaching. This is certainly not unique to these particular teachers. Both older and more recent research on teachers' attitudes and values confirms a sense of mission to be an underlying motivation for many teachers.[2] Nonetheless, the teachers in this book shy away from seeing teaching as missionary work. They see themselves as serving the common good, but without describing themselves as saviors and without the sense of self-righteousness that inevitably dooms good intentions.

They know, however, that they make a difference; for some children, a life-saving difference. Kerri Warfield describes her mission as being a "life-toucher." She asks, "In what other job can we help improve the future, share our knowledge, and learn every day?" Mary Ginley is eloquent in describing her encounter with Steven, a former student who wrote to her years after he had been in her 1st-grade classroom, telling her how she had saved his life ("Foolish child, to think I wouldn't remember him," she writes). Even after an arduous year with Steven, she resisted having him placed in another class because he still needed her. In the same vein, Jennifer Welborn writes, "I may be naive, but I believe that what I do day in and day out *does* make a difference. Teachers *do* change lives forever." Ambrizeth Lima adds, "It is also a mission with a tangible goal: I teach because teaching transforms my students, and it transforms me." And in an eloquent description of what it means to teach with a sense of mission, Ambrizeth says that teaching "has insinuated itself into my very being." When Mary Cowhey described going into school in spite of being sick with the flu to share a Valentine's Day poem with her students, she felt better afterwards. She came to the conclusion that teaching is better than any award. It reminds me of my own cooperating teacher so many years ago, Mrs. Adler, who told me one day, "I'd rather teach than eat!"

Teachers' sense of mission often extends beyond their own specific classrooms to their feelings about public education in general. Stephen Gordon views participation in an intellectual tradition as an essential component of that mission, especially for young people who are generally not seen as capable of participating in the intellectual tradition. He writes, "Ideas sustain, motivate, engage, and enrage—why I teach."

The public good—a term sadly missing in most conversations about education these days—also is implicated in teachers' sense of mission. According to Andy Hargreaves and Michael Fullan, "The most creative and emotionally engaged teachers see themselves not just as educating learners and workers, but as developing citizens."[3] Jennifer Welborn, while admitting that her mission is a personal one (because teachers change lives every day), also views teaching in a broader sense. She writes, "I teach in public school because I still believe in public school. I believe that the purpose of public school, whether it delivers or not, is to give a quality education to all kids who come through the doors. I want to be a part of that lofty mission."

SOLIDARITY WITH, AND EMPATHY FOR, STUDENTS

Another quality that the teachers demonstrate is a combination of solidarity and empathy, which also can be described as love. But "love" is not a word that one hears very often these days when teaching is the topic at hand. In fact, it seems almost maudlin to speak about it, as if it were inconsistent with professionalism and academic rigor. Yet it is well established that teachers who love their students and feel solidarity with them also develop strong and consequential relationships with them, an essential ingredient for students' affiliation with school.

The teachers' essays make it eminently clear that caring is necessary for both teachers and the students they teach. A nationwide survey of several hundred 13- to 17-year-old students asked whether they worked harder for some teachers than for others. Three out of four said yes, and the reason was that these were the teachers who cared most for them. The survey authors concluded that effective schooling relies almost entirely on creative and passionate teachers.[4] While it is problematic to place the entire responsibility for student achievement on teachers—as if issues of inequality, structural barriers due to racism and other biases, lack of resources, poor infrastructure, unfair bureaucratic policies, and so on, did not matter—this finding nevertheless underscores the fact that care is an essential quality for teachers to have.

Nel Noddings has defined this quality as the "challenge to care" in schools, and Angela Valenzuela has termed it "the politics of caring."[5] For these researchers, when students experience school as a place where they belong and are welcome, they are more likely to take on identities as "school kids" rather than as "street kids," terms coined by Nilda Flores-González based on her research in a Chicago high school.[6]

Love is not simply a sentimental emotion, especially when defined within schools. For teachers who think deeply about their work, love means having genuine respect, high expectations, and great admiration for their students. There are numerous examples throughout these essays about how teachers demonstrate their love. Bob Amses, for instance, writes, "Teaching is based on trust, and when students see me as a real person who genuinely wants them to succeed, strong bonds are formed." Sandra Jenoure, eloquent in defense of her students, offers another example: "I know it's easy to sit back and listen to the gossip in schools. 'These kids can't learn,' is what you hear. The truth is they can and do. We have to see and believe." This is what it means to have solidarity with, and empathy for, students.

Having solidarity with students also means remembering what it was like to be a child. Mary Cowhey remembers, and so do her mother and aunt. Mary wants to create a classroom that she would have wanted to be part of, and that her mother and aunt would have enjoyed. For Mary, having solidarity also means forming a community of learners. According to her, there is far too much to learn to try to do it alone. She could, she says, read books every day until she dies, but it wouldn't be as exciting because she would be doing it alone, and there would be no one to share it with. "You just cannot beat being part of a learning community," she concludes, even if that learning community is composed mostly of 6-year-olds. It is this sense of community that is at the heart of solidarity.

Mary Cowhey points out another significant way in which teachers express empathy and solidarity with their students: They value students' families. The tone she uses to speak about the families of the children she teaches is one of respect and affection. She sends home a weekly letter to parents, a long and detailed account of what has taken place that week in school and of what to expect the following week. Every August, she visits the home of each of the children she will be teaching in September, and these visits prove to be invaluable in her quest to understand both the children and their families. It is no wonder that parents and families feel so affirmed in her classroom, and that they volunteer to help even years after their children have been in her class.

In his essay, Stephen Gordon, an English teacher and 35-year veteran of the Boston public schools, reflects on teaching as loving both his students and his subject matter. This was evident when Tashia, a student who had been reluctant to recite a poem, recited, after prodding from him and one of his co-teachers, "Phenomenal Woman" by Maya Angelou. Stephen concluded that the reason to be in school was "to hear poetry, to be moved by language, to be together in a place where young men and women express the words that they have taken to their hearts—beautiful, powerful words of identity, hope, and learning."

Laila Di Silvio, a fairly new teacher, also knows what it means to feel solidarity with students. Roscoe, the student who gave her more sleepless nights than any other, was also the one who won his way into her heart. The poignant incident when he lent her his copy of a Harry Potter book is one of those moments that all teachers hope for.

Solidarity with students also means that teachers value students' lives and carefully think about how to include them in their teaching. Nowhere is this more evident than in the essay by Ayla Gavins, who chuckles when she thinks about the antics of some of her students. Ayla says that she has met many people she admires who have contributed to her life and character. Many of them, she admits, "just happen to be under the age of 13." Stephen Gordon explains solidarity by saying that meeting up with former students "makes me feel I have done right by them, that they remember that I cared about them, that I respected their identity and intelligence, their hopes and difficulties."

We also are reminded by researcher Barbara Comber that "students' lives are not 'background' to what occurs in school, since it is imperative for teachers to understand what life is like for different children and to anticipate the worlds children will live in later in their lives."[7] In her essay, Judith Baker shies away from understanding students' lives as "background." In thinking about the qualities that would characterize the teacher she wants to be, Judith writes, "I also would study my students carefully, hoping to get the clues that would guide me away from destructive, harmful attitudes and practices, knowing too that students are different and they change."

THE COURAGE TO QUESTION MAINSTREAM KNOWLEDGE

Unless they have access to contexts, experiences, or texts that challenge conventional knowledge, and unless they engage in deep reflection and serious dialogue about their own knowledge and the curriculum they teach, many teachers do not develop the practice of questioning mainstream knowledge. This is a good reminder that teaching is always about learning and relearning, a point made by Mary Cowhey. One day a few years ago, I ran into Mary and her family at Old Deerfield, a reconstructed colonial town in western Massachusetts. She had been on a tour of the town, particularly interested in the Native American experience in the town, and in how it's depicted. Mary told me that, after fielding many of her questions during the tour, the guide had said to her, "You sure ask a lot of questions!" to which she responded, "I have to! I'm a 1st-grade teacher."

The point, as Mary knows, is not simply knowing how to ask questions, but more important, knowing how to read answers and keep questioning them. It is, according to Ambrizeth Lima, about "truth telling in the classroom." Educational philosopher Maxine Greene, addressing this issue in the aftermath of September 11, 2001, when asking questions began to be seen with greater suspicion, wrote, "The curriculum has to leave so many questions open so that children will explore and wonder and not believe there is a final answer, because they can only be devastated when they find out there isn't."[8] Hence, even though she could have avoided broaching the Iraq War with her 2nd graders, Mary Ginley decided not to do so. In her case, even reading a children's book about a family in Iraq was an act of courage.

The challenge for those who work with teachers—including teachers themselves—is to encourage them to develop the courage to confront what philosopher Michel Foucault has called "regimes of truth," that is, the kinds of discourses promoted by each society as truth, and produced, transmitted, and kept in place by systems of power such as universities, the military, and the media.[9] The result of these regimes of truth is that perspectives and realities different from those that are officially sanctioned, tend to remain invisible. In teacher preparation, this situation can be confronted by including multiple perspectives in courses and other teacher preparation experiences.[10] Such diverse perspectives include different ways of looking at knowledge and truth. Presenting new knowledge and perspectives may upset students' taken-for-granted assumptions about reality, including their biases and stereotypes about certain groups of people, an uncritical acceptance of what they read and hear, and a limited understanding of history, both national and international. In the long run, however, if we are to develop more-nuanced understandings of complex issues, it is necessary for everyone to confront different perspectives.

Jennifer Welborn provides a vivid example of doing so in her essay. It was the book *The Mismeasure of Man* by Stephen Jay Gould that helped change how she looked at science.[11] The book became the impetus for a unit on scientific racism and the social construction of race that she has taught every year for the past 10 years. In her essay, Jennifer writes that she wants her students to "learn to be skeptics," to "differentiate between good science, bad science, and pseudoscience." She also wants students to think about the advantages and disadvantages that race automatically confers on individuals and groups, because, according to Jennifer, "it is through this knowledge and dialogue that students can understand the complexity of racism in our country." For Yahaira Marquez, the very subject matter of English helped her see the world in its tremendous complexity. As she explains, she wants to do the same for her students: "I'd like my students to learn to see the world differently, with a new set of eyes, and to leave my classroom conscious of the fact that not everything is clear-cut and fixed, and knowing that their voices are just as important as anyone else's."

In another example, Laila Di Silvio describes how Travis, a previously unengaged student, became animated and eager to learn when the subject matter—Native American mascots and "dysconscious racism"—were the topics at hand. These topics, typically disallowed in school, riveted him and caused a dramatic turnaround in his connection with school.

Challenging mainstream knowledge, and conventional ways of doing things in general, is not easy. Seth Peterson captures the inevitable contradiction in this situation when he writes, "We, who do this work, are caught in a conundrum, working within the system to create change." Yet wrestling with this seeming contradiction is precisely what it will take in order to improve the system, in this case, schools.

When students and teachers are not encouraged to challenge mainstream knowledge, or when they are prohibited from doing so, democratic principles can be thwarted. Lack of access to knowledge of all kinds has negative outcomes not only for schools in general, but also for students specifically. Judith Baker worries that, even through their well-intentioned questions, teachers are always interrupting students' own thinking. She writes, "'Think this' and 'think about that' are not-so-subtle incursions into a vulnerable, precious mental territory." "If this goes on for many years," she concludes, "the K–12 interruption of thought must be truly debilitating." Her solution? She's tried to stop asking questions ("test questions, homework questions, 'raise-your-hand-and-answer-this' questions") and instead asks students to *notice*. In her English classroom, this means noticing what is important in a particular text. For those who teach other subject matter, it can mean noticing different things. Adopting this stance in teaching certainly will challenge conventional wisdom and mainstream knowledge.

IMPROVISATION

Educator, artist, and performer Theresa Jenoure views jazz improvisation not only as a form of music, but also as aesthetic outlook and pedagogy. In music, jazz improvisation is a system of composing, but beyond music, according to Jenoure, it is "a way of thinking and behaving."[12] In teaching, she sees jazz improvisation as a metaphor for creativity within structure. This happens through interaction among artists, opportunities for self-defining, and transcendence, that is, making the extraordinary out of the ordinary. In the same way, caring and committed teachers use improvisation to see beyond frameworks, rubrics, and models. Katina Papson, also an artist, frames the description of her childhood as a "play of opposites" that helped her learn how to negotiate teaching. As Judith Baker so aptly states, many schools are in "template heaven," viewing templates as the end rather than the means to effective instruction. Using improvisation means learning to go beyond the template, or even to question the template. This is not to say that templates or other models in and of themselves are useless. On the contrary, they are often necessary as a foundation for creativity.

The same is true of jazz. According to Jenoure, most definitions of jazz as simply creating music on the spur of the moment fall short because they fail to take into account the tremendous amount of preparation needed for it to be successful. In the same way, teachers need to know the basics before they can build on them. But if all they use are the basics, or if they stay stuck in the same models, little creativity will result.

Using improvisation is learning to "think on your feet." It is not surprising that teachers view this aspect of teaching in terms that are themselves artistic: They see it as a "collage," as "weaving," as creating. This is certainly the case in Patty Bode's classroom because, after all, she is an art teacher. But it is true for those who teach reading or math or anything else as well. Melinda Pellerin-Duck likens teaching to a Kente cloth, and writes about the "colors and strands" of teaching. Improvisation also means taking advantage of the moment, even putting aside the planned lesson for the time being. It is, according to Elaine Stinson, "teaching outside the lines," building on what excites and energizes students.

Improvisation also means being prepared for uncertainty, both the joy and the frustration of it. This requires a great deal of elasticity, and the teachers in this book show many ways in which they are up to the task. Not only are they up to it, but they consider it one of their greatest strengths. Yahaira Marquez, for instance, writes, "I go into class every morning not knowing what kind of day it will be. . . . It is that uncertainty, that element of surprise, that I think drives me even harder." Likewise, years ago Nina Tepper told me she was astonished to hear another teacher boast about being on *exactly the same page* as the previous year in her plan book! In contrast, Nina said that of all the qualities she has adopted on her quest as an educator it is the ability to listen to her students and grasp a teachable moment that is most important.

Elaine Stinson explains the ability to adapt in the following way: "I must be willing to allow the content of the day to unfold." She recognizes, she says, that "there is no manual with all the answers." So, even though it was hard to teach without a curriculum when she began her career, in retrospect she says it was fortunate because it offered her the possibility "to weave a social justice perspective into most of the guidelines provided by the administration." Patty Bode's essay exemplifies what it means to improvise in teaching.

When Andrew and Damon got into a fight over what one of them thought was landscape colors and the other viewed as racism, she immediately changed course midstream. Rather than sticking to a lesson that would have been meaningless for the students at that point, she abandoned the landscape lesson—at least for the time being—and developed an entire curriculum based on skin color and race. This curriculum not only changed her life and the way she teaches, but it has deeply affected the lives of many of her students, the many student teachers she has mentored, and her colleagues as well.

Bob Amses, who in his first year reverted to keeping his students busy as a hedge against losing control, became demoralized because that's not the kind of teacher he had imagined himself being. He thought he had lost his utopian ideals. On reflection during his second year, he writes, "As I've gained experience, however, I recognize that I never abandoned my ideals at all. I just had to shove them out of the way for awhile so I could survive the transition." He learned that being flexible also means admitting to mistakes, and this can be humbling. Not everyone can do this, but Bob writes that freeing himself from what he calls the "twisted wreckage" of mistakes "underscores precisely what I love about teaching: Through my mistakes, I learn how to be better." Kerri Warfield probably expresses the wishes of many teachers who view teaching as improvisation, by saying, "I hope that my students will remember my class not because it was perfect, but because of its unique flaws."

A PASSION FOR SOCIAL JUSTICE

Teaching, according to Ambrizeth Lima, is always about power. That is why it also must be about social justice. As Mary Ginley, who now teaches children who are for the most part privileged, writes, "If I just teach them how to survive in this inequitable society, how to get along, I am doing them a tremendous disservice."

Although all the attitudes and values the teachers articulate in their essays are vital, perhaps the one issue that connects them all is their sense of teaching as a vocation in the service of social justice. All of them write in one way or another about this. Katina

Papson, for instance, says that early on in life she started to question disparities she saw around her and she brought these questions with her to her art and her classroom. Her intention, she writes, is to help students discover the "grey" areas, both in their photographs and in their lives, where they will find voice by sharing their perspectives. "There," she concludes, "in that circle of young creative minds, is a revolution."

Teachers demonstrate their motivation for social justice in different ways, depending on their own attitudes, autobiographies, and experiences. For some, social justice has to do primarily with racial, ethnic, and economic equality. Yahaira Marquez, in her first year of teaching, is working in a school where she can personally relate to the experiences and backgrounds of her students. In order for students to feel that they can achieve, Yahaira believes they need to have positive role models, and she wants to be one of them. And although Seth Peterson does not share the race, ethnicity, or social class of the majority of his students, he is keenly aware of and sensitive to their realities, most of whom he says were born "on the wrong side of the poverty and race lines." He learned even before becoming a teacher, while in college and working as a tutor, that "building trust across years and cultures is a slow business." Trust is at the core of a commitment to social justice.

Social justice also means mentoring students, particularly those who have been shortchanged by society, so that they realize they are capable and worthy. This was the case for Kristen French, whose beloved mentor Dale gave her "the courage to succeed," a model she carries with her in her work with her young students. Her social justice projects with them are a reflection of her view of teaching as empowerment, love, and mentoring. Beth Wohlleb Adel described how coming out of the closet as a lesbian—although she had wanted to do so at some point, the way it happened was quite unplanned—served as a catalyst for creating a loving and compassionate learning environment in her classroom. Beth encourages her students and their families to become involved in the curriculum by suggesting issues that are meaningful in their lives. It is by sharing their own identities, by learning about the varied realities of others, and by recognizing how oppressive attitudes and behaviors often get in the way of both personal and collective development that this transformation could take place.

Activism is at the core of how some teachers include a social justice perspective in their teaching. For some, it is their own activism, as in the case of Nina Tepper who views teaching as risk taking. Several years ago, she nearly lost her career because she believed strongly in the curriculum she had designed and in the intelligence of her students to engage with it. Judith Baker is also an activist for social justice, most recently in an exchange project with South African teachers. For some teachers, student activism is also an important part of their mission. Patty Bode, for instance, integrates her art lessons with students' concerns for social justice, and this link is evident in everything from the questions they feel empowered to ask in her classroom (Why is it hard to talk about race? Why are we in Iraq?) to the art they produce (for example, one year in her class, students made bowls to sell as a fund raiser after a devastating hurricane in Puerto Rico). In Mary Cowhey's case, this means involving her students in Thanksgiving community dinners, collecting needed items for a food bank, and establishing relationships with students in a number of schools in South Africa. Melinda Pellerin-Duck's students became the catalysts for helping to keep the Springfield public libraries open. Although the city's libraries had been slated for closing because of budget cuts, the students campaigned to change this decision by using civil rights strategies of organizing: speaking at demonstrations; sending letters to key politicians, including the mayor; and speaking to community groups. The students learned an important lesson through these activities: Not only did they sharpen their skills in writing, speaking, and reading, but they also learned that their voice can make a positive difference.

For some teachers, social justice is closely tied to economic and resource issues that lead to educational inequality. Social justice, in this sense, might mean taking things into one's own hands. Thus, Sandra Jenoure spent her educational career in Harlem concerned about the educational injustices faced by her students. She knew they did not have adequate resources to help them achieve in science. "In East Harlem," she writes, "my students didn't have what they needed. I learned that if I wanted those things, I had to get them myself. *I* had to make my classroom equal."

Mary Cowhey combines all these reasons to teach with a social justice perspective when she says, "I teach because I am part of a community, a country, and a world that could be better." And Ambrizeth Lima asks what to her is a fundamental question in teaching: "Is it morally right for me, as a teacher, to witness injustice toward students and remain quiet?" One of the most powerful essays in this regard is the one by Bill Dunn. His passion for social justice is based both on his own autobiography as a working-class kid from a working-class town and on his long experience as a teacher working in the same town with poor kids, most of whom are now Puerto Rican. A veteran teacher of English and social studies in a struggling mill town in the northeast, Bill knows the reality of his students' lives all too well and he fiercely defends his students against those who do not. Having spent most of his career in an urban vocational school, he also has spent much of his time fighting for fairness for his students. In his essay, Bill focuses on the MCAS, the high-stakes test in Massachusetts that he says is leading to *less* educational opportunity, not *more*, for his students. He ends his compelling essay in this way:

> So why do I teach? I teach because someone has to tell my students that they are not the ones who are dumb. They need to know that only the blissfully ignorant and profoundly evil make up tests to prove that they and people like them are smart. . . . My students also need to know that 4 days of reading in a second language under high-stakes testing conditions would shut down even Einstein's brain. . . . I teach because the people who make up these tests don't know these things or, worse, they do.

FINAL THOUGHTS

Once considered "the great equalizer," today public schools no longer seem to even entertain the illusion that they provide all young people with an equal and high-quality education. In actual fact, the ideal of equality seems curiously out of sync with the reality of public schools today. Not only are public schools more segregated by race, ethnicity, and social class than at any time in the recent past, but the conditions in schools attended by students of various backgrounds differ radically in such respects as per-pupil expenditure, qualifications and experience of teachers, type and rigor of curriculum, science labs available for instruction, kinds of playgrounds, and even cleanliness of halls and bathrooms, among other differences.

Inequality in schooling is nothing new, unfortunately. It has been recognized as a problem since the beginning of the 20th century when John Dewey warned:

> It is not enough to see that education is not actively used as an instrument to make easier the exploitation of one class by another. School facilities must be secured of such amplitude and efficiency as will in fact and not simply in name discount the effects of economic inequalities, and secure to all the wards of the nation equality of equipment for their future careers.[13]

As a result of the continuing inequality in schooling, children in our nation attend vastly different schools based largely on where they live, and where they live is based largely on their social class and race. Given the situation of immense inequality in our public schools, we no longer can naively state that equality is a driving force of our educational system. It is for this reason that, probably more than at any time in our recent past, the question of why people enter teaching has become so vital. Nothing less than the future of public education is at stake.

At the same time, we must remember that many teachers have not had sustained contact with people of diverse backgrounds, nor have they learned about people different from themselves in other ways. As a result, it is no surprise that some teachers have negative perceptions, biases, and racist attitudes about the students they teach, and about the students' families, cultures, and communities. These things also must be challenged. Nevertheless, it will do no good to either moralize or blame teachers for their negative attitudes and biased behaviors. Teachers are not superhuman; they pick up the same messages and misconceptions that we all do, and it is only by confronting the ones that get in the way of student learning that change will occur. This means encouraging prospective and practicing teachers to reflect deeply on their beliefs and attitudes so that a shift can take place. Taking part in an isolated workshop, attending a yearly conference, or taking one university course a year is not enough. Teachers need to give sustained attention to these questions, and this implies that schools need to provide them with the resources and support they need for doing this kind of difficult but, in the long run, empowering work.

The most significant implication of the thoughts of the teachers in this book is that as a nation we need to get back to the task of educating young people in our public school system. The current policy climate at both state and national levels is permeated by a profound disrespect for teachers, especially teachers who work with poor students and students of color. Over a decade ago, Henry Giroux characterized the situation in public education as "a retreat from democracy," an apt description for a system that was supposed to be at the core of democratic values.[14] Yet current reforms in education that focus on recruiting "highly qualified teachers" and on developing "best practices" will not adequately prepare teachers to be effective with their students. According to a study that analyzed teacher quality and how it is linked with teacher performance, researcher Jennifer Rice concluded, "Teacher policies need to reflect the reality that teaching is a complex activity that is influenced by the many elements of teacher quality."[15]

Subject-matter knowledge is important, of course, but if teachers do not learn how to question it, they simply replicate conventional wisdom and encourage students to be docile learners. A grasp of pedagogy is also vital, but if teachers do not develop meaningful relationships with their students, they will not succeed. If they do not understand the life-and-death implications of the work they do, no amount of certification requirements will help.

In my ongoing work with teachers, I am finding instead that, in addition to subject-matter knowledge and a mastery of pedagogy, the qualities that teachers develop before they enter the profession, as well as through their practice, are just as significant and in some cases even more so. Those who enter teaching need to be encouraged to delve into life before, during, and after their teacher preparation. Courses alone cannot teach them the qualities they will need in order to sustain their idealism and commitment. On the other hand, a combination of university, school, and societal policies and practices that foster such qualities can indeed help. These might include a broad liberal arts education, a rigorous curriculum in all subjects, serious recruitment of teacher candidates of diverse backgrounds and experiences, ongoing support for their professional development and the encouragement to challenge conventional wisdom, the opportunity to form close and successful learning partnerships with their peers both before they become teachers and in their schools after they enter the profession, meaningful compensation for their work, and the opportunity to continue to learn throughout their careers.

Many of these policies and practices require no additional resources; others do require such resources, particularly those that support consistent teacher learning and renewal, and equitable funding for all schools. Spending such resources makes good sense for many reasons, including a more robust economy and more involved citizens. According to a report from the Economic Policy Institute based on a compelling body of research, adequate and effective funding of education is the *best* way to achieve faster growth, more jobs, greater productivity, and more widely shared prosperity.[16]

Economic growth, however, should not be the only, or even the main, reason for investing in education. As it now stands, wealthier school districts can afford to buy the best education; poorer school districts cannot. A 2004 editorial in the Sacramento *Star Tribune*, for example, summed it up well. Sharply critical of the current policy in many school districts to engage in fund-raising campaigns to stave off teacher layoffs and to fund other educational needs, the editorial concluded:

> Therein lies the most disturbing problem with the creeping reliance on private fundraising for schools. Public education lies at the heart of what America does for the common good. Well-educated children and teens are an asset to all of society; everyone should contribute through taxes to the common goal of ensuring that education. The core premise of American public education is threatened if only rich districts, or ones with successful fundraising machines can have more.[17]

The teacher qualities we have reviewed in this chapter, and throughout the book, define what I believe are "highly qualified teachers." Supporting public education means supporting them and their colleagues by committing the nation's moral and economic resources to changing the current situation. As it now stands, too many young people and their families have lost faith that the public education system is worth fixing. The question to be addressed, then, is this: Is it worth the trouble to commit both moral and material resources to the task of providing all young people with the best teachers among us? Our answer to this question may well determine the future of public education in our nation.

Notes

Preface

1. K. Carter, The place of story in the study of teaching and teacher education, *Educational Researcher, 22*(1) (1993), p. 9.
2. F. M. Connelly & D. J. Clanindin, Stories of experience and narrative inquiry, *Educational Researcher, 19*(5) (1990), p. 8.

Chapter 1

1. National Education Association, *Status of the American public school teacher, 2000–2001* (Washington, DC: Author, 2003). Also see O'Neil, J. Who we are, why we teach: A portrait of the American teacher. *NEA Today, 22*(1) 2003, 27–32.
2. S. Farkas, J. Johnson, & T. Foleno, *A sense of calling: Who teaches and why* (New York: Public Agenda, 2000), p. 36.
3. National Education Association, *Status of the American public school teacher, 2000–2001* (Washington, DC: Author, 2003).
4. S. Nieto, *What keeps teachers going?* (New York: Teachers College Press, 2003b).
5. S. W. Freedman, E. R. Simons, J. S. Kalnin, A. Casareno, & the M-CLASS Teams (Eds.), *Inside city schools: Investigating literacy in multicultural classrooms* (New York: Teachers College Press, 1999); S. Intrator, *Tuned in and fired up: How teaching can inspire real learning in the classroom* (New Haven, CT: Yale University Press, 2003); G. Ladson-Billings, *Crossing over to Canaan: The journey of new teachers in diverse classrooms* (San Francisco: Jossey-Bass, 2001); S. Nieto, Challenging notions of "highly qualified teachers" through work in a teachers' inquiry group, *Journal of Teacher Education, 54*(5) (2003a), 386–398; P. J. Palmer, *The courage to teach: Exploring the inner landscape of a teacher's life* (San Francisco: Jossey-Bass, 1998); M. Rose, *Possible lives: The promise of public education in America* (New York: Penguin Books, 1995).
6. U.S. Bureau of the Census, *USA statistics in brief: Population and vital statistics* (Washington, DC: U.S. Department of Commerce, 2000b). (available at http://www.census.gov/statab/www/popppart.htm).

7. U.S. Bureau of the Census, *Profile of the foreign-born population in the United States: 2000* (Washington, DC: U.S. Department of Commerce, 2002).

8. National Center for Education Statistics, State nonfiscal survey of public elementary/secondary education, 2000–2001, *Common core of data (CCD)*. (Washington, DC: Author, 2002).

9. G. Orfield, *Schools more separate: Consequences of a decade of resegregation* (Cambridge, MA: Civil Rights Project, Harvard University, 2001).

10. U.S. Bureau of the Census, *Current population reports, Series P-60, No. 188* (Washington, DC: U.S. Government Printing Office, 1995); U.S. Bureau of the Census, *Poverty in the United States: 2000* (Washington, DC: U.S. Government Printing Office, 2000a).

11. D. Hare & J. L. Heap, *Teacher recruitment and retention strategies in the midwest: Where are they and do they work?* (Naperville, IL: North Central Regional Educational Laboratory, 2001).

12. National Education Association, *Status of the American public school teacher, 1995–96* (Washington, DC: Author, 1997); National Education Association, *Status of the American public school teacher, 2000–2001* (Washington, DC: Author, 2003).

13. National Partnership for Excellence and Accountability in Teaching, *Projects and activities* (2000) (available at www.web3.educ.msu.edu/projects/html#recr)

14. S. M. Wilson, R. E. Floden, & J. Ferrini-Mundy, *Teacher preparation research: Current knowledge, gaps, and recommendations* (Seattle: Center for the Study of Teaching and Policy, 2001).

15. See National Commission on Teaching and America's Future, *What matters most: Teaching for America's future* (New York: Columbia University, Teachers College, 1996); W. L. Sanders & J. C. Rivers, *Cumulative and residual effects of teachers on future student academic achievement* (Knoxville: University of Tennessee Value-Added Research and Assessment Center, 1996). For a cogent review of related research, see M. Cochran-Smith, Teaching quality matters [Editorial], *Journal of Teacher Education, 54*(2) (2003), 95–98.

16. For the discrepancy in quality among teachers who work with diverse populations, see K. Haycock, C. Jerald, & S. Huang, Closing the gap: Done in a decade, *Thinking K–16, 5*(2), pp. 3–5.

17. See L. Darling-Hammond & B. Falk, Using standards and assessments to support student learning, *Phi Delta Kappan, 79*(3) (1997), 190–199.

18. For a fuller discussion on this point, see S. Nieto, Challenging notions of "highly qualified teachers" through work in a teachers' inquiry group, *Journal of Teacher Education, 54*(5) (2003a), 386–398.

19. U.S. Department of Education, *Meeting the highly qualified teachers challenge: The secretary's annual report on teacher quality* (Washington, DC: U.S. Department of Education, Office of Postsecondary Education, June 2002). However, this is not to discount the importance of such things as superior verbal ability. For instance, tests that assess the literacy levels and verbal abilities of teachers have been shown to be associated with higher student

achievement. See J. K. Rice, *Teacher quality: Understanding the effectiveness of teacher attributes* (Washington, DC: Economic Policy Institute, 2003). Also see, for instance, commentaries in M. Cochran-Smith, Reporting on teacher quality: The politics of politics [Editorial], *Journal of Teacher Education, 53*(5) (2002) and in L. Darling-Hammond & P. Youngs, Defining "highly qualified teachers": What does "scientifically-based research" actually tell us? *Educational Researcher, 31*(9) (2002), 13–25.

20. See, for instance, E. E. García, *Student cultural diversity: Understanding and meeting the challenge* (Boston: Houghton Mifflin, 1999); G. Gordon, Teacher talent and urban schools, *Phi Delta Kappan, 81*(5) (1999), 304–306; M. Haberman, *Preparing teachers for urban schools* (Bloomington, IN: Phi Delta Kappa Educational Foundation, 1988); J. J. Irvine, *Educating teachers for diversity: Seeing with a cultural eye* (New York: Teachers College Press, 2003); M. S. Knapp, P. M. Shields, & B. J. Turnbull, Academic challenge in high-poverty classrooms, *Phi Delta Kappan, 76*(10) (1995), 770–776; G. Ladson-Billings, *The dreamkeepers: Successful teachers of African American children* (San Francisco: Jossey-Bass, 1994). T. Lucas, R. Henze, & R. Donato, Promoting the success of Latino language-minority students: An exploratory study of six high schools, *Harvard Educational Review, 60*(3) (1990), 315–340; M. Rose, *Possible lives: The promise of public education in America* (New York: Penguin Books, 1995); A. M. Villegas & T. Lucas, Preparing culturally responsive teachers: Rethinking the curriculum, *Journal of Teacher Education, 53*(1) (2002), 20–32.

21. R. V. Bullough, Jr., *Uncertain lives: Children of promise, teachers of hope* (New York: Teachers College Press, 2001).

22. See, for example, the work of J. J. Irvine, *Educating teachers for diversity: Seeing with a cultural eye* (New York: Teachers College Press, 2003); G. Ladson-Billings, *Crossing over to Canaan: The journey of new teachers in diverse classrooms* (San Francisco: Jossey-Bass, 2001); A. M. Villegas & T. Lucas, Preparing culturally responsive teachers: Rethinking the curriculum, *Journal of Teacher Education, 53*(1) (2002), 20–32.

23. Some of these critical treatments of education in a sociopolitical context include J. Anyon, *Ghetto schooling: A political economy of urban educational reform* (New York: Teachers College Press, 1997); A. Hargreaves & M. Fullan, *What's worth fighting for out there?* (New York: Teachers College Press, 1998); P. Lipman, *Race, class, and power in school restructuring* (Albany: State University of New York Press, 1998); J. H. Spring, *Deculturalization and the struggle for equality: A brief history of the education of dominated cultures in the United States* (Boston: McGraw-Hill, 2001).

24. J. Dewey, *Democracy and education.* New York: Free Press, 1916, pp. 119–120.

Chapter 2

1. S. J. Gould, *The mismeasure of man* (New York: Norton, 1981).

Chapter 5

1. J. E. King, Dysconscious racism: Ideology, identity, and the miseducation of teachers, *Journal of Negro Education*, *60*(2) (1991), 133–146.

2. T. Kidder, *Among schoolchildren* (New York: Houghton Mifflin, 1989).

Chapter 6

1. P. Bode, A letter from Kaeli, in S. Nieto, *The light in their eyes: Creating multicultural learning communities* (pp. 125–129). (New York: Teachers College Press, 1999).

Chapter 8

1. M. Angelou, Phenomenal Woman, in M. Angelou (Ed.), *And still I rise* (p. 8). (New York: Random House, 1978).

Chapter 9

1. P. Freire, *Pedagogy of the oppressed* (New York: Continuum, 2001).

Chapter 10

1. A. Lima, Voices from the basement: Breaking through the pedagogy of indifference, in Z. Beykont (Ed.), *Lifting every voice: Pedagogy and politics of bilingualism* (pp. 221–232) (Cambridge, MA: Harvard Education Publishing Group, 2000), p. 222.

2. Ibid., p. 231.

3. P. Freire, *Teachers as cultural workers: Letters to those who dare teach* (Boulder, CO: Westview Press, 1998).

4. J. Ward, Raising resisters: The role of truth-telling in the psychological development of African-American girls, in Leadbeater & Way (Eds.), *Urban girls: Resisting stereotypes, creating identities* (New York: New York University Press, 1996).

5. J. W. Loewen, *Lies my teacher told me: Everything your American history textbook got wrong* (New York: New Press, 1995).

Chapter 12

1. B. Bigelow, B. Miner, & B. Peterson, *Rethinking Columbus: Teaching about the 500th anniversary of Columbus's arrival in America* (Milwaukee: Rethinking Schools in collaboration with the Network of Educators on Central America, 1991).

Part IV

1. P. Freire, *Pedagogy of the oppressed* (New York: Continuum, 2001).

Chapter 13

1. L. Christensen, *Reading, writing, and rising up: Teaching about social justice and the power of the written word* (Milwaukee: Rethinking Schools, 2000).

Chapter 14

1. N. E. Arbulú, "I knew very early on": Honored teacher credits her upbringing, *The Republican* (November 14, 2003) (available at http://www. masslive.com/search/index.ssf?/base/living-0/1068799703140141.xml).

Chapter 17

1. J. Kozol, *Death at an early age: The destruction of the hearts and minds of Negro children in the Boston public schools.* (Boston: Houghton Mifflin, 1967).
2. W. Ryan, *Blaming the victim* (New York: Vintage Books, 1976).
3. P. Freire, *Pedagogy of the oppressed* (New York: Seabury Press, 1970).

Chapter 19

1. J. King, *A family from Iraq* (Austin, TX: Raintree, 1998).

Chapter 20

1. B. Dunn, Mi semester de español: A case study on the cultural dimension of second language acquisition, in S. Nieto (Ed.), *The light in their eyes* (pp. 146–152) (New York: Teachers College Press, 1999).

Chapter 22

1. J. Lester, *From slave ship to freedom road* (New York: Penguin, 1998).

Chapter 23

1. See, for instance, A. L. Amrein & D. C. Berliner, High-stakes testing, uncertainty, and student learning, *Education Policy Analysis Archives, 10*(18)

(2002) (available at http://epaa.asu.edu/epaa/v10n18/); M. Neill, L. Guisbond, B. Schaeffer, J. Madison, & L. Egeros, *Failing our children: How "No Child Left Behind" undermines quality and equity in education* (Cambridge, MA: FairTest, 2004). In addition, both teachers and researchers have criticized the focus on testing as leading to a narrowing of the curriculum. See, for example, J. J. Pedulla, L. M. Abrams, G. F. Madaus, M. K. Russell, M. A. Ramos, & J. Miao, *Perceived effects of state-mandated testing programs on teaching and learning: Findings from a national survey of teachers* (Boston: National Board on Educational Testing and Public Policy, Boston College, 2003); J. W. Pellegrino, N. Chudowsky, & R. Glaser, *Knowing what students know: The science and design of educational assessment* (Washington, DC: National Academy Press, 2001).

2. Various examples over the years confirm this to be the case. See, for example, M. M. Cohn & R. B. Kottkamp, *Teachers: The missing voice in education* (Albany: State University of New York Press, 1993); S. Farkas, J. Johnson, & T. Foleno, *A sense of calling: Who teaches and why* (New York: Public Agenda, 2000); M. Haberman, *Preparing teachers for urban schools* (Bloomington, IN: Phi Delta Kappa Educational Foundation, 1988); M. Rose, *Possible lives: The promise of public education in America* (New York: Penguin Books, 1995).

3. A. Hargreaves & M. Fullan, *What's worth fighting for out there?* (New York: Teachers College Press, 1998), p. 33.

4. S. Crabtree, Teachers who care get most from kids, *Detroit News* (June 4, 2004), p. 9.

5. N. Noddings, *The challenge to care in schools: An alternative approach to education* (New York: Teachers College Press, 1992); A. Valenzuela, *Subtractive schooling: U.S.–Mexican youth and the politics of caring* (Albany: State University of New York Press, 1999).

6. N. Flores-González, *School kids, street kids: Identity and high school completion among Latinos* (New York: Teachers College Press, 2002).

7. B. Comber, What *really* counts in early literacy lessons, *Language Arts*, *78*(1) (2000), p. 40.

8. M. Greene, Reflections: Implications of September 11th for curriculum, *Division B: Curriculum Studies Newsletter.* (Washington, DC: American Educational Research Association, 2001).

9. M. Foucault, Truth and power, in C. Gordon (Ed.); C. Gordon et al. (Trans.), *Power/knowledge: Selected interviews and other writings 1972–1977* (pp. 107–133) (Brighton, UK: Harvester Press, 1980).

10. In teacher preparation, books that include multiple perspectives are rare. Some of those that take on "mainstream knowledge" include J. W. Loewen, *Lies my teacher told me: Everything your American history textbook got wrong* (New York: New Press, 1995); J. W. Loewen, *Lies across America: What our historic sites got wrong* (New York: Touchstone Books, 2000); J. H. Spring, *Deculturalization and the struggle for equality: A brief history of the education of dominated cultures in the United States* (Boston: McGraw-Hill, 2001). In addition, books such as H. Zinn, *A people's history of the United States, 1492–present* (New York: Harper Perennial, 1980/2001) are often helpful in giving pre-

service and practicing teachers (and indeed all students) a different way of looking at history.

11. S. J. Gould, *The mismeasure of man* (New York: Norton, 1981).

12. T. Jenoure, *Navigators: African American musicians, dancers, and visual artists in academe* (Albany: State University of New York Press, 2000), p. 16.

13. J. Dewey, *Democracy and education* (New York: Free Press, 1916), p. 98.

14. H. A. Giroux, Educational leadership and the crisis of democratic government, *Educational Researcher, 21*(4) (1992), p. 4.

15. J. K. Rice, *Teacher quality: Understanding the effectiveness of teacher attributes* (Washington, DC: Economic Policy Institute, 2003), p. vii.

16. W. Schweke, *Smart money: Education and economic development* (Washington, DC: Economic Policy Institute, 2004).

17. Buying teachers/lawmakers must fund K–12. [Editorial], *Star Tribune* (June 20, 2004). (available at http://www.startribune.com/stories/561/4835721.html).

References

Amrein, A. L., & Berliner, D. C. (2002). High-stakes testing, uncertainty, and student learning. *Education Policy Analysis Archives, 10*(18). Available at http://epaa.asu.edu/epaa/v10n18/

Angelou, M. (1978). *Phenomenal woman.* In M. Angelou, *And still I rise* (p. 8). New York: Random House.

Anyon, J. (1997). *Ghetto schooling: A political economy of urban educational reform.* New York: Teachers College Press.

Arbulú, N. E. (2003, November 14). "I knew very early on": Honored teacher credits her upbringing. *The Republican.* Available at http://www.masslive .com/search/index.ssf?/base/living-0/1068799703140141.xml

Bigelow, B., Miner, B., & Peterson, B. (1991). *Rethinking Columbus: Teaching about the 500th anniversary of Columbus's arrival in America.* Milwaukee: Rethinking Schools in collaboration with the Network of Educators on Central America.

Bode, P. (1999). A letter from Kaeli. In S. Nieto, *The light in their eyes: Creating multicultural learning communities* (pp. 125–129). New York: Teachers College Press.

Bullough, R. V., Jr. (2001). *Uncertain lives: Children of promise, teachers of hope.* New York: Teachers College Press.

Buying teachers/lawmakers must fund K–12 [Editorial]. (2004, June 20). *Star Tribune.* Available at http://www.startribune.com/stories/561/4835721 .html

Carter, K. (1993). The place of story in the study of teaching and teacher education. *Educational Researcher, 22*(1), 5–12, 18.

Christensen, L. (2000). *Reading, writing, and rising up: Teaching about social justice and the power of the written word.* Milwaukee: Rethinking Schools.

Cochran-Smith, M. (2002). Reporting on teacher quality: The politics of politics [Editorial]. *Journal of Teacher Education, 53*(5).

Cochran-Smith, M. (2003). Teaching quality matters [Editorial]. *Journal of Teacher Education, 54*(2), 95–98.

Cohn, M. M., & Kottkamp, R. B. (1993). *Teachers: The missing voice in education.* Albany: State University of New York Press.

Comber, B. (2000). What *really* counts in early literacy lessons. *Language Arts, 78*(1), 29–49.

Connelly, F. M. & Clanindin, D. J. (1990). Stories of experience and narrative inquiry. *Educational Researcher, 19*(5), 2–14.

Crabtree, S. (2004, June 4). Teachers who care get most from kids. *Detroit News*, p. 9.

Darling-Hammond, L., & Falk, B. (1997). Using standards and assessments to support student learning. *Phi Delta Kappan, 79*(3), 190–199.

Darling-Hammond, L., & Youngs, P. (2002). Defining "highly qualified teachers": What does "scientifically-based research" actually tell us? *Educational Researcher, 31*(9), 13–25.

Dewey, J. (1916). *Democracy and education.* New York: Free Press.

Dunn, B. (1999). Mi semester de español: A case study on the cultural dimension of second language acquisition. In S. Nieto (Ed.), *The light in their eyes* (pp. 146–152). New York: Teachers College Press.

Farkas, S., Johnson, J., & Foleno, T. (2000). *A sense of calling: Who teaches and why.* New York: Public Agenda.

Flores-González, N. (2002). *School kids, street kids: Identity and high school completion among Latinos.* New York: Teachers College Press.

Foucault, M. (1980). Truth and power. In C. Gordon (Ed.); C. Gordon et al. (Trans.), *Power/knowledge: Selected interviews and other writings 1972–1977* (pp. 107–133). Brighton, UK: Harvester Press.

Freedman, S. W., Simons, E. R., Kalnin, J. S., Casareno, A., & the M-CLASS Teams. (Eds.). (1999). *Inside city schools: Investigating literacy in multicultural classrooms.* New York: Teachers College Press.

Freire, P. (1970). *Pedagogy of the oppressed.* New York: Seabury Press.

Freire, P. (1998). *Teachers as cultural workers: Letters to those who dare teach.* Boulder, CO: Westview.

García, E. (1999). *Student cultural diversity: Understanding and meeting the challenge.* Boston: Houghton Mifflin.

Giroux, H. A. (1992). Educational leadership and the crisis of democratic government. *Educational Researcher, 21*(4), 4–11.

Gordon, G. (1999). Teacher talent and urban schools, *Phi Delta Kappan, 81*(5), 304–306.

Gould, S. J. (1981). *The mismeasure of man.* New York: Norton.

Greene, M. (2001). Reflections: Implications of September 11th for curriculum. *Division B: Curriculum Studies Newsletter.* Washington, DC: American Educational Research Association.

Haberman, M. (1988). *Preparing teachers for urban schools.* Bloomington, IN: Phi Delta Kappa Educational Foundation.

Hare, D., & Heap, J. L. (2001). *Teacher recruitment and retention strategies in the midwest: Where are they and do they work?* Naperville, IL: North Central Regional Educational Laboratory.

Hargreaves, A., & Fullan, M. (1998). *What's worth fighting for out there?* New York: Teachers College Press.

Haycock, K., Jerald, C., & Huang, S. (2001). Closing the gap: Done in a decade. *Thinking K–16, 5*(2), pp. 3–5.

Intrator, S. (2003). *Tuned in and fired up: How teaching can inspire real learning in the classroom.* New Haven, CT: Yale University Press.

Irvine, J. J. (2003). *Educating teachers for diversity: Seeing with a cultural eye.* New York: Teachers College Press.

Jenoure, T. (2000). *Navigators: African American musicians, dancers, and visual artists in academe.* Albany: State University of New York Press.

Kidder, T. (1989). *Among schoolchildren.* New York: Houghton Mifflin.

King, J. (1998). *A family from Iraq.* Austin, TX: Raintree.

King, J. E. (1991). Dysconscious racism: Ideology, identity, and the miseducation of teachers. *Journal of Negro Education, 60*(2), 133–146.

Knapp, M. S., Shields, P. M., & Turnbull, B. J. (1995). Academic challenge in high-poverty classrooms. *Phi Delta Kappan, 76*(10), 770–776.

Ladson-Billings, G. (1994). *The dreamkeepers: Successful teachers of African American children.* San Francisco: Jossey-Bass.

Ladson-Billings, G. (2001). *Crossing over to Canaan: The journey of new teachers in diverse classrooms.* San Francisco: Jossey-Bass.

Lester, J., & Brown, R. (1998). *From slave ship to freedom road.* New York: Penguin.

Lima, A. (2000). Voices from the basement: Breaking through the pedagogy of indifference. In Z. Beykont (Ed.), *Lifting every voice: Pedagogy and politics of bilingualism* (pp. 221–232). Cambridge, MA: Harvard Education Publishing Group.

Lipman, P. (1998). *Race, class, and power in school restructuring.* Albany: State University of New York Press.

Loewen, J. W. (1995). *Lies my teacher told me: Everything your American history textbook got wrong.* New York: New Press.

Loewen, J. W. (2000). *Lies across America: What our historic sites got wrong.* New York: Touchstone Books.

Lucas, T., Henze, R., & Donato, R. (1990). Promoting the success of Latino language-minority students: An exploratory study of six high schools. *Harvard Educational Review, 60*(3), 315–340.

National Center for Education Statistics. (2002). State nonfiscal survey of public elementary/secondary education, 2000–2001. *Common core of data (CCD).* Washington, DC: Author.

National Commission on Teaching and America's Future. (1996, September). *What matters most: Teaching for America's future.* New York: Columbia University, Teachers College.

National Education Association. (1997). *Status of the American public school teacher, 1995–96.* Washington, DC: Author.

National Education Association. (2003). *Status of the American public school teacher, 2000–2001.* Washington, DC: Author.

National Partnership for Excellence and Accountability in Teaching. (2000). *Projects and activities.* Available at www.web3.educ.msu.edu/projects/html1#recr

Neill, M., Guisbond, L., Schaeffer, B., Madison, J., & Egeros, L. (2004). *Failing our children: How "No Child Left Behind" undermines quality and equity in education.* Cambridge, MA: FairTest.

Nieto, S. (2003a). Challenging notions of "highly qualified teachers" through work in a teachers' inquiry group. *Journal of Teacher Education, 54*(5), 386–398.

Nieto, S. (2003b). *What keeps teachers going?* New York: Teachers College Press.

Noddings, N. (1992). *The challenge to care in schools: An alternative approach to education.* New York: Teachers College Press.

O'Neil, J. (2003). Who we are, why we teach: A portrait of the American teacher. *NEA Today, 22*(1), 27–32.

Orfield, G. (2001). *Schools more separate: Consequences of a decade of resegregation.* Cambridge, MA: Civil Rights Project, Harvard University.

Palmer, P. J. (1998). *The courage to teach: Exploring the inner landscape of a teacher's life.* San Francisco: Jossey-Bass.

Pedulla, J. J., Abrams, L. M., Madaus, G. F., Russell, M. K., Ramos, M. A., & Miao, J. (2003). *Perceived effects of state-mandated testing programs on teaching and learning: Findings from a national survey of teachers.* Boston: National Board on Educational Testing and Public Policy, Boston College.

Pellegrino, J. W., Chudowsky, N., & Glaser, R. (2001). *Knowing what students know: The science and design of educational assessment.* Washington, DC: National Academy Press.

Rice, J. K. (2003). *Teacher quality: Understanding the effectiveness of teacher attributes.* Washington, DC: Economic Policy Institute.

Rose, M. (1995). *Possible lives: The promise of public education in America.* New York: Penguin Books.

Sanders, W. L., & Rivers, J. C. (1996). *Cumulative and residual effects of teachers on future student academic achievement.* Knoxville: University of Tennessee Value-Added Research and Assessment Center.

Schweke, W. (2004). *Smart money: Education and economic development.* Washington, DC: Economic Policy Institute.

Spring, J. H. (2001). *Deculturalization and the struggle for equality: A brief history of the education of dominated cultures in the United States.* Boston: McGraw-Hill.

U.S. Bureau of the Census. (1995). *Current population reports, Series P-60, No. 188.* Washington, DC: U.S. Government Printing Office.

U.S. Bureau of the Census. (2000a). *Poverty in the United States: 2000.* Washington, DC: U.S. Government Printing Office.

U.S. Bureau of the Census. (2000b). *USA statistics in brief: Population and vital statistics.* Washington, DC: U.S. Department of Commerce. Available at http://www.census.gov/statab/www/popppart.htm

U.S. Bureau of the Census. (2002). *Profile of the foreign-born population in the United States: 2000.* Washington, DC: U.S. Department of Commerce.

Valenzuela, A. (1999). *Subtractive schooling: U.S.–Mexican youth and the politics of caring.* Albany: State University of New York Press.

Villegas, A. M., & Lucas, T. (2002). Preparing culturally responsive teachers: Rethinking the curriculum. *Journal of Teacher Education, 53*(1), 20–32.

Ward, J. (1996). Raising resisters: The role of truth-telling in the psychological development of African-American girls. In B. Leadbeater & N. Way (Eds.), *Urban girls: Resisting stereotypes, creating identities* (pp. 85–99). New York: New York University Press.

Wilson, S. M., Floden, R. E., & Ferrini-Mundy, J. (2001). *Teacher preparation research: Current knowledge, gaps, and recommendations.* Seattle: Center for the Study of Teaching and Policy.

Zinn, H. (2001). *A people's history of the United States, 1492–present.* New York: Harper Perennial. (Original work published 1980)

About the Editor and the Contributors

Sonia Nieto is Professor of Language, Literacy, and Culture at the University of Massachusetts, Amherst. A teacher at elementary and middle school levels for several years and a teacher educator for the past 30, she has written extensively on diversity and teacher education. Her books include *Affirming Diversity*, *The Light in Their Eyes*, and *What Keeps Teachers Going?* She has received many awards for her scholarly work, advocacy, and activism, including two honorary doctorates. Recently, she was named the 2005 Outstanding Educator by the National Council of Teachers of English.

Beth Wohlleb Adel has taught middle and high school students for 10 years in many capacities: as a GED instructor for gang-involved youth, as a community service leader for urban youth in Boston, and as a Social Studies teacher in a public high school and middle school. She started and co-led one of the first gay-straight alliances in a public middle school. She is an adoptive and foster mother in a racially diverse family, and promotes awareness of all types of diversity and justice in the schools. She recently published curricula in the user guide for the exhibit "In Our Family: Portraits of All Kinds of Families" by Family Diversity Projects (http://www.lovemakesafamily.org).

Bob Amses teaches fifth grade at Kyrene del Milenio Elementary School in Phoenix, Arizona. Bob has been cited by Intel for his integration of technology in the elementary classroom, and was the subject of an article in their Autumn 2004 online education journal. Born and raised in New Jersey, Amses is a graduate of the State University of New York College at Brockport and received his postgraduate education degree from Arizona State University.

233

Judith Kauffman Baker is a secondary English teacher in the Boston Public Schools where she has taught since 1971 and has coached basketball for 20 years. Judith collaborates with South African educators in projects supporting rural teachers in the teaching of writing, critical thinking and HIV/AIDS education. Her major influences have been the Boston Writing Project, the anti-apartheid movement and anti-racism campaigns in her community. Judith has published articles in books by Lisa Delpit and Sonia Nieto. She is a National Board-certified teacher and has been recognized for excellence in teaching.

Patty Bode has been teaching art for 15 years in the public schools. Her classroom focuses on critical pedagogy through the arts in social action. She is a doctoral candidate with a concentration in Language, Literacy, and Culture at the University of Massachusetts, Amherst. The recipient of numerous awards and grants for her efforts in anti-racist curriculum reform in art education, she is currently an art teacher at Amherst Regional Middle School in Amherst, Massachusetts. She can be reached at pbode@comcast.net.

Mary Cowhey has been teaching first and second grade at Jackson St. School in Northampton, Massachusetts for 8 years. Before becoming a teacher, she was a community organizer for 14 years. Her essays have been published in *What Keeps Teachers Going?* and *Teaching With Fire: Poetry That Sustains the Courage to Teach*. She is a recipient of the 2002 Milken National Educator Award.

Laila M. Di Silvio currently teaches World Geography to sixth graders in Springfield, Massachusetts. A returned Peace Corps Volunteer and avid traveler, she seeks to prepare her students to be compassionate, knowledgeable, and just global citizens.

Bill Dunn is an English teacher at an inner-city vocational school in Massachusetts. He is a lifelong resident of the working-class town where he teaches. He is a vocal critic of "high stakes" testing and an advocate of vocational-technical education as a viable option for poor and working-class kids. He also coordinates an alternative evening program for struggling students.

Kristen French is a doctoral student in the Language, Literacy, and Culture program at the University of Massachusetts–Amherst. She has been a teacher and teacher educator for over a decade. Kristen is currently working in an urban elementary school, where she is a theater and writing teacher.

Ayla Gavins is currently an academy director at the Orchard Gardens Pilot School in Roxbury, MA. A teacher for 12 years, Ayla spent the last 6 of those years teaching at the Mission Hill School, a progressive K–8 school founded by Deborah Meier. During those years she joined many other progressive educators in forums and collaboratives to sustain authentic assessments, project-based, and experiential learning in schools.

Mary Ginley is a fifth-grade teacher in Longmeadow, Massachusetts. A teacher for more than 30 years in both urban and suburban schools, she has spent most of her career with five-, six- and seven-year-olds. She recently changed grades and has fallen in love with ten-year-olds. She has also served as an adjunct professor of education at the University of Massachusetts, Springfield College and Bay Path College in Longmeadow. She was named the Massachusetts Teacher of the Year in 1997 and received National Board Certification in 1999.

For 30 years **Stephen Gordon** taught English in Boston high schools, followed by work with Boston teachers to support their craft development. He currently works in the National Writing Project initiatives on new teacher retention and student reading improvement, and with Snowden International School teachers and students on the transition from high school to college writing. His experiences also include teacher-research through the Boston Writing Project and participation in school-site and across-school teacher-inquiry groups, including Sonia Nieto's "What Keeps Teachers Going" group.

Sandra Jenoure was born and raised in New York City. She received a B.A. in Sociology from Hunter College, in 1972, and began teaching right out of college; she taught in East Harlem for

25 years. During those years she taught science to grades 2 through 6 and worked as an administrative assistant to the principal. She has an M.A. in Early Childhood Education, an M.A. in Administration and Supervision, and an M.S. in Environmental Studies. She has received the Presidential Award for Excellence in Science and Mathematics Teaching Certificate of Honor. For the past 13 years she has taught graduate courses at Hunter and City Colleges of the City University of New York.

Ambrizeth Lima is an immigrant from the Cape Verde Islands. She has been a teacher for 14 years and is presently writing her dissertation on the socialization of Cape Verdean boys in the United States. She is an active member of her community and is always involved in issues that concern immigrant youth and their well-being in the United States.

Born and raised in Brooklyn, **Yahaira D. Marquez** has always been interested in reading and expressing herself through writing. After graduating with honors from Boston University and volunteering her time at various educational institutions across Boston, Massachusetts, she knew her decision to teach was well worth it. After teaching 9th grade English in Brooklyn, she moved to Virginia Beach, where she is currently working toward a Master's Degree.

Katina Papson is an artist/photographer who is currently in her fifth year of teaching visual art and social justice performance at Amherst Regional High School in Massachusetts. An advocate for youth-initiated projects, Katina's activism manifests in her classroom practice as well as through after-school and community wide organizing. She directs an alternative summer arts camp and has worked in nonprofit programs for teens.

A teaching veteran of 23 years, **Melinda Pellerin-Duck** was nominated Massachusetts State Teacher of the Year in 2004. As a high school teacher in Springfield, Massachusetts, she has taught law, history, and technology. Pellerin-Duck's accomplishments include working with the New England School of Law so that high-school students can learn with first-year law students. In addition, she successfully worked in tandem with students and social activists to prevent closure of several local public libraries.

Seth Peterson has just completed his first decade of teaching at Snowden International School, where he has been the grateful apprentice to a faculty of dedicated educators. The past 10 years of working and learning in the Boston Public School System have convinced him that choices, creative autonomy, and human interactions—for teachers and students—are the forgotten treasures that just might save public education.

Elaine Stinson is an elementary educator for Amherst Public Schools in western Massachusetts. Elaine holds a Master's Degree in Education from the University of Massachusetts. Her field of study was within the Bilingual, ESL, Multicultural Education Program. She has also earned National Board Certification and has been teaching young children for 11 years. Elaine's passion is finding ways to weave social justice education into the mainstream curriculum.

Nina Tepper has taught in the inner city public schools for over 20 years at both the elementary and middle-school levels. Currently, she provides school embedded staff professional development, teacher mentoring, and direct student instruction as a literacy Colloborative Professional Development Teacher in the Springfield Public Schools. As a consultant with the Western Massachusetts Writing Project since 1993, she has facilitated workshops at schools and conferences statewide. Nina was honored by the Massachusetts Department of Education as a Semifinalist for Massachusetts Teacher of the Year 2000.

Kerri Warfield is a graduate from the University of Massachusetts, Amherst, with both a Bachelor's Degree in Fine Arts and a Master's Degree in Multicultural Education. She has taught visual arts to High School and Middle School children for the past 6 years and is currently teaching at North Middle School in Westfield, Massachusetts. Along with her teaching profession, she is also a commissioned artist, mentor, participant in the Foundation for Excellence in Schools (2005), and has guest-lectured at the University of Massachusetts.

Jennifer Welborn has been teaching science to all ages of students for over 18 years. She holds a Masters Degree in Education and a Bachelors Degree in Wildlife Biology. She was awarded the Anti-Defamation League's World of Difference Teacher Incentive Award and The Pioneer Valley Woman of Distinction Award for the anti-bias curriculum she has developed and taught. Currently, she teaches eighth-grade science in Amherst, Massachusetts.

Index